FIVE-STAR

Celebrating 25 Years of History, Legends, and Instruction from the Nation's Premier Basketball Camp

FIVE-STAR

Celebrating 25 Years of History, Legends, and Instruction from the Nation's Premier Basketball Camp

Michael Ryan

MP

MASTERS PRESS

Published by Masters Press, 5025 28th Street, S.E.,
Grand Rapids, Michigan 49512

© Copyright Masters Press, 1990

Printed in the United States of America
First edition

All photographs reproduced courtesy of Five-Star
Basketball Camp

Library of Congress Cataloging-in-Publication Data

Ryan, Michael, 1951 Jan. 15—
    Five-star: celebrating 25 years of history, legends,
    and instruction from the nation's premier basketball
    camp / Michael Ryan.
        p   cm.
    ISBN 0-940279-30-4
    1. Five-star (Pa. and Va. : Basketball camp)—History.
    I. Title.
    GV885.72.P4R93   1990   90-37521
    796.323′0973—dc20   CIP

DEDICATION

The author dedicates this effort to all the players at Catskill High who didn't understand their gift and the ones who hopefully will; to his mother, Dorothy Ryan, who loves her five kids (and their kids); to his father, Patrick Ryan, who loved long walks; to his father-in-law, Joe Segelman, who died before this book's completion but is proud; to his mother-in-law, Nina Segelman, who shared her home; to his mentor, Charles E. Dornbusch; and mostly to a shared red rose and Bonnie, who keeps him interested.

Michael Ryan

You can't pick up a newspaper or magazine or turn on a television without the sport of basketball being trashed. It seems as if half the media is on a crusade against the game. True, much of their ammunition is supplied by the dopers, dumpers, and cheaters themselves, but the nefarious ones are just a fragment of the hoop population.

The good feelings about Five-Star Camp, on the other hand, remind us of all that is great in basketball: the hard work and team play needed for a winning season; the love of a coach for his players; the respect and admiration of players for their coach; the enduring friendships among teammates and respected opponents; the development of sound bodies and minds; the building of character, discipline, and self-confidence; the sacrifice of the individual for the good of the team; the brotherhood of players who don't see race, religion, color, or creed; and the camaraderie that only caring teammates can feel.

Then there are the selfless individuals: the Jack Twymans with the Maurice Stokes Fund; Bob Knight and his Landon Turner Relief Fund; Hank Carter's "Wheelchair Classic" for the benefit of Goldwater Memorial Hospital; coaches like Dave Maggarity (St. Francis of Loretto, PA) and Roy Williams (Kansas) who granted four-year scholarships to Les Jasicek and Chris Lindley, respectively, when pre-freshman tragedies abruptly ended their playing careers; pioneers like the late Ollie Edinboro, whose community organizations help thousands of teenagers across America; the Zelda Spoelstras, whose support of the NBA's Player Pension Plan is legendary; and countless other "Citizens of Hoop" who never get their names in print. It's to these positive influences that we sincerely dedicate this book.

Will Klein and Howard Garfinkel

CONTENTS

PART THREE *Pitt*

PART FOUR *Honesdale*

Epilogue

ACKNOWLEDGMENTS

Hubie Brown was right when he told the Five-Star campers that saying thank-you to someone for their help costs nothing, but is the only way to pay for something priceless. I want to thank the following people for their help: Cliff Wexler, Jill Busby, Michael Rozen, Alan Wexler, Don Conover (who is hopelessly "Back in '54"), and Diana Balta (wherever she is) for encouragement and advice; Louise Havens and John Griffin from the *Daily Mail* newspaper for granting me time away from the office; fellow basketball officials Whitey Raymond (IAABO Board #114) and Roger Casey (CDBWBO) for letting me work without fining me; Evy Alger, Sonja Demakos, John Smith, Jim Tyrrell, Sandy Zensen, and Bob Zimmerman for taking an interest; and Laura Goff, Elizabeth Guenther, and Jennifer Pros for constantly disrupting my work, which I hope they continue to do.

I want to thank Howard Garfinkel and Will Klein for their trust; Tom Bast, Amy Wolterstorff, and Anne Shuart for their patience; Mrs. Eva Garfinkel, Hubie Brown, Bob Cremins (who called me back after I lost my notes), Chuck Daly, Mike Fratello, Bob Knight, Moses Malone, John Paxson, Rick Pitino, Dave Pritchett, George Raveling, Ron Rothstein, Gordie Van Buren, and Rick Evrard and Bob Minnix from the NCAA for making time to talk; George Rivenburg, the longtime caretaker at Lake Bryn Mawr, for finding my car keys; Five-Star staffers Bill Lily and Angie Butterey for their assistance; and in New York City for the use of their premises for lengthy interviews: Milton Palmer and Fred Klein at the Carnegie Deli; Ralph Scotto at Sasha's Restaurant; Jerry Shaw at Wylie's Ribs II; and the Hilton Hotel at 54th Street and 6th Avenue.

I apologize to anyone mistakenly left out of the book and for any and all inaccuracies.

FOREWORD

I'm happy to have the opportunity to say a few words about Five-Star, which I consider to be one of the finest basketball teaching camps in the country.

There are exactly 324 players in the NBA. Some of them are stars, some are superstars, and some just sit on the bench, but all of them are very, very good basketball players. And they all have one thing in common: They were all ten years old once, bouncing a basketball in their driveways or on a playground, like tens of thousands of other youngsters who shared the same dreams, but who weren't quite as fortunate or blessed with quite the same talent. There are more than 250,000 kids playing organized high school basketball in the United States today, which means that the odds of making it to the NBA are a little better than one in one thousand.

I am very privileged, and deeply grateful, to be one of those who did make it. Why am I one of the lucky few? I really don't know; my story isn't too different from thousands of others. I grew up in Chicago, the youngest of nine children, and in fact my goal was to go to law school. I do know that I worked very hard, but even with all the hard work and long hours of practice, I could never have done it alone. Many other people, too numerous to mention here, helped make my dream become a reality.

Two of those people were Howard Garfinkel and Will Klein, co-directors of the Five-Star Basketball Camp. I think I had heard about the camp from Gene Pingatore, my high school coach at Westchester St. Joseph's, but I sure wasn't prepared for the regimen that greeted me as a high school junior in 1978! You'll read about that regimen, as well as a lot of other things, in this book, and I envy you the pleasure you have in store. If you have attended the camp, this book will awaken many pleasant—and some not so pleasant!—memories, and if you haven't, it will serve as a wonderful introduction to one of the nation's finest basketball camps, which, I'm glad to acknowledge, was a formative influence on my basketball career.

Isiah Thomas

DRIVING MR. ISIAH: *Coach Buddy Gardler (Cardinal O'Hara H.S.) says "See ya later" as he gives a tired Isiah Thomas a spin to the canteen following a tough NBA game in July of '78. Gardler always had an eye for future Academy Award winners.*

INTRODUCTION

"Argue for your limitations and sure enough, they're yours."

– Author Richard Bach

In the summer of 1989 I went to Five-Star to write a book thinking I didn't have it in me.

I'd been there the previous summer putting together a series of articles for a small weekly newspaper in Catskill, New York. Actually that was an excuse to get to the camp.

I'd taken an interest in a talented kid who'd run out of room on the playgrounds in his hometown with no idea where to turn next. Five-Star, by reputation, was a bottom-line type of place. It was where high school basketball players went to find out if they were as good as they thought. The kid was willing to risk it so we went. He learned things well beyond the game of basketball.

I got to meet Howard Garfinkel, the colorful and (though he'll argue this) occasionally cantankerous co-director of Five-Star. He gave me free rein, asking only that I send him a copy of the completed articles. I did, he liked what he saw, and, with Five-Star's 25th anniversary approaching, mentioned an idea being tossed around for a history and was I interested?

Newspaper articles were one thing, but a book, well— but for some reason I told him "Sure, why not," and at a springtime meeting in New York City between Garfinkel (affectionately known as Garf), his partner Will Klein, publisher Tom Bast, and me, it was decided. I would visit the camp throughout the summer and use what I found as a backdrop for the story.

Five-Star, it turns out, is an itinerant concept. The camp materializes for seven separate weeks, from June to early September at three different sites: along the quieting New River at the university in Radford, Virginia; on the campus of Robert Morris College in Coraopolis, a suburb of Pittsburgh, Pennsylvania; and at Lake Bryn Mawr summer camp in northeastern Pennsylvania, not far from Honesdale, an old coal town.

Each spot is distinctive. Radford draws the down-home southern boys who know how to run a pick-and-roll, stick the open jumper, and answer "Yes, sir" and "No, sir." It's where Five-Star's summer begins.

Coraopolis, nicknamed Pitt in honor of its Steel City neighbor, is a melting pot. East Coast man-to-man toughs check out the laid-back West Coast types with their finesse defenses and three-point shots and no one can believe the Midwest kids who show up pristine and pure as new corn and leave with court burns and raggedy sneakers. All through humid July, young men drift in from Texas, Alaska, and even overseas to find out if the rest have got something they don't.

Lake Bryn Mawr is the closest thing to home Five-Star knows, where a light is left burning. It is always, in deference to the year-round residents, referred to as Honesdale and tradition demands that summer end there. Twenty-five years ago a hearty bunch of New York City and New Jersey coaches and players got things started at Camp Orin-Sekwa, a similar but considerably more rustic hideaway in Niverville, New York, a stone's throw south of Albany.

Guys hardly anybody had heard of like Hubie Brown and Marv Kessler and Chuck Daly spent a week in the woods teaching basketball to inner-city and suburban kids thrown together for the first time in their lives. They moved to Camp Rosemont the following year, not far from Lake Bryn Mawr, staying there nine summers.

Dear old Camp Rosemont—where a young Bob Knight disciplined the troops and where upstart coaches such as Rick Pitino and Mike Fratello and growing boys like Mel Davis and Moses Malone matured. Those original bunkmates and many since have left their mark on the game.

Part One of this book chronicles those early years, 1966-1976, and Five-Star's emergence as a basketball phenomenon. To achieve historical accuracy, I spent numerous hours talking to Garf, Will Klein, and other prime movers in the camp's growth. Legend and truth shamelessly overlap.

Part Two takes a closer look at the expansion years and what camp life is like today. To get a feel for the place, I spent a week at each site. Basketball, indeed, has very little to do with what really happens at Five-Star. It is the reason everyone goes but also the means to a much different end.

My first stop was Radford. It was the second week in June and hot. There was a noisy train yard outside the dorm room window and teenagers in rooms on either side of mine and across the hall. Given more to privacy and with self-doubt settling in hard, I was sure this book thing would never pan out. I took a nap, hoping to find a respectable way to tell Garf he'd picked the wrong man.

Instead I had this strange dream. In the dream, Garf was yelling something about missing the greatest scoop ever. Being a newspaperman, I was always interested in breaking a news story first and fast. Garf said he'd been wrestling on the ground with Adrian Branch, an ex-camper of his who'd made it all the way to the NBA, and where the hell was I? The photojournalistic opportunity of a lifetime and I'd blown it.

Even in my dream I had to smile, picturing Garf, a dignified but slender-at-best Jewish guy with glasses and slicked-back black hair (though he'll argue the part about the hair) rumbling with the muscular Branch. Impatienty awaiting my explanation, incredulous, incessant cigarette fuming, I noticed he had on the fashionable lime green pants and orange Converses he sometimes wears and he was nothing if not deathly serious.

When I woke up some deep fear of failure was gone, replaced by the reality of a lot of hard work, but I figured I could handle that and went to the outdoor courts to get started. Garf was there amid a swirl of camper activity. Perhaps the greatest evaluator of basketball talent ever, the basis of Five-Star, I could immediately see he was in his element. I also saw he had on those blinding green trousers and Halloween hightops of his.

A little unsure now if I'd dreamt or not, I went to him and half-kiddingly asked if he'd been in my room. Turning toward me, tense, agitated, consumed by the pressure of running the camp smoothly, he said, "What? No. What are you talking about? Why would I be in your room?" I told him my dream and he looked away at the activity surrounding him, then back at me, quizzically attentive and said, "I'm not clairvoyant, you know."

I didn't believe him. He has a way of getting inside your head and besides, others have had other dreams and Garf has been in them.

PART ONE

In the Beginning

ONE
Laying Down Tracks

"If you knew of all the years,
Of hopes and dreams and tears,
You'd know it didn't happen overnight."

— Judy Garland in *A Star is Born*

There was nothing to indicate it would turn out the way it did.

Garf figured it'd be a week of playing basketball and having fun in the countryside, which it was, but then the other thing began happening.

It started before Five-Star was even a gleam in Garf's eye. He was a young boy hiding in the ball shack at Camp Mascoma in Enfield, New Hampshire, with his friend Donald Prenowitz. He spent 15 summers at Mascoma, far removed from his well-to-do New York City family, and was a happy camper. "I'd go back today if they'd let me," he says. One afternoon someone in charge did something that annoyed him, and stuffed in the sweltering shed he swore he'd run a camp someday and run it right. Prenowitz, wanting out, offered little resistance and later unwittingly helped the plan along. That was at Camp Chickopee, another summer hideaway. Garf introduced him to a young girl he was sweet on and Prenowitz eventually married her, which was as close as Garf got to the altar until Five-Star.

* * * * *

There were other loves, such as baseball and Judy Garland.

Garf grew up on Park Avenue, the second son of Stanley and Eva Garfinkel. His grandfather, Morris Garfinkel, was a successful woolen jobber, building M. Garfinkel and Sons in the early 1900s into the largest textile center in New York. Garf's father took over the business when he was 24 and groomed his sons to follow.

Garf was cut from a different cloth. "Howard hated Mr. Garfinkel's business," says his mother, a slight and modestly elegant woman. "His father was angry with him, but Howard did not enjoy sitting around waiting for somebody to come in and buy small lots of woolens. Mr. Garfinkel was very, very angry with him for going into sports. There was a little friction there. He did not think Howard would be a success."

Sports had secretly maintained Garf's spirit from an early age. Born on August 1, 1929, he slipped away from his governess often enough to capture the unofficial wallball championship of 91st Street, subduing pals Edgar Culkin and Stan Gans en route. The soothing voice of Red Barber and subtle grace of Joe DiMaggio filled his summer afternoons.

"I heard Red Barber and that put an end to my dream of being an announcer. I knew I could never be that good," Garf says, although he did add play-by-play listening alone in his room. "Joe DiMaggio was one of my idols. I always wanted to be a baseball player and I was very good at Camp Mascoma and ballparks like that. I was a pretty good athlete, I thought, until I got to high school."

He suited up for the Horace Mann nine, perennial academic powers, before transferring to Barnard High in his senior year. Switching to basketball when the weather changed, he warmed the bench on "the worst team in New York City" but developed a sweet two-hand set shot that would serve him well at Five-Star.

Madison Square Garden, the old Garden at 50th Street, was his winter refuge. His father took him when he was too young to go on his own, paying four bucks for the Side Loge green seats, the best seats in the house. In his teens he went alone or with Prenowitz or some other friends and paid 50 cents for a balcony view. Later, he paid two-and-a-quarter for seats in the End Arena, behind the baskets, which was perfect because he really knew the joint.

He knew every seat number in every section and always bought a corner ticket, five feet and one aisle away from the Side Loge. In the old days there were doubleheaders, and at halftime or between games the regulars would congregate in the lobby or meet elsewhere to sit and schmooze. Among that group were Roy Rubin, the coach at Columbus High in the Bronx who would play a pivotal role in the formation of Five-Star, and Larry Pearlstein.

Pearlstein, raised in Brooklyn, met Garf in the late forties. He had a knack for spotting talent and his friends called him "Scout." He did some bird-dogging for Bud Milliken at the University of Maryland before helping the New Jersey Nets and owner Joe Traub make the transition from the American Basketball Association to the National Basketball Association, doing everything from bottle-washing to making trades. He would always keep an eye on Five-Star.

Garf left his strategic End Arena seat briefly to attend Syracuse University, acquiring an affinity for the color orange but little else. He was an assistant manager for the basketball team, feeding All-American Bill Gabor, another boyhood idol, his daily dose of one hundred foul shots. Loyal to the bone, when Garf departed the upstate university after less than two semesters, he continued to keep close track of Gabor's college career and rise to the NBA Syracuse Nationals.

Things were not much changed on his return to the city. He tried different jobs, making shoulder pads for suits and working as a travel agent, among other things, but says he "hated them all." He was well aware that he stood to inherit the family woolen business, but the idea offended him. The popularity of man-made fabrics eventually resolved the problem, forcing his father to liquidate the firm and open a stock brokerage, another successful venture, and in the early fifties, Garf was adrift.

He sort of fell into his future. On a lark, with a nudge from Mike Tynberg, he agreed to coach a winless YMCA basketball team in Queens. "I've asked myself a thousand times why I did that," Garf says. "I guess I did it because Tynberg asked me to. I first met him at Camp Mascoma. He was my bunk counselor. Later, I used to watch him coach city all-star teams, 'outside' teams, we called them, high school kids mostly. After the games we'd grab a bite to eat and BS. We became friends.

"I had never coached before, but I had nothing to do and I was floundering. The regular coach couldn't make it and Frank Tempone, who was organizing the games, asked Tynberg to find someone. Part of the fun of watching had always been second-guessing coaches, so it was a challenge for me. I felt I knew the game." A team with four players, led by twin brothers Vin and Frankie Quarto of Elmhurst, Queens, stomped his team by 50 points.

Undaunted, he accepted an invitation to coach in a season-ending Rotary/YMCA tournament for boys 15 years of age and under. His first move was to recruit the Quarto brothers. It was the beginning of a beautiful relationship. The Quartos, on their way to becoming outstanding college players, Vin at Adelphi and Frankie at Manhattan, delivered Joe Daley. Garf picked up Kenny Harrison from New Jersey, who brought along future Holy Cross star Jack Whalen. There was an Irish kid named Tom Rooney, and Aemon Killoran, Larry McNeil, Jim Conners, and Jack Corker.

Garf still has the plaque listing all their names. It wasn't exactly a ragtag team, but they hadn't been together long either so nobody expected them to do well, much less win the tournament, which they did. They got a break when the favorites, Tynberg and Joe Mulholland, met in the opening round. Mulholland, the coach at St. Teresa's parish in Queens and presently the Commissioner of Parole in New York State, disposed of Tynberg, and Garf returned the favor by beating him in the finals.

"I got my bug winning that tournament," he says. "It was an honor just to be coaching in it, and then to win it was unbelievable. It was the greatest thrill I've ever had in sports. Forget everything that's happened since. Forget the camp, forget all the great players and coaches that have been a part of it. There's never been another feeling like that in my life and there never will be again."

Coaching the New York Nationals came close. Stirred by his success, Garf kept the nucleus of the team together, borrowing their new name and orange and black uniform style from his hero Bill Gabor's Syracuse Nats. Dan Palmer, an Astoria bar and grill owner, provided burgers and financial backing. Wexler's Formal Wear, a tuxedo place in Jamaica, Queens, also sponsored the team.

The Nationals, no matter who paid, were awesome. Garf was beginning to know the local talent and had a knack for blending it well. It seemed to come naturally to him and he rose quickly in the ranks of outside coaches. Rivalries, friendly and otherwise, grew as he consistently held his own against the Gems, coached by his mentor Tynberg, and other blacktop teams such as the Reliables, coached by insuranceman Walter November.

Satch Sanders, destined for the Boston Celtics, anchored Garf's most memorable Nationals quintet. Future St. John's All-American Al Seiden was the glue at point guard, steering the offense after driving everyone else to the court. His backcourt mate was Art Benoit, with collegiate All-Americans Tony Jackson (St. John's) and Cal Ramsey (NYU) at the forward spots. They played at Grover Cleveland Park in Ridgewood, Queens, "the longest court in the history of basketball," according to Garf, and wherever else they could find good basketball.

That bunch, with Long Beach import Larry Brown and future pro Art Heyman coming off the bench, won 33 of 34 games and two straight mythical city titles. Brown, coach of the 1988 NCAA champion Kansas Jayhawks, made the first in a succession of notable exits shortly thereafter, defecting to Tynberg's Gems with Hayman and drawing Garf's ire. The perceived disloyalty was not soon forgotten.

Garf felt better about it after he was chosen over Tynberg and November to coach an all-city team at a tournament in Allentown, Pennsylvania in the early sixties. A forerunner to national all-star events, it matched the best players from New York City, central Pennsylvania, the city of Philadelphia, and Washington, D.C. Garf's crew beat Morgan Wootten's Capital City boys in the finals, giving him a still coveted 1–0 edge over Wootten, the legendary head coach of DeMatha High in Hyattsville, Maryland. They would cross paths many times in the future.

In the meantime, the poor little rich boy from Manhattan had become known as a purveyor of fine players. He knew the five boroughs like the back of his hand. If a college coach came to him searching for a particular type of player, he usually knew where to look. He got good at it and it was something he liked doing. It helped the kids too, and word got around that he had connections and would put in a good word for a guy who kept his nose clean.

Gradually his word became respected throughout the business. When the Dapper Dan Tournament got started in Pittsburgh in the mid-sixties, pitting Pennsylvania's best high school players against the rest of the country, organizer Sonny Vaccaro asked Garf to pick the New York and New Jersey entries. A rift over the selection process led to a split with Vaccaro, who subsequently joined forces with the upstart Nike sporting goods company, and Garf, never far from the game, got in on the ground floor of the McDonald's All-American Game with Wootten and others.

He helped pick the team and, in a style fairly reminiscent of the great Red Barber, delivered eloquent and occasionally lengthy player introductions, including one or two a shy southern kid named Moses Malone would never forget.

* * * * *

Vic Bubas had long since learned to appreciate the talents of Howard Garfinkel. Bubas, then an assistant coach at North Carolina State, marveled at Garf's knowledge and keen eye during his own recruiting trips to New York in the early 1950s. He made it his business to exchange notes whenever he was in town, and in 1955, with the blessing of his boss Everett Case, put Garf to work as a Wolfpack scout.

It was an unofficial and unpaid position, but it suited the wandering city kid to a T. "I was a pipeline," Garf says. "Everett Case told me they wanted big bastards and clever little shits. I never found any big bastards, but I found a lot of clever little shits. It was something that was always in me, I guess; I just needed a chance to find it."

He didn't develop the skill entirely on his own. He'd been preened for the job by his mother. Garf's uptown upbringing had exposed him to the cream of New York society and the brightest stars in show business. On his fifth birthday, Al Jolsen kneeled and sang "Sonny Boy" to him, and celebrities like Sophie Tucker, Henny Youngman, Ted Lewis, and Milton Berle performed at his bar mitzvah. The family held box seats at the Metropolitan Opera House and the Garfinkels were admired patrons of the arts. Garf's mother went beyond being an observer and helped launch the singing career of superstar Eddie Fisher.

Fisher, on his way up the ladder, worked as a singing waiter at Grossingers in the Catskills. Garf's parents dined there regularly and were joined one evening by megastar entertainer Eddie Cantor, their good friend. Engaged in conversation, neither Garf's father nor Cantor took notice while Fisher strolled the room in song. Mrs. Garfinkel, recognizing a good thing when she heard it, interrupted their chat to make them listen. Cantor signed Fisher to a night club tour right then and there.

Fisher might have been discovered anyhow, but as Garf is fond of saying, "You can never tell in this world. It's all timing." One of his earliest finds was Mark Reiner out of Lincoln High in Brooklyn. "He was all set to play for Fred Schaus at West Virginia, but Everett Case told me he needed a guard who could shoot. I told him about this kid, so he came up to watch him in a summer game.

"Reiner hit about eight jumpers in a row and I'll never forget it. Case looked at me like he was in shock and said, 'Does he always shoot like that?' I told him, 'No, just most of the time,' and he gave Reiner a scholarship on the spot. Fred Schaus hasn't talked to me since. I can't win."

Garf was unknowingly serving his Five-Star apprenticeship. Watching for potential Wolfpack recruits, as well as players for his Nationals and the high school all-star teams, he was absorbing the experience of not only Bubas and Case, but also young basketball wizard Walter Lee Terrill, an assistant at North Carolina State and his main contact.

"Terrill had the greatest basketball mind I'd ever seen. I'd never met anyone like him in my life. He would sit in a place all night and take salt and pepper shakers and forks and knives and maybe a few pickles and move them around, running plays, creating new ones, and going over the old ones. I was surrounded by brilliant basketball minds. I knew some things, but he really taught me how to evaluate a player, what to look for, little things."

The bubble burst in 1961. College basketball, for the second time in 10 years, endured a major point-shaving scandal. "I was just a kid during the '51 scandal. That one was staggering, but 1961 was a killer," Garf says. He had had his suspicions. There were a lot of easy shots missed and some funny bounces at the end of close games, so when the scandal finally broke he was not totally surprised. Still, it was a cruel blow. "I was in mortal shock. I couldn't believe that the kids I sent to State, my kids, would dump a game."

Terrill, totally devastated, quit the game. North Carolina State "de-emphasized" its basketball program, cutting scholarships and limiting recruitment to within state lines. Garf's services were no longer needed. Now and then, he would send a kid to Bubas, who relocated at Duke University, and he was always ready to help one of his Nationals get into a good school, like Satch Sanders at New York University, or find a prospect for a friend, like Roy Rubin after he got into the college ranks, but for all intents and purposes, his scouting days were over.

More or less. With a return to cozy Camp Mascoma out of the question and time on his hands, Garf, in the summer of 1963, migrated upstate to Saugerties and Jack Donahue's Friendship Farm. Donahue coached at Power Memorial in Manhattan, in the rugged Catholic High School Athletic Association (CHSAA). Every summer he trundled next season's starting five up to Friendship Farm to get acquainted. He figured it was an edge, and so did coaches like Archbishop Molloy's Jack Curran, who was on the staff at the time and became the "winningest" high school coach in state history.

Anyone was welcome to bring their players, provided they could play. The coaches would roust them out of bed, teach them a few moves, and then roll out the basketballs. Garf was a resident coach, keeping an eye on his share of the campers while coaching a team. He was disappointed that Lew Alcindor, Donahue's heralded center, had left already. But Garf was coaching, occupied with the game, and content.

It was a great way to get the kids out of the city for a few days and get them in shape. College coaches would stop by and spend a day or two ogling the talent and lecturing on some phase of the game like man-to-man pressure defense or setting offensive screens, heady stuff like that, and then leave. Occasionally they'd be asked to stay around to fill in for someone who had to take care of personal business away from camp, which is how Garf got to lock horns with the young ram Robert Montgomery Knight.

Knight, then at West Point, had already earned a reputation as a tough disciplinarian. His cadets were always scrappy, and although they had no business being there, every year it seemed like they ended up in the National Invitational Tournament, driving the favorites crazy or beating one of them. He frequently spoke at Friendship Farm and that year he showed the kids the right way to do defensive slides, asking his friend Garf to assist and demonstrate.

"He volunteered me," is the way Garf remembers it. "I wasn't about to tell him no. He had me going from sideline to sideline, doing V-cuts, the whole bit. I was in pretty fair shape in those days." Knight, who would one day bring his unique brand of discipline to Five-Star, tells a different story. "If I used Howard, it was only because he needed to have his ass busted a little bit. It certainly wasn't because of any innate ability that he possessed."

Either way, the amicable adversaries—and still good friends—found themselves in opposite corners in the camp championship tilt. Knight built an eight-point lead with two minutes left. Garf took his legions aside and told them to start pressing or else. A couple of Archbishop Molloy kids, Brian Adrian and Kevin Joyce (whom Garf renamed The White Tornado), heeded the warning and pulled it out for him.

That win made Garf 1–0 versus Knight too, but more important, he liked this notion of a basketball camp. There were one or two things he might change, of course, but the theory was great and the timing was perfect. No one else was doing it except The Maestro himself, Clair Bee, at Kutcher's Sports Academy down in Monticello. That was just part of the daily program, though. Garf had something more intense in mind and approached his friend Roy Rubin with a plan.

He laid the whole thing out, explaining how with Rubin's name and his energy they could strike out on their own and maybe make a few bucks. Besides that, it was a great way to pass the time. Rubin, in his final years at Columbus High, half-listened and didn't want to be bothered. Garf figured he couldn't cut it alone and let the idea die quietly. It was the calm before the storm.

* * * * *

Roy Rubin, in truth, was more of an idol than a pal to Garf. Extremely talented, he was preparing to jump directly from Columbus High to the head coaching job at Long Island University, a rare feat. "We were very tight, I thought, but Rubin was the king. The leader. He called me 'Kid' and everyone followed him. He was very charismatic. I don't think a day went by in a period of four or five years that we didn't talk on the phone, not a week we didn't see each other. We were better friends than I want to believe, because we ended up not being friends at all," Garf says.

Rubin loathed "spooks"—strange guys, to his way of thinking, who hung around gyms and playgrounds courting young players for their unofficial all-star teams or, on the QT, for a college. Guys like Tynberg and November and Garf. "Rubin hated outside ball, outside coaches, outside teams, anything not connected with his purity, but it was fraudulent purity. For years I lived and died with Columbus High and LIU, but he did nothing to help me. He attacked everything I was doing, but I was supposed to be loyal to him and help him in his career and with recruiting, which I did. Deep down I knew, but I was a fool."

Rubin would be there for the beginning of Five-Star, but first there was this other idea Garf had for a magazine. He had been thinking about it for quite some time and wanted to pattern it after the popular *Dell Book,* a sort of Who's Who in College Basketball of the times that was published prior to every season. Garf wanted to do the same thing for high school players in the five boroughs, Nassau, Suffolk, and Westchester counties, and northern New Jersey, calling it *High School Basketball Illustrated (HSBI).*

His father deplored the idea, stopping just short of undermining it, but Garf and Morrey Rokeach, the high school sports editor of the *Journal American,* formed a partnership and got underway. Midway through the first edition, Rokeach became ill. He made his office available but had to bow out otherwise, leaving Garf with a staff of one working 20-hour days. That summer, 1964, Garf returned to Friendship Farm facing a November deadline. Lurking there, waiting to add to his miseries, was, he recalls, "one of the most aggravating campers I'd ever met."

In no time they would be like father and son (when they weren't involved in spirited one-upmanship, which was often).

Richie "Rick" Pitino of Oyster Bay, Long Island, "was a total pain in the neck," Garf says, fondly. "He was only a high school sophomore, but he constantly badgered me to get him a scholarship to Rutgers. For some reason that was his dream school. He harassed the shit out of me and was a complete pain in the ass."

The feeling was mutual. Pitino went to Friendship Farm with his entire St. Dominic's team. As was the custom, one coach stayed in the bunkhouse to supervise the campers, and Pitino got Garf. "Across from my bunk," Pitino says, "was this bizarre-looking guy, a tremendous guy, but we broke his balls constantly. We played our Motown records and he played Big Band music, and we'd ask him if he were doing it just to annoy us. He'd get all huffy and say real witty stuff, like 'Yeah, like you're trying to annoy me.' It was great."

Both sides would walk away mentally sticking their tongues out at each other, each thinking they'd won the moment. Little has changed, and to this day it remains a devoted, sticks-and-stones relationship. "He was a very smart player and a great scorer, but I love to kid him that he was a one-on-one dervish who couldn't finish his drives—and still can't," Garf says.

"At camp, Garf's team was horrible, as usual, and mine was in first place," counters Pitino, now the head coach at the University of Kentucky. "He had a hundred team meetings behind the bunkhouse and tried everything, but nothing worked. We used to love bugging him. One day we went through his suitcase and hung his clothes from the trees and windowsills and hid all his *HSBI* papers. When he came in, we pretended to be asleep and he snapped. From then on, though, everything was fine."

Garf had too many other things on his mind to be bothered with such silliness. He had a magazine to get out. Friendship Farm head coach Jim Herrion did what he could to help, licking envelopes and mailing them out to advertise it, but summer and then autumn came and went with no *HSBI*. In mid-January, 10 weeks late, it hit the stands.

The magazine contained 64 pages with color photos and the first non-newspaper story about schoolboy wonder Lew Alcindor, later known as Kareem Abdul-Jabbar. The timing was excellent. Alcindor was in the midst of leading Power Memorial to 71 straight wins, a streak soon to be halted by Morgan Wootten and DeMatha High. DeMatha had been knocked off the previous season, Alcindor's junior year, but in the winter of 1965 Wootten pulled one out of the hat.

Wootten had been around for awhile. He got started in the business at St. Joe's orphanage in Washington, D.C., taking over at DeMatha in 1956. Thirty-four years and more than 900 career wins later, he is still plugging and has become one of the four greatest coaches in America, according to Garf, right alongside UCLA wizard John Wooden, Princeton's Pete Carril, and Bob Knight. Getting ready for the rematch with Alcindor, Wootten told one of his players to stand on a chair during practice and swat shots away with a tennis racket. The rest was easy.

HSBI's feature article was on John Condon, the revered public address announcer at Madison Square Garden. The write-up was accompanied by a picture of Condon feigning sleep at the microphone during the infamous slow-down game between Roy Rubin's Columbus High team and virtually invincible Boys High, led by the incredible Connie Hawkins. "It was a much-talked-about game, and going into it Rubin said the only way to beat Hawkins was to hold the ball," Garf recalls. "That Boys High team was perhaps the greatest high school quintet ever, and Rubin thought the strategy was brilliant." The score at halftime was 8–3, but Boys High managed to up the tempo in the second half, winning 21–15.

The magazine's main thrust was a listing and an analysis of the players and teams in and around the city. Garf picked players he thought would star and highlighted their abilities. He broke down their strengths and weaknesses on defense, offense, attitude, and every other phase of their game. In addition, he made special note of any improvements they'd made since the end of the previous season. He also predicted which teams he thought would be the ones to beat in each league.

HSBI had taken eight months to assemble. It was professionally done from cover to cover, but with the season half over Garf felt certain it would be a tough sell. He was right. Fifty thousand copies were printed and twelve thousand got sold. The rest were heaved into the river by distributors who took 31 cents from the 50-cent cover price to circulate them in North Jersey. Garf and Paul Lizzo, a personal friend and an assistant to Roy Rubin, tried hand-delivering copies around the city, but many of the high schools, his major market, had lost interest.

There was one brief moment of exhilaration. "A day or so after the magazine was published, while Lizzo and I were still racing around trying to sell it, I went to a night game at East Side High in Paterson, New Jersey," Garf says. "The gym had a track running around the top like old-time courts used to have. I looked up at the kids leaning over the railing and every one of them had a copy. The feeling of conquest was thrilling, and dollar signs went off in my head. I soon found out it was only one school, but I will always have a warm spot in my heart for East Side High."

Halfway through his appointed rounds, thoroughly exhausted and frustrated, Garf hurled his watch against the side of a building. It shattered. Garf had reason to be discouraged. He barely broke even after paying the printer, Gene Chichura, his $1,000 and paying back his mother, who had fronted him $5,000 more. "When Howard tried to do his magazine, he went to his father's friends for help, but they weren't very solicitous," Mrs. Garfinkel recalls. "They weren't very nice about it. I guess they did not want to invest in something they would not get dividends from, but I think it would have worked out very well if they had.

"Howard stayed up all night working on his sheets about the players. Mr. Garfinkel couldn't get him up in the morning, and when he did get him down to the office he was very tired and evidently didn't do well. If Mr. Garfinkel had known Howard was going to be a success he might have respected him more, but he was very angry when he finally found out what Howard had been doing."

Stanley Garfinkel wasn't the only one upset. Paul Brandenburg, an assistant coach at Citadel, wasn't pleased with Garf either. Out of a job (he'd been fired from a travel agency for losing clients), thoroughly at odds with his father, and feeling totally defeated, Garf had decided to discontinue *HSBI*. Once was enough. Brandenburg told him he was making a mistake.

"Thank God for Paul Brandenburg," Garf says. "If it weren't for him, I'd probably be a bum sleeping in the streets. One night, early in the spring of 1965, I was sitting with him in his car. He was getting ready to go on a recruiting trip and had a copy of my magazine with almost every name circled. He said it was the greatest recruiting tool he'd ever seen." Completely by accident, Garf had created a Yellow Pages on the best players in the metropolitan region.

Brandenburg said rather than terminate the magazine, he should expand it. He should make it a "scouting service," a ready reference for coaches and recruiters that would give an in-depth evaluation of every quality high school player in the area. He was sure every college would buy into it. Garf consulted another friend, Seattle University assistant Vince Cazzetta, who agreed, saying he should charge each college $50. Garf mailed letters to several colleges and immediately received eight checks, including one from his loyal friend at Duke University, Vic Bubas.

"I knew if Bubas liked it, everybody would," Garf says. "Suddenly I had a fortune. Four hundred dollars. I felt rich, but I still had no job. To put a roof over my head and cake on the table, I figured I'd try again to do the camp." He went to Rubin a second time, spelling it out in detail. They could get ten coaches who would bring five or ten players each. The coaches could work with their own kids to gain an edge for their season, which would have to be their incentive for coming because Garf couldn't afford to pay them. And they would teach the game.

"Teaching was important, even back then," Garf says. "I wanted to emphasize it, but at the same time I didn't have any big dream of any giant camp. I was anticipating nothing. I was hoping we'd make a little money and have some fun in the sun."

Rubin balked. He liked the sound of it but said they needed a famous name to help sell it. Garf contacted Satch Sanders, in his third year with the Celtics, and got "a positive no." Sanders thought it would work, but he couldn't give it proper attention. Rubin, meanwhile, discussed the idea with Will Klein, his assistant at Columbus. Klein, a provident soul, worked summers as the head counselor at Camp Orin-Sekwa in upstate New York to help make ends meet. His dream was to run a summer camp.

Garf says, "Rubin and I talked again and he said, 'Kid, I been thinking it over and I think you've got something there. My assistant may have a place. Let's have a meeting.'" Rubin, Klein, Garf, and Estelle Kazer, the owner of Camp Orin-Sekwa, met that fall. They set the camp up for the following summer, running from the last week of August into early September, 1966.

"Kazer said it would cost us this much and that much and the food, she wasn't sure how much the food would cost, we'd just have to judge it by what everyone ate," Garf says. "She said she would show us the bills at the end of the week, and all I knew was we were going to have a basketball camp and I loved it."

TWO
All Aboard for Orin-Sekwa

"He gave me a look at myself I've never had before.
He saw something in me nobody else ever did.
He made me see it too. He made me believe it."

> – Judy Garland in *A Star is Born*

As things turned out, Garf ran the show. Will Klein made sure the show went on. Klein's quiet strength and common sense would become the substance of Five-Star. A decent man of few words, white-haired now, he never seemed to be around until he was needed.

Klein, born in Brooklyn and bred in the Bronx, was a playground rat, a weathered gym rat. He knew his place at the old Garden, the end balcony, never bumping into Garf there though their love of the game was equal. A 5'2", barely 100-pound teenager, he didn't make the basketball team at mighty DeWitt Clinton High but grew to 6'2" and learned to handle himself. He played some hoop and coached a little in the Army, later meeting his wife Vera at summer camp.

Before taking the teaching job at Columbus High, where he met Roy Rubin, Klein taught at a rough school in the South Bronx. Every so often he'd have to take the toughest kid in class out to the courts for a one-on-one whipping. He'd beat him, then tell everyone else he'd lost. The kid, most times, saw things differently after that.

Life wasn't quite as simple for Garf in the early part of 1966. He was scrambling for coaches and campers and it was, he recalls, "kinda slow going." He was getting worried. He would get that way a lot over the next 25 years.

Rubin, busy settling in at LIU and organizing a series of clinics he would give in Spain that summer, was largely indisposed. He didn't mind lending his name to the camp (it was called the Roy Rubin Basketball School for the first two years) or loaning his Blackbird players as counselors (mainly to let them practice together), but his only other contributions were Martin Van Buren coach Marv Kessler and Bronx Science coach Norm Lefkowitz.

Marv Kessler subscribed to the old school. He mixed a little "nareshkeit," Yiddish nonsense, in with his X's and O's, thinking it stuck better that way. After a shaky start, he'd stick around Five-Star a long time. A frizzy-headed Brooklyn brat, Kessler liked it when guys got on him about being the last great white point guard at bad-ass Boys High in Bedford Stuyvesant. "I was the only kid in the layup line who didn't dunk," Kessler says now. "As long as I fed Solly Walker and Sihugo Green, I stayed in the game though.

Kessler went to NC State on scholarship, getting significant minutes before injuring a disc. He felt guilty sitting the bench and talked his coach, Everett Case, into letting him scout upcoming opponents. He started to study the game seriously after that and hasn't stopped yet.

Kessler schlepped two pretty fair players, John Fosterbay and Ron Johnson, up to Orin-Sekwa, and his buddy Norm Lefkowitz brought along a half dozen more. Mike Cingiser, the coach at Lynbrook High on Long Island, promised a few players, and Dan Buckley, the coach at LaSalle Academy, was ready to deliver his two All-Americans, John Roche and big man Tommy Owens. The camp would definitely have quality but had to have quantity too.

Garf was suffering. Rubin and Klein had other pots in the fire, but this camp was it for him. If the venture failed, it meant going back to his father and meaningless jobs and nothing. Someone he barely knew granted him salvation.

* * * * *

Families aren't always the people we start out with. Paul Brandenburg was already a part of Garf's extended family, having encouraged him to start the successful *HSBI* scouting report. In the spring of 1966 he added another clansman. There was a coach in Fair Lawn, New Jersey, Brandenburg said, who was intense and intelligent and interested in the camp. His school was hosting the state tournament, and although his team wasn't good enough to be in it that year, he'd be there patrolling the premises. Garf should go and ask for Hubie Brown.

Garf had nothing to lose, so he went. When he got to the gym, he was pointed in the direction of a guy holding the restraining rope keeping kids off the court. He was an average-looking guy, but Garf sensed there was more to him than that. "You don't have to be a genius to tell about people," he says. "In about the first 10 seconds, just by the way he said hello and the way he was holding the rope, I could tell he had that little something extra."

Garf's passions were awakened in the presence of "that little something extra." It had been that way since the first time he saw Judy Garland perform. Even when he was a child she stirred something real inside of him, and he adored her from afar. "I have every record she ever made," he says. "When she died in 1969, I didn't play them for five years. I heard about her death while I was at camp. Tom Carmody, now the head coach at Rhode Island, told me. I remember it so clearly. I was on my way to the dining room and I went berserk, and immediately got depressed. I didn't want to work, but I had a camp to run.

"I went into the dining room and I was distraught. The campers were talking like they always did, but I told them to quiet down and they didn't do it fast enough. I could still hear their voices murmuring and it wasn't a good day for that. They wouldn't stop, so I went on a five-minute tirade about what, I don't even remember. If somebody had walked in off the street and heard me they'd have probably called the Section 8 squad from Bellevue."

Garland's artistry, as much as anything, was the inspiration behind Five-Star. For Garf, it was perhaps best symbolized in the film *A Star is Born*. Garland portrayed Vicki Lester, a small-time band singer with big-time dreams. Norman Maine, played by James Mason, was a fading matinee idol with connections. By chance he heard her sing in a roadhouse after hours and was profoundly moved. Garf, watching and listening as Maine revealed Lester's gift to her, was similarly affected:

Maine: "I've never heard anyone sing quite like you." Pausing, reaching for the right words, he went on. "Do you ever go fishing? Do you like prizefighting? Ever watched a great fighter?" Seeing her baffled, blank stare, he explained, "I'm trying to tell you how you sing."

Lester: "You mean like a prizefighter or a fish?"

Maine: There are certain pleasures that you get, little jabs of pleasure, when a swordfish takes the hook or when you watch a great prizefighter getting ready for the kill. See? You don't understand a word I'm saying, do you?"

Lester: "Not yet, why don't you try bullfights?"

Maine:	"You're joking, but that's exactly what I mean. If you'd never seen a bullfight in your life, you'd know a great bullfighter the moment he stepped into the ring, from the way he stood, the way he moved. Or a dancer. You don't have to know about ballet. That little bell rings inside your head. That little jolt of pleasure. Well, that's what happened to me just now. You're a great singer."
Lester:	Who, me?"
Maine:	"Hasn't anyone ever told you that before?"
Lester:	"No, not sober."
Maine:	"You've got that little something extra. That's what star quality is, that little something extra."

Similarly, Garf and Hubie Brown talked after everyone had gone home. "I told Hubie that Vic Bubas, who was still at Duke, was going to be our guest speaker and that we were charging $100 and all the rest and he wanted in," Garf says. By late June, however, Brown hadn't come across. "His kids were involved in a summer league, so I went there a couple of times to pick up the names and at the same time look at players for my HSBI report. It was a double-header.

"Hubie kept saying he's got the kids and he'll get the money, but he kept delaying, and I was starting to panic. We had a total of about 25 kids. One day an oversized manila envelope arrived from Fair Lawn with 24 checks. Overnight, we doubled our enrollment, and from nothing we had a camp. Hubie Brown saved the day."

The number rose to 61 by August. Garf got a handful of kids from another summer league being run on Long Island by Frank Morris, the head coach at St. Agnes in Rockville Center. "Coach Morris had a very nice league going and I would stop out there two or three nights a week to watch games and write kids up in HSBI," Garf says. "I did that for the first 10 years of the camp and was free to roam there and talk to the kids."

He also recruited Tommy Sullivan, an all-city center from St. Helena's in the Bronx, who was bringing a friend, Bobby Benson. Bernard Brown from Long Island City High was coming too. Bernard Brown was built like heavyweight boxer Mike Tyson, except he stood 6'6" and had a scar on his chest. He played like a little explosion, and on the court was as gentle as one of Tyson's punches. Bernard had one problem. He didn't like to get up early. He also liked to play only when he felt like it. He would make that perfectly clear in due time.

Robbie West was coming also and everyone wanted a piece of him. He was one of Garf's original fair-haired boys, the family favorite, although there would be countless others. West eventually did fine. He played for Duke and scored the winning basket against North Carolina the night the Blue Devils dedicated their new Cameron Indoor Arena. Garf did some crowing that night, but it had been a long time coming. By then it was West's senior year and he was finishing an up-and-down college career.

In later years he got into stocks and bonds, which made sense because as a kid his jumper was usually on the money. Nothing went according to plan for him at Orin-Sekwa. He seemed to be rushing his shot and clanging it off the rim a lot. "There's never been a nicer kid than Robbie West," Garf says. "We all thought he was the next coming of Jerry West. He had a beautiful jump shot. The first time I saw him he was making everything he put up, but I learned something. Like they say in the old song from *The Music Man*, 'You gotta know the territory.'

"West played at a great high school, Columbia in Maplewood, New Jersey, but his territory was all suburban white kids. He could get away from those guys easy. But I learned you had to take that and transpose it. In my mind, after that, I would put a quick guard on a player like West, maybe a black kid from the inner city, a street player. Maybe then I would see the kid not being able to get his shot off and I could better evaluate the level at which that kid could play. It took years of experience and not just with West, but that's how I became a good evaluator, the King of Guards. Since then, I've discovered more guards than work at Buckingham Palace."

He could have used some of them on opening night. Rubin was overseas and neither Garf nor Klein had been a head honcho before. They asked Vic Bubas to come early and help out. "Bubas told us he couldn't come early and that in fact he couldn't come at all," Garf says. "He wanted to know if it would be all right if he sent his assistant, Chuck Daly, whom he'd just hired out of Punxsutawney, Pennsylvania." Daly got there, but a day late.

Without a leader, Garf and Klein hoofed it. Klein took care of the niceties—meals, who slept where, homesick campers—and he also ran the canteen, the camp's snack bar. For the right price, campers could get candy, soda, chips, and, on good days, hot dogs and hamburgers. Civilized eats. Food would never be the camp's strong point, and as years passed old wives' tales spread about how Klein, with his frugality, ran the whole operation off his goodie wagon. Everyone was glad it was there, just the same.

Garf handled the nasties. "The camp almost ended the first night," he says. "At Friendship Farm, we had tryouts and I liked that. The coaches watched the players and put them in their right league, according to ability. I wanted to have four 'Pro Division' (NBA) teams for the better players and four 'College Division' teams for the rest, so we had tryouts and held our first draft."

It was the dawning of a Five-Star tradition. All the coaches were there: Kessler, Lefkowitz, Buckley, Cingiser, Brown, and a sixth guy, Gordie Van Buren. In search of an indoor gym for bad weather, Garf and Klein had gone to the local school, Ichabod Crane Central, where Van Buren was the coach and athletic director. He said OK and liked the idea of the camp so much that he joined up. Some of the city slickers figured they'd gotten a country bumpkin, but his Ichabod Crane teams were in the middle of a 12-year stretch as local league champions. What's more, Van Buren won an NBA title at camp before all was said and done, so he was nothing to sneeze at.

Things were going from bad to worse at the draft. "It was going fine until we started getting to Lefkowitz's players," Garf says. "We'd toss a kid's name out and everyone would vote which league he should be in. Every time we'd vote one of Lefkowitz's kids into the college division, he'd raise a fuss, saying, 'No no, no, he's got to be in the NBA. That's why I brought him here, to get some competition.' You gotta understand, Normie was a great coach, but Bronx Science was an academic school. You had to be a genius to get in there. He really had no players.

"Nobody minded what he was doing, but I was starting to cringe every time a Bronx Science kid came up. They weren't good enough for the NBA and I was getting worried about having the right break-down for the leagues. The idea of this camp was equal competition and I was adamant about that. We weren't even picking teams yet, but it was getting annoying because it was obvious some of these guys weren't there for the right reasons. The purpose wasn't for anyone to just work with their own kids. We all wanted that, but the bigger goal was to teach basketball to everybody, not just worry about your own five guys.

"Kessler was voting with Lefkowitz because they kind of came together and Buckley didn't care who played where as long as his guys were in the NBA, which was no problem. Roche and Owens were great players. Hubie was a little intemperate, but he didn't argue until we got to Brendan Suhr, a sophomore, one of his better players. I read off his name and Lefkowitz says, 'College division, college division' and Hubie got pissed. He said his Brendan Suhr was better than all Lefkowitz's players and should be in the NBA, tapping the table for emphasis, and it was starting to get heated.

"I tried to settle everyone down, and Suhr was just a sophomore so Hubie gave in. I agreed with Hubie, but I was panicking by then because we needed guys in the college division or we wouldn't have a good camp. We got to the end and there were two names left. We needed them both in the college division, but one of them was a Bronx Science kid.

"Lefkowitz says, 'No, no, he's my fifth guy, he has to be in the NBA,' and that was it for Hubie. He and Lefkowitz got into it hot and heavy and stood up and there was almost a fight. I tried to calm them down again, but Lefkowitz said something like 'I don't need the aggravation of this freaking camp,' and grabbed Kessler and they both went to their rooms and slammed their doors. They were packing their bags and leaving. They were out.

"Everyone was in shock. Hubie was simmering and I'm dying, because all I can think is that Rubin is going to show up in two days and those guys are going to be gone. The camp is going to be over and if that happens my life is over. I might as well leave the country. As it was, I got a hell of a verbal lashing when Rubin showed up. Naturally it was my fault, but what did I do?

"Luckily, Buckley, whom everybody liked, could make a hell of a frozen daiquiri. He knocked on their doors and brought those guys out and gave everybody a couple of strong ones. Lefkowitz and Hubie were half-drunk but they shook hands and the camp was saved. The next day we went to work."

*   *   *   *   *

No one ever said Camp Orin-Sekwa was made for basketball. Stuck off County Route 28 in Niverville, down a potholed dirt road, it was 30 minutes and light years away from Albany. Built in 1927 as an all-boys camp, Estelle Kazer's family bought it in 1959 and the next year made it coed. When the Five-Star pioneers arrived, there were two regulation courts, miniature by today's standards, a converted shuffleboard court for one-on-one games, and the Orin Rec Hall.

The Rec Hall, a quonset-hut-shaped structure, was plenty long enough for hoops but sadly squeezed for space on the sidelines. Fortunately, it stayed sunny all week, sparing campers the indignity of putting one leg up on the wall, doggie-style, to inbound the basketball. Campers slept in cabins scattered throughout the property, cooling off in milkweed-edged Knickerbocker Lake.

There is no Orin-Sekwa today. It is now 15 rental residences the Kazer family hopes to turn into a retirement community. The original dining hall was declared a hazard and torched by the local fire department in the mid-eighties. The cabins are boarded shut. There is only the wind whistling through rusted metal backboards, and cracked blacktop courts, everywhere overgrown and weeded-in, except in the lane. It is perpetually bare in the paint, the Five-Star war zone.

* * * * *

By the time Chuck Daly arrived, the camp was in full swing. He got into the flow quickly as its first guest lecturer. "Orin-Sekwa was awful," Daly says now. The coach of the 1989 NBA champion Detroit Pistons, Daly is Garf's friend and still a frequent Five-Star visitor and lecturer. "It was cold and there were spiders on the ceilings and snakes in the bushes. I remember my first lecture was about offensive basketball. I remember talking about the violent pump fake, which was a key phrase in coaching back then.

"Camps were new to the basketball world, but we all knew Garf had been in touch with all the best players since the beginning of mankind, so there'd be some great talent there. It hasn't changed in that regard. When I go there now I go just for an hour or two to speak, but in the beginning I spent the whole week. At night we'd get a couple of bottles of wine or whatever. We had some great times."

Out on the courts, something unforeseen was happening. Nobody had expected it or was even aware it could occur, but hitherto ungathered forces were colliding and taking a shape of their own. Everybody knew that West and Roche and Bernard Brown and the rest would be intense, but no one expected every single camper to be that way. They were feeding off each other.

It seemed normal enough at the start. Borrowing the Friendship Farm setup, everyone assembled for morning and afternoon lectures on offense or defense and afterwards the coaches went over them in greater depth with their teams. Every camper played three games a day and the rest of the time was their own to take a dip in Knickerbocker Lake or do some bird-watching. Typical camp stuff.

"The premise was just playing games," recalls Hubie Brown, who is still very much a part of Five-Star, "but what happened was all that great talent wanted to be coached. It wanted to be harnessed."

It was as if the talent were floating above the courts waiting to be gathered in and molded. The air was electric. As soon as the kids walked on the court they could feel it and so could the coaches. It swept everyone up and slowly transformed them.

"It was amazing how much talent there was, and the coaches soaked up that great talent and worked with it," Brown says. "The coaches were all outstanding teachers. The better players started to really push each other, competing hard, and the other kids were forced to develop their individual games to survive in that atmosphere. The ego factor of the coaches also started to become a pulse beat of the camp. It was not only who would be the best player, but also who would be the best teacher, the best coach. That fostered enthusiasm and forced the kids to respond. Everyone was forced to excel."

Forced. Two abounding energies melding and changing, like igneous rock masses coming together with nowhere to go but up. It was unusual and no one was sure where it would lead, but it was custom-made for Hubie Brown. "Even as a high school coach, I used to get annoyed at guys who didn't pay attention to their good players, didn't prepare them for the next level," he says. "Kids from systems like that would come to camp, especially in later years but that first year too, thinking they just had to do their thing to get by. They were forced to learn. For many of them, the camp would be the only true coaching they'd ever get. We gave them the opportunity to be coachable, *forced* them to be coachable.

"Another bone-crushing thing with me were the coaches who would send a kid to a college where he was going to receive the biggest bonus, the car, the biggest monthly payment, the apartment, the clothes, or whatever it took to get him there. He was back on the same corner he came from, and I can't just lump black kids in there, although you hear about them more today. It happened to white kids too. The camp tried to make kids aware of that."

There had never been anything like it before and Bernard Brown wanted no part of it. The burly fella could tolerate the accommodations and didn't mind the brutal basketball—it was the frequency of the games and falling out of bed before noon that bothered him. On the second day of camp, he decided not to show up for his night game. There was nothing in the bylaws to cover it, so Garf and Hubie Brown played it by ear.

"The word is he's tired and in his cabin, so Hubie and I went to get him and he's there lying on his bunk," Garf recalls. "I'll never forget it. This guy is an enforcer on the court, but he's also kind of a pain in the rear end, so Hubie says to him, 'C'mon baby, you've got a big game' and Bernard says, 'Man, you don't understand. I can't play three games a day. My body won't take it. I play hard.'

"Hubie says, 'We told you about that before you got here,' and Bernard says, 'Yeah, but you don't understand. Did you ever hear of a guy named Tynberg? Ever hear of the Gems? Yeah, well look, man, I play for the Gems and Tynberg pays me five dollars a game, and I ain't coming to no camp and playing three games a day for nothin'.'

"Hubie was shocked. He stormed off, and Bernard never did

show up for the game. Hubie traded him for Tom Owens, which has to be one of the biggest robberies since the Brinks Job. Bernard ended up leaving early, and just before he left, he said, 'If I wanted to die, I wouldn't have come to camp.'

"The funny thing is, he ended up having a good college career. I didn't see him for 22 years, then in the spring of 1989 I got a phone call from him. He wanted to send his son to Five-Star, and he didn't even know it was my camp. It was still the Roy Rubin School when he was there. We had a nice talk, and I got to meet him at the bus station, sending his son off, and he was an absolutely fantastic person. I couldn't believe it was the same guy, he was so far from that first image. He appeared a little disabled, though. He was a transit cop and became a hero stopping a holdup."

The rest of the campers managed to last it out. Tommy Sullivan, now an assistant coach at Seton Hall, vividly recalls the final day of that first week. He and his buddies Roche and Owens, both bound for the University of South Carolina and professional careers, still had Garf's wrath ringing in their ears. A few days earlier they'd pulled the first heist in camp history, raiding a nearby apple orchard in the moonlight.

"The farmer figured it had to be those crazy boys from the camp," Sullivan says. "He told Garf he hadn't seen their faces, but one of them had feet a long way from his knees. We tried to hide him, but Garf knew it was Owens. It was hard to hide a 6'11" kid. The most memorable thing for me, though, was listening to Hubie Brown speak. He was so energetic. Every kid wanted to hear him. You could hear a pin drop when he talked."

Brown wasn't supposed to be the closing speaker. That honor belonged to Roy Rubin, who'd returned from Spain. At Garf's behest he gave up his spot to a relative novice. "Mike Cingiser pointed out that Hubie hadn't done a lecture," Garf says. "I'd seen him coach and liked that, but I didn't know if he could lecture. I wasn't a big fan of lectures. Most of them bored me, like they probably still do the campers, but it was the only way to get into teaching.

"I had heard maybe one guy, Al Lobalbo, do a lecture I liked. That was in the late fifties at a summer coaching clinic being run at Adelphi College by the head coach, George Faherty. To my knowledge it was the first clinic of its type, and today there are thousands patterned after it all over the world. Faherty asked me to get some players together to use for demonstration purposes. It was like an all-star game after a while, and coaches would come not just for the clinic, but to watch the players too.

"Lobalbo, now an assistant at St. John's, did a lecture one year on defense called 'Ball, You, Man.' Anyone who heard it copied his style, and listening to him thrilled me, really. I didn't get that feeling again until I heard Hubie Brown. The first time, though, I was afraid he might bore the campers. On the other hand, he'd brought 24 kids and saved the camp, so I figured he could do any damn thing he wanted.

"Usually everybody sat on the ground casually leaning back on the fences, but that morning I was eating breakfast and I could see Hubie and Cingiser setting up some benches in an L-shape. I thought to myself, 'Oh, oh, we've got a production going on,' but right away I knew there was some thinking going on, some organization. That was my first inkling this might be better than I thought.

"So he starts with his six one-on-one moves in dramatic fashion, doing the jab step, the rocker step—and he's unbelievable. It was like watching a Fred Astaire choreography. It's hard to explain but it gave me goosebumps. Hubie spoke for two minutes and I just knew it was there. The way he's moving, his voice. It's something you never heard before."

Midway through, Brown had his cheek split open by Kessler's kid, John Fosterbay. Lecturers used campers to demonstrate points, demanding they take it seriously. Fosterbay did. Clearing space on a rebound, he nailed Brown, who was wearing sunglasses, with an errant elbow. Brown needed stitches but waited. "I didn't want to sit down. I was thinking this might be my only opportunity to speak to a group of kids with this kind of talent," he says.

Hundreds of lectures later, he hasn't forgotten that fleeting chance. Brown's career took off after that first summer. He became an assistant at William & Mary College, then Duke. He was an assistant with the NBA Milwaukee Bucks and as a head coach won an ABA title and rebuilt the NBA Atlanta Hawks and New York Knicks. Corporations and basketball clinics wait in line for his services as a motivational speaker today and he provides color analysis for network TV college and NBA games. He remembers how he got there.

"It's an old story. You can have all the ability in the world, but if you only stay in your own little cubbyhole, no one knows about you," Brown says. "I have a hard time with coaches who have benefitted from their exposure at Five-Star and who have now made it so-called big and don't understand where their exposure came from. Their egos can say they had that talent all along but the opportunity came about because of Five-Star; whether they want to say Howard Garfinkel or Will Klein gave them that opportunity, the Five-Star family gave them that opportunity and that's what it's all about."

In ways not expected, the campers benefitted too. "Over the

years we've had great players come from Five-Star who never panned out, who've been shot, or overdosed, who broke coaches' hearts and got coaches fired," says Brown. "But there have been a lot of guys who got to college on scholarships and got their degrees. Some got to the pros, but more important, they got to go to college. Free. To me, Five-Star will always stand for that first year of the camp. When it was over, Howard got three kids from Wingate High School into junior college. He gave them a chance to get an education, something they never imagined being able to do."

It wasn't the last dream Garf would enter. His word, his positive or negative input on a player, had begun to carry considerable weight. There was no schoolyard too big or too small for him to check out. Mainstream recruiters, on the other hand, in those days were often afraid to infiltrate the troubled inner cities and had overlooked three of coach Jack Kaminer's Wingate players, all from Bedford Stuyvesant. Garf knew their every waking move.

"He was not in the limelight, but a lot of kids were very thankful to have someone like Garf to count on," Kaminer says now. "He helped a lot of kids that otherwise would have been passed by." Sam Samuel, Ron Louder, and Eddie Agard went to Ellsworth Community College in Iowa. Samuel transferred to the University of Texas El Paso where he was teamed in the backcourt with Nate "Tiny" Archibald. Louder moved on to Rhode Island. Agard shipped out to Hawaii where he set an assist record. Those three, and five others Garf helped, Vernon Cowan, Bernard Hardin, Antonio Lewis, Robert Murphy, and Mo Rivers, all graduated.

None of this was helping Garf's wallet. "I wasn't making anything with *HSBI* yet, even though more schools were subscribing, so at the end of the week we went to Estelle Kazer to collect our money," he says. "I'm thinking this is my big chance to get rich. We knew what the rental was and we figured we'd make about $1,000 each. Then she hit us with the food bill and we went nuts. The bottom line is we divided $993 three ways: Rubin, Klein, and I got $331 each.

"Klein and I worked our asses off for that and I'm thinking, 'There's no money to be made in this business.' Then I start to figure, 'Maybe if we get a hundred kids next time,' but the place isn't big enough and besides Kazer wants to charge us a thousand dollars to blacktop some ground for a new court. We decided to leave there. Klein talked to a friend of his, Hank Jacobsen, then the head coach of DeWitt Clinton High, who also worked as a regular counselor every summer at Orin-Sekwa. Jacobsen knew about another camp, Camp Rosemont, somewhere in Pennsylvania. He said it would fit our needs, so that's where we went."

THREE

Rumbling into Rosemont

"You had to want to find the place. The only way in was by private plane, and then to get back out you had to go by way of New Jersey."

– Al McGuire remembering Camp Rosemont

Camp Rosemont took some getting used to, but for the next nine summers it would be home for Five-Star, which was still known as Roy Rubin's baby although that would soon change. Other things never changed.

Dear old Camp Rosemont. It got into your bloodstream. Hilly, rolling Route 371 took you most of the way there if you couldn't afford air fare. From the east and the city, you passed through towns like Damascus, where common sense tells you how Hillside Cemetery got its name. It was common sense country and neighborly too, with signs in the front yards telling you everyone in the family's first name, not just their last. It was beautiful country, where clean, wild, mountain lakes suddenly leaped at you, like flushed-out partridges, from the Pennsylvania thickets.

Harry Silverman ran the place, which was tucked in the upper right-hand corner of the state, on the northern fringe of the Poconos. It was built in 1926 alongside Rose Lake, which was called Rose Pond until somebody changed it for the advertising brochure. Across the lake was Camp Summit, a girls' camp. On rainy days Harry bused Garf's kids over there to the dry gym. Harry kept things going for years before finally selling out, and he died in the mid-eighties. Local people swear that when the wind is right, they still hear Harry and his bulldozer out howling at one o'clock in the morning trying to get Rosemont ready for Five-Star.

There was a lot to do, and Harry didn't always keep up. The bunkhouses tended to lean as if they were rectangles turned triangular. The road leading in from the main highway was rutted from years of spring rains, and it was dark and downright scary, especially for the city kids. And it wasn't Harry's fault, but the nighttime air tended to linger, mountainous and frosty, until almost mid-day.

"It was a real trip with him," Garf says. "He was a very good man and very interested in the kids. He spent time with them. He loved basketball and would sit in the stands and watch the games, but it was very difficult, very hard to make any money with him. In the dining room the napkins were stapled together at each table. They were counted out to make sure everybody got one and don't even ask for a second one. It was like you were stealing from him.

"The gym, it was like a barn really, was on a slant. Every year we had to crawl in and put wooden planks under the floor. It kept collapsing. It was unbelievable. There was a huge fireplace at one end and a stage at the other end. The roof beams hung down and Eddie Biedenbach, who coached at Davidson at one time, used to demonstrate rafter shots off them. There were no overhead lights, only little side lights. Robert Parish of the Boston Celtics was a counselor that year and he played there. It was like watching him play in candlelight."

Despite the lack of modern conveniences, the enrollment doubled. The ubiquitous Garf, simultaneously scouting summer leagues for his *HSBI* report and recruiting players for camp, was meeting more people, making more connections. He was proficient and possessed. He had no car then or now—"I might be the only person left in America who can't drive," he says—so it was not unusual for him to walk blocks or miles in the snow and sleet and then change buses twice to arrive at some remote high school to see one player, like Chris Ford, the current assistant coach of the Boston Celtics.

There was method in his madness. He was still selecting players for the Dapper Dan Classic and needed one representative from New Jersey. "I'd gotten a tip about a kid in Abescon whom I'd never seen," Garf says. "It might have been my last chance, because Ford's team was in the state semifinals, so I made the horrendous trip. Maybe I was nuts, but I always wanted to make sure I got the right kid. It was worthwhile. I picked him."

Such ardent fervor inevitably attracted young Dave Pritchett, a madcap recruiter's recruiter, but that was yet to pass. For the time being, news of the camp was still spreading. "In the beginning we just tried to do everything right. When we started out, don't forget, we didn't know what we were doing. If we were total businessmen, we could have made double the money, but we weren't. Most summer camps were six days, but we had an eight-day camp, which was crazy. When you're paying by the head, every day can add up, but the kids were coming and we figured that was one reason why. They knew they were getting their money's worth.

"The college coaches being there the first couple of years, watching the games, helped put the camp on the map too. We had clocks, score sheets, shirts, everything. The only thing we wouldn't do was put the kids' names on the shirts. We didn't want to become a meat market. The intent wasn't to showcase players, even though that happened along the way. We wanted to be a basketball camp, not a meat market. The early success, I would say, was due to the players, their names, and the competition.

"Also, we tried to be organized." Being organized meant one thing—that Will Klein was entrenched in bookwork. It was only one week and less than 100 campers per summer, but Klein was laying the groundwork for what would eventually become seven weeks and nearly 3,000 campers every year. "Howard had no head for numbers," Klein says, humbly. There was also Silverman to dicker with, as well as contracts to negotiate, transportation arrangements to make, and little things, lots of little things. Klein did them all expertly, keeping the camp solvent.

* * * * *

Making it past the first night was never easy. The draft had begun to assume legendary proportions. Garf mediated as best he could, but that second year there were rumors that someone stuffed the hat, trying to steal the first pick, and there were claims that somebody, no one was saying who, was telling kids to dog it at tryouts. They should try to look bad so nobody would notice them and when the time was right, that unmentionable somebody would pick them like a ripe peach.

It went on like that for hours, and around three in the morning Garf tried to break it up so Claire and Hubie Brown—coaches brought their families in those days—could celebrate their wedding anniversary. A beautiful white cake had been bought, but the coaches, like rabbis in Talmudic discussion, gazes fixed and hands jabbering, never noticed.

The quarreling carried over to the games. No one could keep the clock right, of course, especially in the precious closing seconds of a tight game, and there were accusations of fraud. Every kid in camp played two quarters a game. There would never be any leeway there, but sometimes the teams had an odd number of players, seven or nine, so every team was allowed a "horse." A big gun. The franchise player. He could stay in all day as long as everybody else got their minutes, or he could go in for anyone who got hurt or fouled out, which of course gave rise to stories of faked sprains and inexplicable blatant pushes in front of the referees.

It was family, though, and things got hashed out, which is still the way it's done after 25 years. Everything was fine when Al McGuire arrived to lecture. McGuire had heard about the place and didn't expect much, but he was pleasantly surprised. "Before Garf came along, there were more token, specialty camps where you built birdhouses out of popsicle sticks and spent an hour a day on basketball," McGuire says. "His was the first true thoroughbred camp. It was legit.

"There was a gunslinger type of thing going on there, to find out who was the best and who just thought they were. And his camp allowed fresh air to blow into the Boys Club level, giving a lot of young guys who would have been lost in the playgrounds an opportunity for broader exposure.

"It's a new world today and there are not as many sleepers, but there is still an undercurrent of conversation at conventions. Whenever guys from Tark to PJ to Pitino talk about players, the name Garf comes up. There's an old saying that 'When the genius is in the fool's home, the fool is always the smartest' and you can never be sure with someone, but Garf knows young talent. His seal of approval definitely moves a kid from Division III or Division II to Division I, and his lack of approval can move a kid down.

"If anyone has not been well known in the game, been like a shadow, it's been Garf. He lives for the summer. When he walks around the camp, he's like a Frank Sinatra in his day or even like a Tom Cruise today. That is his turf. His stage. He doesn't want each session to end. He doesn't want each day to end."

Those feelings of wanting the camp to go on endlessly had been welling up in Garf, maybe since Camp Mascoma, maybe since the YMCA team had given him that unforgettable chill. He was putting his heart into this camp like nothing before. He would watch the campers as they listened to Al McGuire or Hubie Brown speak. He would watch their eyes. "Their eyes would be on the guy, reacting," he says. "They would be paying total attention. They were enjoying it, getting something out of it. I don't know if it was pleasure, but they were learning in an enjoyable way.

"They were getting that and I was producing it for them. That was a pleasure for me, and it is a little selfish thing too because it is a nice feeling watching the kid you helped do something good for himself later on, and if you can go through life with that nice feeling every three or four days, what's wrong with that?

"I would like my epitaph to read, 'Five-Star: He—and they—worked every session as if it would be their last.' If the camp ended in the middle of next summer, I would want it to be the best session in the history of Five-Star. I learned that by watching the great ones, great singers like Judy Garland. When she did a concert there were no throwaways. She sang every song like it was her last, and all the great players and coaches and lecturers at Five-Star leave their guts on the court that same way."

* * * * *

Roy Rubin was more interested in trophies. "A lot of the glamour was starting to wear off him," Garf says. "The last day of camp that year, it was raining and it was impossible, busing kids around, and the mud. I was drenched and hadn't shaved in three days. Klein was doing all the inside stuff, and everybody was working their asses off, everybody except Rubin. He just wanted to lecture and have fun.

"We weren't getting along at all. I walked into the gym, exhausted, and it was loaded with kids and there were balls flying all over the place, but Rubin was just sitting there. There was an old upright piano at one end of the gym, and on top of it were the trophies we were going to give to the Most Valuable Player in each league. As I walked past Rubin he barked, 'Kid, get those trophies off the piano before some balls hit them and break them!' He'd seen them there for at least a half hour, so I said a few things to him, and told him if he was so worried about the damn trophies, he should move them himself—but I knew that was it."

It wasn't like it hadn't been brewing. Rubin had never given his blessing to Garf's "outside basketball" activities, despite making the most of them. He'd always shied away from congregating with Garf and his spook sidekicks at the old Garden cafeteria, preferring to meet at Rudley's, a less-haunted coffee shop up the block. He had even gone so far as to keep Garf's name off the camp brochure the first two years, something Garf says didn't bother him that much. "I wasn't doing it for the ego thing, and besides everyone who went knew I was involved."

More than anything, it was that dratted *Sports Illustrated* article that never stopped eating at Rubin. Garf had been embarrassed by it himself, stunned actually. It had come out in the late fifties, and it was about college basketball's "Underground Railroad": the recruiting train taking New York City and New Jersey kids south, mainly to what is now the Atlantic Coast Conference. Garf and his friends were the conductors.

"It exposed the so-called nefarious characters, which we really weren't, who scouted for those schools," he says. "Larry Pearlstein was doing it for Maryland, Mike Tynberg worked for Marquette, and Harry Gotkin scouted for Frank McGuire at North Carolina. McGuire got all the Catholic school kids. All he had to do was touch them and they'd kneel. Walter November scouted for Loyola of Chicago."

And there was Fred Steigman, who worked the marketplace, the back alleys. It was said that if you needed a player he'd shop around, barter a little here, deal a little there, and find you something. For two dollars he could get you a nice little point guard. Then you had to have a center to go with him, maybe a tall, skinny boy from a good family who could go strong to his right. For ten dollars, he was yours. Oh, if you wanted him to go both ways and maybe get you some rebounds too, well, that would cost you twenty.

"Steigman may have taken a dime or two in his day, but compared to what goes on today he was like a puppy dog," Garf says. "Why did we do it? It was an obsession. For me, it was thrilling to be involved with people who, in my mind, were bigger than life. We did it for the love of the school too. For years, when NC State lost I didn't sleep and when they won I was euphoric. I got attached and became attached to the players I recruited."

The *Sports Illustrated* deal started after Garf got a call from a friend of his, Aldo Leone, a waiter at Leone's Restaurant and a third cousin of the famed Mama Leone. Garf liked Aldo. He'd coached in the Daily Mirror League, an outside league with teams a step slower than Garf's Nationals, until he got tired of it. His English was a little weak in spots, so Garf and Vic Bubas used to love teasing him about it. They would eat at Aldo's place and ask him if he'd gotten back into coaching. "I'm not interesting in basketball anymore," Aldo would always say.

Aldo had gotten in touch with Garf to tell him about a Columbia University student who was doing a term paper on recruiting. The kid, Dick Schaap, wanted to follow Garf and his Nationals around for a week or two to get a feel for the territory. "I met Schaap and he was a nice, personable kid, so I said yes and over the next few weeks we became very close," Garf says. "He'd stay at my place sometimes and we would talk about the business and his project."

When the term paper showed up as a feature article in *Sports Illustrated,* Garf knew it wasn't just dumb luck. He started to put two and two together and figured that had to be Schaap's plan the whole time. The article had photographs of Garf and Tynberg and the rest of the Underground Railroaders standing in the lobby at Madison Square Garden and he didn't remember posing for them. Schaap got a nice job with the *Herald Tribune* shortly after that and later became a mover and shaker working in major network television. Garf came out looking all right in the article and was mildly amused, but the experience left a bad taste in his mouth for the print media.

Schaap, aside from the clever disguise, had slipped up on a very important detail, in Garf's opinion. One of Garf's best players at the time was York Larese, who played for Lou Carnesecca at St. Ann's Academy (which later became Archbishop Molloy) on his way to the University of North Carolina. Garf liked Larese. Not only was he good for 30 points a night, he was a good kid.

One night after the Nationals won a tournament, the three of them went out for a victory dinner and Larese caught sight of an unusual pen Garf had in his pocket. "It was a white pen with three ink fills with red, green, and black ink," Garf says. "You pressed down whichever color you wanted and it would write that color. It was a novelty back then and Larese said, 'What a great pen; I'd love to have one of those.'

"I had two of them so I said, 'Anything for you, Yorky, you're the greatest and you're my friend,' and I gave him one. That was the first thing I'd given him in all that time. He had played for me three years and I gave him a pen he liked. One single, solitary pen. In his story, Schapp recounted the dinner and he got it fine until the last sentence. He told about the pen but quoted me as saying, 'Anything for a basketball player,' and that's not what I said or meant. There's a big difference."

The whole thing gave Roy Rubin the heebie-jeebies. Garf could live with that and he could overlook his lack of involvement in the camp's daily affairs, but something had to give when Rubin hassled him about the Sammy Davis, Jr. charity basketball game. It wasn't the game that Rubin objected to as much as Garf having asked one of his star Long Island University players, Larry Newbold, to take part.

Garf originally organized the Sammy Davis, Jr. game with Dick Vitale, who was a long way from where he is now. They'd met when Vitale was coaching a high school team in East Rutherford,

New Jersey. Garf heard him speak at a banquet, felt that little jolt, and told him he belonged elsewhere. He passed the word around to his friends and Vitale landed an assistant's job at Rutgers University. Vitale, a vital voice in college basketball announcing today, says, "If someone doesn't open doors for you, you can stay right where you are. Garf opened doors for me."

Garf, Vitale, and a friend of Vitale's, Tom Ramsden, wanted to raise money for a New Jersey kid who'd been named after the famous song-and-dance man. He needed artifical limbs because he'd had an accident in which he'd been pinned by a train. The fund raiser worked out well and they kept it going for years. Pros like Willis Reed and Earl Monroe of the Knicks, Wes Unseld of the Bullets, Calvin Murphy of the Houston Rockets, and Julius Erving of the Philadelphia 76ers always made it their business to show up.

Larry Newbold played in the game in 1967, a few weeks before camp got started. "Rubin was out of the country, but when he got back and found out, he went berserk," Garf says. "Newbold had already graduated. I'd helped recruit him for Rubin, but that didn't matter. I could sit outside Newbold's home for hours waiting for him to show up to talk to him and I could personally deliver a kid from New Jersey he'd never heard of, Cliff Culuko, who became one of his better players, but whatever else I did was wrong.

"I could do things for Rubin, but it all had to be private. It couldn't be talked about because I was the nefarious and infamous recruiter. He did nothing to help me with what I was doing, except lend his name to the camp, but my name couldn't go on the brochure with his. I guess deep down it did bother me. I was supposed to be loyal to him and be in his corner, but he was never in mine."

In the rickety gym, in the rain, at Rosemont, it all fell apart. The two old friends parted bitterly and haven't spoken since. Five-Star's gestation period was over.

FOUR

Meet Me at the Stations

"The food was terrible. I may never have eaten worse food."

                    – Bob Knight remembering Rosemont

The split with Rubin was painful for Garf. It wasn't exactly easy for Will Klein. He'd kept Garf and Rubin apart for two years and suddenly had to make a choice. He liked running the camp. It fulfilled his fantasy. Besides, they'd cleared $1,000 each that summer and the future looked promising. He'd taken over Rubin's head coaching job at Columbus High and they were friends. Rubin told him the camp wasn't a priority with him, that he was thinking of starting his own anyway, and that Klein should do whatever felt right.

Thinking about it, Klein realized he and Garf might make it work. They had their moments. They would argue vehemently, usually about something minor, like the file cards that listed every camper's name, age, school, position, and whatever. Klein wrote them all. He still does. In a rush sometimes, he'd type the name too close to the corner. If something got stapled to it, the name would get blocked and Garf would holler. He still does. He's a fanatic for detail.

They didn't always see things eye-to-eye, but there was an undeniable chemistry between them. "Howard has his share of flaws, I can tell you that," Klein says. "Generally when he yells, something else is bothering him. We talk it out. I've never said he doesn't work hard. No one puts in 24 hours like he does. Howard does everything he can for the kids and always had a knack for making each person feel like he was the reason the camp worked. There was a loyalty that developed."

It worked both ways. "Will Klein is the greatest partner a human being can have because he is exceedingly intelligent and does his job," Garf says. "We don't interfere too much in each other's end and never did. I am shabby and disorganized when it comes to finances, and if it weren't for Will, the camp would have gone under a long time ago. People joke about him being too thrifty, but all the money goes through him and if it didn't, there'd be no camp because I'd have absconded the funds or screwed it up somehow."

Perfect mom and pop ownership. Next, the store needed a name. Gil Glass, a scout for Rhode Island University and fellow aficionado of the game, came up with one. "We were sitting in a car one night after a game. It seems like I was always in a car going somewhere to scout. I told Glass I needed a name," Garf recalls. "He thought for a minute and said, 'There's five guys on a team, right? And all of them are stars in a way, right?'

"I said 'Yeah' and it sounded good and then I had a flash. The first two years of my *HSBI* scouting report, I'd rated players as having either major college or small college potential. That was the way all the recruiters and magazines did it back then.

"The third year I realized that wasn't right because there were levels within each level and then pluses and minuses within each different level. UCLA and Yale were both major college teams, but if they played 50 times, UCLA would win by 30 points every time. This was when UCLA was in the middle of their incredible run of 10 NCAA titles in 12 years.

"I invented a new system using stars. I made any kid that I thought had the potential to contribute to a Division III team by his sophomore year a one-star player. A good Division II or small Division I player got two stars. The big-time Division I programs, the perennial NCAA Tournament teams, I broke down into three categories.

"Colleges like Yale were low-major. Players who could go there and contribute were three stars. Then there was a level between Yale and UCLA, mid-major, and those kids got four stars. The best big-time players, kids who could contribute to a perennial Division I Top Twenty team, got five stars.

"It became the standard in the business. After that, all the best prospects became known as five-star players. Also, borrowing the idea from then-NYU head coach Lou Rossini, I started using terms like 'point guard' and 'off-guard,' 'power forward' and 'small forward' to describe the positions of the players in more detail. Before that, everyone was just a guard or a forward. Those terms are part of everyday basketball lingo nowadays, but I had no clue that would happen sitting there that night. Glass said that Five-Star would be the perfect name for the camp. Combine five stars on a team and a five-star rating in *HSBI*."

Five-Star. "I called Klein the next day and told him the idea. He didn't give a damn as long as we got kids. I was still dreaming that maybe someday we'd have 300 kids and make $5,000 a week."

The camp was becoming more widely known, and Garf's reputation as a country-fair evaluator was no longer in doubt. *HSBI* had grown from eight subscribers to over 100. It peaked at 200, paying $200 apiece, all of which left Garf feeling nervous and irritated.

Déjà vu. "I felt we needed a head coach, a name guy, a draw. I felt neither Will Klein nor I had enough stature to run it right. The logical guy was Bob Knight. He was tremendously respected by the inner circle of coaches. He could lead and he was a figure the kids would respect. That's what we needed in camp." Knight, in seven days, transformed Five-Star from a street camp into the best teaching camp on the planet. There had been learning going on with Hubie Brown and the other coaches, but it was still raw. Knight refined it and gave it more direction.

Garf and Knight first began running into each other during the formative years of *HSBI*. They crossed paths on the circuit for some time before being formally introduced by a mutual friend, Bob Lapidus. Dismissing his defeat at Friendship Farm as "something only Howard could remember," Knight says. "Back in the early sixties, Bob Lapidus was about the only guy who really knew the names of a lot of kids playing basketball around the country.

"He was in the jewelry business in New York City. He also wrote a weekly basketball column for *Scholastic Coach* magazine and supplied names for the *Parade* All-American teams. That was an avocation for him. He had a little apartment, he and his wife Sophie, not too far from Columbia University. I used to go down there and read through the stacks of papers that he collected from all over the country. That's how I got started with our recruiting at West Point.

"His papers were categorized by state, so we, my assistant coaches and I, would pick out every kid who had made an all-conference or an all-county team in any state and send that kid a letter and a questionnaire to see if he might be interested in West Point. Through that I got to know Howard, who right about that time was getting into his *HSBI* thing.

"I would check through Lapidus' papers and then go down and copy all the names out of Howard's *HSBI* Blue Books, which was just great for me because they had the names of all the City and Jersey kids. Of course he had no idea if they could play or not, so that was up to us to find out. But 95 percent of the players we checked out came from either Bob Lapidus or Howard during those years."

On one of Knight's visits, Garf hit him with the idea of running Five-Star. They settled on 50 bucks a day. "Everything ran like clockwork at camp, maybe because of Knight's intimidation factor, which is why we got him in the first place," Garf says. "Unlike the media image he has gained at Indiana University, he was extremely cooperative all week long. Except for one area."

Stations. "Before camp opened Knight asked me what we did for stations. I had no idea what he was talking about. I said to him, 'What's a station? What do you mean, a train?' He told me he meant teaching stations. He wanted to know what we did to teach the kids basketball.

"We thought we were doing pretty good. We were doing what we'd always done. We were still having 30-minute lectures in the morning and afternoon and then breaking into teams to drill on the lectures. Knight came to camp and said we weren't going to do that anymore. We were going to put in stations. He didn't ask me. He told me. I protested, but he stopped me. He said they were the best. It was the only time he was vehement all week and he was totally right."

There's a joke about a Protestant kid who got kicked out of every school he went to. No one could get through to him until the kindly old Catholic nuns of St. Mary's agreed to try, right around Lent. They took him to chapel, where he immediately saw the light. Amazed, his parents asked him what happened. "It was those Stations of the Cross," the lad said. "When I saw what they did to that other poor guy, I knew they were serious."

Stations at Five-Star have become no less religiously pursued and persuasive. Stations: the rudiments of basketball reduced to their simplest form. The essence of shooting, passing, rebounding, dribbling, defense, conditioning, and you-name-it presented on a silver platter. Garf's daily bread. Wholesome morning chores and come hell or high water, they must be done.

"No one was sure exactly what to do, so we made things up on the fly in the beginning," Garf says. "We decided on 10 fundamentals, 10 minutes each with a different coach at every station. Knight had the kids running through tires like Marines and all kinds of things, and after two days I loved the stations. They were far better than anything we'd done.

"There was something else too. Walking around I could see that every coach seemed to have a specialty. I found out what each one liked to do, and that became their station. Instead of being taught 10 different ways, every kid was taught the same by an expert, a stationmaster. Over the years that's what we've continued to do."

Garf thought stations were the greatest thing since sliced bread, but it was just another day at the office for Knight. "We weren't dealing with rocket science, for cris'sake," Knight says good-naturedly. "If you're going to do a camp the right way you have to teach, and teaching the kids in a rotating situation, where they are involved for 10 minutes or so with one thing and then another and another is an ideal way. It was pretty simple to set up."

No one had come up with the idea before, though, and in the years that followed, stations became Five-Star's hallmark. Each one is like a compressed pearl of wisdom. They are Garf's pride and joy. He fine-tuned them so there are 12 today. Campers go through four every morning for three days and then go through again. The second time through, coaches expand on what was taught the first time. Each station takes 20 minutes with one minute in between to shift. They run 90 minutes a day for six days, and on the seventh day, imitating the first great creation, the campers rest.

*   *   *   *   *

Bobby Cremins liked the part about resting. Originally from the Bronx, he was a counselor at Rosemont in 1968 and eons away from becoming head coach at Georgia Tech (with a trip to the NCAA's Final Four in 1990). He was paid to keep his eyes open for errant campers, but preferred keeping them closed, mostly around sunrise when he should have been rousing the regular campers and the camper-workers.

The camper-workers were the closest thing Five-Star had to scholarship players. Marv Kessler hatched the idea and Garf unofficially started the program back at Orin-Sekwa when kids like Ron Johnson and a few others couldn't raise the hundred bucks needed to enroll. He let them in for half price. In exchange, they toiled in the dining room, serving food, setting tables, and cleaning up after meals. It was and still is a position of honor. By the third year, Garf expanded the plan so he could recruit players.

Garf's recruits were usually kids with big reputations, well-known players who would raise the camp's intensity even more and, it was hoped, increase attendance. When word hit the streets that so-and-so was going to Five-Star, everyone wanted to be there to teach him a thing or two, to show him how it was done. "There were no cut-and-dried rules in the beginning, but you had to have talent, financial need, and be in the camp's NBA league," Garf says.

Mel Davis met the criteria. Even if he hadn't, no one would have said anything. Davis is a pussycat today, the overseer of six pizza restaurants in upstate New York. His pet name at Five-Star was "Killer." He played at Boy's High, in the Public School Athletic League's "Suicide Division." He was bad looking. Not ugly, bad. He was 6'7" tall, weighed 230 pounds, was bald, and had a scar on his face from nobody knew where.

Knight decided it would be a terrific idea to dump ice water on Davis' head. And not just his, but Bobby Cremins' and Ed Searcy's too. Searcy was Mel Davis' best friend. He grew up in Harlem and played at Power Memorial, but spent the better part of his youth getting chased out of Brooklyn. He and some of the homeboys would cruise on over there, bend a few rims, and then have to exit in a hurry. At Five-Star he was in no rush to do anything, especially wake up.

"Howard almost had apoplexy over this," Knight recalls. "At that time, and this is still a big thing for him, he really enjoyed having the best players, in his mind anyway, at camp. His ego gets in this a little bit and I understand it, but that never to me has been the essence of his camp. That's just been all bullshit to me.

"But anyhow, Howard had all these New Jersey and New York kids working in the dining room as waiters and busboys, and they were all his best players. So one of the first things he tells me was he's never been able to run the program on time. I said to him, 'Well, why is that, Howard?' and he says he could never get the waiters up in the morning. I said to him, 'Howard, this thing is gonna run on time and those son-of-a-bitches will be there.'

"Well, what I did," says Knight, laughing impishly, "was take a bucket of cold water and a cup and I went through the cabin and woke 'em all up. I said that the first guy who wasn't out there could get his ass on the next bus back to New York. I thought Howard was gonna have a cardiac arrest because he thought they'd all quit and go home. Well, we lost one kid over it and the camp ran right on time. Bobby Cremins was in that bunch."

It was a rude awakening. "Little did I know that would be my foundation for coaching," Cremins says today. "There's more to the story. John Roche and I were both there from South Carolina, where we were playing ball at the time. Coach Knight said he wanted us up by 6:00 a.m. and that we were going to work harder that week than we'd ever worked in our lives. We told him we weren't getting up at six o'clock. Actually, John told him. He had more guts than I did. Knight didn't like it and he stared at us and said, 'What did you say?' He didn't wait for an answer. He came right after us.

"Luckily, Howard was there. He jumped in between us. We never did get up at six o'clock, but we worked diligently. What I remember most, though, is the first clinic I saw Coach Knight give. He asked the campers whether they liked offense or defense. One kid said offense, so he hit him with the basketball. Right then and there, I became a fan of Bob Knight.

"It amazed me how he stressed the defensive part of the game. That was my game, defense, and the guys who play tough 'D' don't always get credit. I think I would have liked playing for Coach Knight. He was the first guy I'd ever seen who loved defense as much as offense. All the coaches, Hubie Brown, Al McGuire, were great. It was incredible being there."

Mel Davis dried off, went to St. John's, and was the Knicks' first-round draft choice in 1974. "Garf playing that damn bugle at seven o'clock in the morning in the freezing cold" is another of his vivid Five-Star memories. "It was some kind of Boy Scout bugle," Davis says. "He used to blow it through a huge microphone." Actually, it was Garf doing his impression of post time at the races, his special way of waking up the rest of the camp.

He uses tape recordings of Frank Sinatra or Shirley Bassey or Benny Goodman nowadays, but in Davis' day, decked out in starched white shorts and white sports shirt, he'd crank up the PA system and call the horses. Literally. He'd hum the post time theme loud and clear through his nostrils, as smooth as jockey silks, then announce, "This is the human bugle coming to you from Rosemont. Everybody up." He eventually went hoarse, which got him into Sinatra and the rest.

Most of the campers can't abide the stuff, but Garf is just trying to be nice. "The reason I play the music is the same reason I bring in great speakers, the same reason we have the best coaches, the best stationmasters, the best balls I can get, and the best courts I can find. I want to share with the kids whatever is best in basketball and out of basketball," he says.

A lot of it rubs off. "When I left Five-Star, I knew I could play with anybody," says Mel Davis. "It was the true beginning of my career. While I was at camp, I reached a point where I stopped second-guessing myself. As a matter of fact, all of us there were working it out together. Nothing had to be said. After a while, there was a real clear understanding of where we would all take our talents."

It was the same for his buddy Ed Searcy. Searcy made it from the streets of Harlem to the parquet floor of the Boston Garden. An executive at Columbia University today, he won a championship ring with the Celtics in 1975. "The thing that was so valuable for me about Five-Star was that I kind of knew how I stood in the city as a player, but not outside it. Going against players from other areas let you really know if your moves were still good outside the neighborhood. And Coach Knight inspired me when he talked about great players being the ones who can play defense as well as score. That's how I was able to make the pros."

*   *   *   *   *

Knight's sage counsel didn't help Itchy and Twitchy. They came to camp as Andy and Jeff Diamond, twin brothers from Forest Hills, Queens. They were hotshot counselors at Rosemont before Five-Star got there, blowing away wimpy campfire kids. When kids like Mel Davis and Ed Searcy arrived and started swatting their offerings into the trees, the twins got nervous. Andy itched. Jeff twitched.

"When the guys from Bed Stuy showed up, the atmosphere became very different from normal summer camp," says the Twitcher in an understatement. "It was like a culture shock for us Jewish kids. We just stood there and stared. One day Coach Knight used Mel Davis to demonstrate a boxing-out drill and couldn't move him. I couldn't believe it. Davis had to be over 6'10". He was awesome."

The fidgety twins bunked with Rick Pitino, who'd tailed Garf to Five-Star. "Pitino had his little record player and his Motown platters, stuff like the Four Tops. He was a good player but a better card shark. He'd hustle the kids from the suburbs. If they didn't have any money, he'd beat them out of their new Chuck Taylors. We knew he wasn't going to be a star player, but we knew he would make it somewhere. He was so focused, always talking basketball."

Itchy and Twitchy were somewhat forgettable as hoopsters, but they gave birth to a Five-Star tradition when they hauled Garf's two-hand set shot out of the crypt. "We discovered Garf and the three-point shot," says Twitchy. "He was always a charismatic guy, but we didn't know if he could play ball. No one had ever seen him do it. One day he had a basketball in his hand and we got the whole camp chanting 'Shoot, shoot,' trying to make him show us what he had. There were no three-pointers back then, but he stood at the top of the key where the three-point line is today and shot. He missed, but everybody clapped and cheered anyway. It was great."

The act has since taken on mythical proportions. The campers still do it, and for an instant Garf becomes the symbolic underdog. It is like the kid with glasses coming off the bench with a minute left in the game, his team down by 40 points and him giving it all he's got while looking less than graceful doing it. At least he's in the game, though, so when he gets the ball everyone yells for him to *"shoot."* It becomes each person's innermost moment of truth. If he misses, everyone misses. Making it is the same—everyone makes it. But either way, what matters most is that he "shoot."

Itchy and Twitchy and the rest of the Rosemont campers ate it up. Something had to get their minds off the food. Victuals are a touchy subject with Garf. He says that's not why kids come to camp. But a person's gotta eat and what they got at Rosemont depended on the mood of the cook. Moses Malone, a fairly intimidating figure himself, remembers the cook as "bald-headed and not worth messing with," and Moses didn't arrive until 1973, after the guy had a few years to mellow.

There were rumors he'd get drunk and chase his wife around with a butcher knife. Those were the nights everybody kinda picked at their plate, not sure what they were looking at, and by the end of the week, everyone knew why signs had been hung on the dining room walls telling you what to do for choke victims.

Maybe that's what did it. Maybe everyone was united against the chef. A burnt food brotherhood. Whatever it was, something else very strange started to happen at Rosemont. The racial thing. The black and white thing. The tension. It was gone. Walk into camp and it fell off like an old snakeskin and it wasn't something you thought about again until you got home.

You'd be back in the neighborhood or sitting on your front porch and all of a sudden realize who your teammates had been, who you'd been eating and rapping with all week, sweating with. You'd seen their faces; they were the type of people you and your friends had maybe hassled before. Playing on the same court, under one set of rules, you hadn't noticed. Maybe you noticed a guy's "J" or his handle and you asked him about it, but that was all.

Everyone had been accepted on his own merits. Nobody had to live up to or lower himself to someone else's expectations. A guy could either play ball or he couldn't. That was all there was to it. Word. Back home it all seemed strange. It was easy to fall back into the same old tensions and get tough-skinned again. If you tried to explain it to anyone, they looked at you like you were nuts. That's the way it had been, though. No hassles just because of a guy's skin.

It might have been the food, but more likely it was Garf, or a mishmash of him and everybody else. Garf was enmeshed in Five-Star and buried under *HSBI* and his outside teams, but he found time to help organize the City Game. The goal was simple: run the best game in town to showcase the best kids. Match the public school all-stars versus the Catholic and private school all-stars. Get them seen. Maybe get them some money for college. His partner, Bob Williams, established Sports Foundation Inc., a group that counseled black athletes and lassoed straying youths. Any profits went to them. The first game was played at Xavier High School on 15th Street in Manhattan. The gym only seated 800 and Garf still remembers a newspaper photo showing kids hanging from the transoms and air-conditioning vents trying to get a peek.

If he could have frozen that moment in time, he would have. "I love basketball," Garf says. "The movement, the athletic ability, the teamwork. When it's done right, with five guys passing to one another, guys from different backgrounds patting each other on the back, it's a thing of beauty. That's the feeling we try to capture at Five-Star. Basketball is America's game and it should mirror the country, but it doesn't always.

"It sounds crazy, but in that little week we have at Five-Star, I get a kick out of at least trying to make the whole world a better place to live. The only things that count there are whether you're a good person and whether or not you can play. That's it. Catholic, Jew, Protestant, white, black, doesn't mean shit. What should happen is that racists should be made to go to Five-Star and watch what goes on every day, and maybe we could change some of their thinking."

FIVE
Making Connections

"There were nights a bare-naked woman could have walked through here and the coaches wouldn't have noticed. That's how focused they were on basketball."

– Fireside Inn proprietor Joe Ranner II

By the fourth year, 1969, time had started to stand still at Five-Star. You would arrive one weekend and leave the next and it was as if no time had passed, except inwardly, where change was being measured differently. Inwardly, everything was soundless growth, a continuous process of failing and succeeding until the two were the same.

Roundball romance. It was a phenomenon worth repeating, so that summer Five-Star added a second week. They would keep the traditional August closing week and run an opening session the third week in June. The camp needed to expand its horizons anyway. Kids were wandering in from out-of-the-way places with just a toothbrush and a spare pair of sneakers in their packs. Greg Hawkins, a 6'3" swingman from Huntington, West Virginia, won Player of the Week honors that first June week and as usual, Garf's timing was impeccable.

Maybe the June week would warm up the place too. You only had to see someone like Mel Davis wrapped in a blanket at stations once to know it could get cold in the Poconos. August sounded hot but the wind kicked up at night, especially when the week stretched into early September. Even the changing leaves shivered. Guys would sell their mothers for some heat. Anything.

Setting a building on fire was carrying things a bit too far. "The Great Camp Fire was one of the five worst scares in my life," Garf says. It was actually an accidental drama with frigid campers playing the part of Mrs. O'Leary's cow.

There are different versions. Garf says he saw "flames shooting over the treetops" as he was returning from a local watering hole. "I thought the whole camp was burning. Until I got there, I thought the whole thing was over for us." It was arduous making time on the rutted roadway, but when he made it he saw it was only the laundry going up in smoke.

Standing helplessly nearby, in their pajamas, were Hubie Brown and his wife Claire. "It was very cold that night," Claire Brown recalls. "When the kids got finished with their games they wanted hot showers, but they kept running out of hot water. They went to the boiler shed, cranked the dial as far as it could go, and the tank exploded."

Nobody got hurt, and only one building burned, which was a miracle considering that the flames spread to some frayed, funky electrical wires running from the laundry to the coaches' quarters. Local firemen hadn't arrived yet, so somebody else managed to put out the flames.

"The whole thing became kind of comical," Will Klein says. He first saw the glow through the hole in his bedroom wall, supposedly put there by the brawling camp cook and his wife. "The Honesdale Volunteer Fire Department, five guys in a pickup truck with their wives in the back, showed up eventually, but they didn't have any equipment. There wasn't much they could have done anyway, but they stood there with the rest of us watching it burn, saying stuff like, 'Yup, that's quite a fire you got there.'"

The friendly folks of Honesdale were used to this sort of thing. The closest large town to camp, Honesdale was raised on coal. In the mid-1820s it was the main link connecting the northeastern Pennsylvania coalfields to coal-hungry New York City via the Delaware & Hudson Canal. Residents can boast that in 1829 the first steam locomotive run on an American commercial railroad rolled through their town and that they once had the largest stockpile of coal in the world.

Twice, in 1840 and again in 1851, large sections of town were destroyed by fire so people there have learned to take certain things in stride. Sports, like coal, are part of their heritage. Major League Baseball Hall of Famer Christy Mathewson, a native of nearby Fac-

Fig. 1 **ONE OF A KIND:** *Co-director Will Klein's first, last, and only lecture at Five-Star, Camp Orin-Sekwa, Niverville, New York, August 1966.*

Fig. 2 *Co-director Howard Garfinkel about to drill his patented 21-foot, two-handed set shot for the traditional opening of camp.*

Fig. 3   Tom Owens (left) and John Roche (red shirt) were two of the original campers at Orin-Sekwa in 1966.   Both had lengthy NBA careers following All-American stints at South Carolina.

Fig. 4   That's Mike Fratello, teaching his lungs out as an assistant at James Madison University. "The Gator" helped Rollie Massimino win the 1985 NCAA title for Villanova before engineering four straight 50+ win seasons at the helm of the Atlanta Hawks. The camper in the background to Fratello's right is Terry Tyler, who played 11 NBA seasons with the Pistons, Kings, and Mavs. Tom Zaliagiris, of Catholic Central H.S. (Redford, MI) and North Carolina fame, stands to Tyler's right.

Fig. 5 **TIME-OUT AT ROSEMONT:** *Mike Cingiser (far right, Lynbrook H.S. and Brown University) gives last-minute instructions to Paul Victores (left), Pete Braverman (center), and Pro League MVP Mel Davis in 1968.*

Fig. 6 **SNEAKER DARK AGE:** *Hubie Brown (left) and Mike O'Koren (North Carolina, New Jersey Nets) at Rosemont in 1975, the era before color photography and $175 basketball shoes. O'Koren, Five-Star's first two-time Most Outstanding Player, was Hubie's favorite demonstrator.*

Fig. 7 At Camp Rosemont, 1974, George Raveling (left, USC) cradles his famed clipboard (and yellow legal pad), which helped revolutionize recruiting. Then head coach at Washington State, he poses with his former boss, the legendary Lefty Driesell of Maryland and James Madison University.

Fig. 8 **"AND A CHILD SHALL LEAD THEM"**: "Wonder Boy" Rick Pitino (grad. assistant-to-be at the Univ. of Hawaii) teaches "One-on-One Moves Facing" to a talented group of NBA players at an a.m. station, June Honesdale session. Fifteen years later he would capture the imagination of the basketball world.

Fig's. 9 & 10

GUESS WHO'S COMING TO DINNER?: *Two unexpected guests surprise campers with delicious morsels of Individual Instruction at Station 13: Willis Reed (left) and Connie Hawkins (below).*

Fig. 11   Tom McCorry (asst. Wichita State) instructs two rising superstars: Alonzo Mourning (Georgetown) and Christian Laettner (Duke), at Robert Morris College.

Fig. 12   "Crazy George" Schauer in action. That ball's spinning, folks!

Fig. 13 Moses Malone, whom Garf once termed "the only camper in the history of Five-Star who was too good for the camp," leads his team to an undefeated (11–0) camp championship. There's no truth to the rumor that Malone's five were unscored upon.

Fig. 14 Inventive Dayton assistant Tom McConnell beats a path through his basketball obstacle course in Honesdale.

Fig. 15 "THE VAN GOGH OF THE HARDWOOD": 25-year Five-Star fixture Billy Aberer (La Salle Acad., New York City) is an artist on and off the court. Here, he paints a picture of "Back-to-Basket Moves" at a.m. stations in Pittsburgh. Commissioner of the camp's N.I.T. League in both Bryn Mawr sessions, Billy is also Five-Star's "chart man," and drew many of the diagrams for the best-selling **Five-Star Basketball Drills** handbook.

Fig. 16 "THE DOG BARKS BUT THE CARAVAN MOVES ON": Unsuspecting campers huddle with their stationmaster (who is hidden in the crowd) before breaking for the next station in Radford.

toryville, pitched for the Honesdale nine in the late 1890s, just before joining the New York Giants, and it is the home of Masters golf champion Art Wall.

Basketball first came to the area in 1902 when Vernon Riefler, a transplanted Wyoming Seminary student, married a local belle and brought along a newfangled game. Residents approached the game seriously and the Scranton *Tribune* described an early contest between Riefler's Company E firehouse five and the rival Carbondale Swiftwinds as follows: "The big burly lads of Company E took advantage of the Swiftwinds, who were only learning the game, and proceeded to run it to the very marrow of their bones."

In no time the Honesdale High girls caught on, putting together a string of unbeaten seasons in the 1920s before winning a state championship in 1929. It came only after considerable brabbling, however. Bucktown, another perennial power, laid claim to the title without ever having proved it on the court until, after months of haggling, the teams met properly. Honesdale's 23–19 victory left the 1,000 or more hometown rooters "in the most pleasant of spirits," according to one report, and afterwards, "Pandemonium broke loose and the spirit of noise was in unchecked sway."

Five-Star, amid such vim and vigor, felt right at home and quickly became attached to the town. Whenever Garf or anyone else talked about the camp, they always called it Honesdale. The name rolled off the tongue easily. Even after Five-Star left Rosemont and went to Lake Bryn Mawr, it was Honesdale.

* * * * *

Bob Knight, asking for $100 per day, had priced himself out of a job, but was never far from Five-Star. Headed for Hoosier country, he stopped by to lecture. His subject was motivation, and he picked out a kid from western New York, Mel Montgomery, to serve as his guinea pig. Montgomery barely had time to say hello when he was sent scurrying down a hill for a blade of grass. He had no idea what that had to do with basketball, but he did as he was told.

Garf knew. He had seen the routine before. Usually a kid hustled down the hill and back and Knight would send him again, running alongside him shouting. Most times, the kid moved even faster. "Knight was making a valid point," Garf says. "The point was that when you have a coach who's a prodder, he gets a kid to play harder. Why do we need inspiration to play as hard as we can? I don't know. That's not the way it should be, but that's human nature. Kids play harder if someone is intimidating them, encouraging them."

Mel Montomery was missing the point. "He went real slow, just sort of trotted for the grass the first time and Knight got pissed. Usually a kid ran at least semi-fast, so when Montgomery got back Knight looked at him and said, 'Wrong blade.' He told him to get the right one and Montgomery split. He was scared to death. He took off into the woods and we didn't find him until about four-thirty that afternoon."

Hubie Brown became the new man in charge and Five-Star immediately improved. "We had discipline under Knight, but not totally organized discipline," Garf says. "We were getting 200 kids a week and we were still running around, coming and going. We weren't really sure who was going to what. The coaches were supposed to keep track, but they didn't have to report to anyone. Hubie said that to keep order and to know if someone was sick or hurt, we had to know where the kids were all the time.

"He said we should start taking attendance. I didn't want to turn this into a quasi-military operation, but that became one of the big things in the history of Five-Star. Now we have three attendances every day: one at stations, one at the afternoon lecture, and one before our night program. If a kid isn't there and doesn't have a good excuse, he is docked his next game. If he misses consistently or isn't where he's supposed to be, he's out of here. He's out of the camp.

"If a kid ever skips stations, he is barred from camp too. The only way around it is if a kid who's going to be a senior skips out. He wouldn't be coming back anyway because we don't take kids after their senior year. If that happens there's nothing we can do, but if it happens a lot with kids from the same school, we bar the school. Fortunately, we're in a position to do that. We turn away a thousand kids a year, but I think I'd be brave enough to do it anyway. The day the kids decide not to go to stations on the last day as a group is the day I'm not in the camp anymore.

"Nowadays too we have a guy we call 'The Writer' whose job it is to keep track of attendance. If a kid is missing, he writes him up and finds him. Most of the time kids are in the infirmary getting their ankles taped or whatever. They're not skipping out. Campers have to respond because we are very tough on this."

Forced to respond. Forced to be responsible and to realize that ultimately they have to answer to themselves.

* * * * *

Five-Star continued to change and was slowly becoming impenetrable. There were no fences or walls surrounding the camp.

You could walk right in and out, but if you were anything less than incredibly intense the vibrations spit you right back out. Forced you out. If you weren't tuned in it looked weird, watching 200 kids at stations take jump shots without a ball, perfecting their follow-through. And it was even weirder watching the coaches, in broad daylight, do their schtick, their act, coaching like there was no tomorrow.

They were becoming a peculiar lot, these Five-Star guys, but they were the only kind Garf wanted. He wanted guys who could convince a kid that if he did something, the only way to go about it was fully. From the heart. He wanted guys who could get a kid to play like he'd never played in his life, guys who could give a kid something to take home with him that would last.

Rumple-haired Marv Kessler could do that. He'd become a regular and even the other coaches liked his routine. They'd laugh along with the kids when he'd tell them his stories, like the one about Ira Shapiro, his reluctant center at Van Buren High. Shapiro was 6'6" but had never played for the team. His father wanted him to be a rabbi. Shapiro wanted to become an accountant, which he eventually did.

Kessler convinced him to try basketball in his senior year. He introduced him to the court and went over all the lines and measurements and then told him he couldn't stand in the blue area underneath the basket. Shapiro asked why and he explained that was the three-second lane and that he couldn't stay in there any longer than that. "Well, that's not a very long time," Shapiro said, all nasally and like that would have to be changed, of course.

Kessler told him he'd just have to get used to it. He taught him how to cut through the lane and how to yell *"Don't throw it"* when he did. Shapiro did beautifully for about 10 games, but then he grew suspicious. He asked why he was doing that, so Kessler told him. If he didn't, someone might pass him the ball, he'd shoot, and probably miss. It was better this way. Shapiro was happy after that. He knew his role. Everyone needs to know where they fit in.

*　*　*　*　*

Five-Star was comforting like that but it had one major problem. Actually, a couple. With all that energy being spent, guys had to get out of there sometimes. Have a little fun. Do something uncomplicated. Get their minds off basketball. There was the floor show at the Concord Hotel, but that was way up in Monticello. It was a trek. The other problem was the food. It hadn't improved. No one was dying from it, but the cook was getting some nasty looks.

Old Fuzzy's place, the Fireside Inn, saved the cook's hide and a lot of people's sanity. Two seconds after lights out, there'd be a line of coaches' cars leading to the front door. The Fireside cured what was ailing them. Joe Ranner I doesn't mind being called Old Fuzzy. He says he's been called worse. Not in his place he hasn't, at least not by anyone who stuck around.

Joe has never forgotten what it was like coming over from Germany in the late twenties. He worked on a farm. He couldn't speak the language, so some other hired hands taught him to say "Go to hell," and told him to say it to the boss after daily inspections. Being the trusting sort, he did. He didn't get fired, but you'd better watch your lip in his establishment. The Fireside, just down the road from Five-Star, is part of the landscape around Honesdale these days.

It is famous for its meals and deals. "Just about everyone imaginable in basketball has been in here," says Old Fuzzy's son, Joe Ranner II. "It's not the same anymore with the new NCAA recruiting rules, but the coaches used to pack the place. One of my favorites was Pete Carril. One night, Pete was sitting at the bar with Dean Smith and a few others. They were all bragging about their programs and Smith says to Carril, 'Name one thing you can do at Princeton we can't do at North Carolina.' Pete rolled his cigar, thought for a second, then sort of grinned, and said, 'We can outspell you.' They don't make coaches like him anymore. They're almost all gone. Al McGuire was good too. He always told me, 'The best deals for finding players are cut at the Fireside.'"

*   *   *   *   *

In the early days of Five-Star, college recruiting was a year-round circus. Competition for prime athletes went on nonstop, and in order to survive, recruiters had to be colorful characters who could sell their school's wares. The process was costly, especially for smaller programs, and occasionally criminal, at least by NCAA standards. By the mid-1980s, new regulations aimed at controlling costs and abuses had been put in place.

The chief targets were the evaluation and contact periods, the times recruiters could observe and talk to high school athletes. A calendar was drawn up strictly limiting those times. Those who wanted to found ways around them, but the intent was to give everyone, the so-called haves and the have-nots, an equal shot and to bring order to the system. It has become known as the "Live/Dead Period," and the argument over its success is a continuing one.

Five-Star, internally, was unaffected. Garf, years before the NCAA coaches began policing themselves, had declared his own hands-off policy. Coaches could exchange hellos with a kid at camp if they knew him, but that was all, and no bumping into each other accidentally-on-purpose outside the main gate either. Garf's eyes were everywhere. He started it after Louisiana State University coach Dale Brown, then at Utah State, took Rick Pitino out behind the gym one afternoon for a friendly chat.

Pitino, already committed to the University of Massachusetts, was having a hot day, hitting jumpers from everywhere. The LSU coach didn't do anything devious, he just buzzed in Pitino's ear about the Beehive State and what a nice nest he could have out there, but Garf put the kibosh on it.

Garf never said the coaches couldn't talk among themselves, though, and they did, half the night down at Old Fuzzy's. They'd eat, sit back and relax, and pontificate. "The Fireside was where it came down to short strokes in the coaching world," remembers Al McGuire. "It was like at a convention where you pick up the real knowledge in the hallways and side rooms. Nothing gets done at the main seminars and lectures. It was the same way at the Fireside.

"There were a lot of guys faking each other out, saying this kid or that kid didn't look good. There was a lot of joking going on and meanwhile they're really thinking the kid is a mint-in-the-box. It was a case of always knocking the product until you owned it and then the value tripled. The kid became one of a kind."

The chatting, not limited to recruits, could get heated. "I cannot believe how many fistfights got broken up at the Fireside," says Hubie Brown, laughing about it now. "We have had total egomaniacs come to Five-Star, who thought that their way was the only way to play basketball. When a guy is young he might honestly think that. When you become a national college recruiter, though, you go into a lot of gyms, baby, and you find out this game is played differently.

"The confrontations came at the Fireside because people were thrashing new ideas against other people who didn't believe they worked. Over a period of time you would see these people mature. Five-Star, by branching out and bringing coaches and players from other parts of the country together, brought about a maturity in the philosophies of a lot of basketball coaches and players."

From the conflicts grew comaraderie. "Five-Star to me will always be Honesdale," Brown says. "I loved the intimacy of the old place; taking on the cold, the rain, the food, the outdoor courts. Today, there is no going in the army like my generation did, so kids miss that two years of regimentation, discipline, and growing up. It was like that and still is like that at Five-Star. Sucking it up, gutting it out. When you're there, you appreciate everything. There's a bond that happens."

And from comaraderie grew loyalty. The Five-Star Connection. "Guys helped one another, Brown says. Guys who were recruiting might ask Garf about a kid. At the same time they'd pass along the name of a good coach they'd seen working in some gym in Anywhere, USA. Garf would hire him and he'd add something special to the camp. He'd be seen too and maybe move on to higher things. Lasting friendships developed between coaches and also between coaches and players.

"The players would go on to college and come back as counselors. They wanted to pass on what they'd learned. If they didn't play in the pros, some would come back as coaches. That's the way it worked. I can't speak for anyone else, but my father, when he needed work, was an assistant trainer at the camp and my wife was the first nurse. Five-Star becomes almost a part of you that way."

Such loyalties fortified Five-Star. Later, in more careworn times, they would be seriously questioned.

SIX

Good Times and Bad Times, Wild Times and Quiet Times

"Piss on it, there's ball to be played."

    – Dave Pritchett, basketball scout extraordinaire

Five-Star, unexpectedly, had become a proving ground for coaches as well as players. Every summer it was Orin-Sekwa all over again. Guys grinding it out on the sidelines, yanking and tugging at their insides, constantly reaching their limit and rushing past it. Competing, struggling to excel. But it wasn't the usual competition. You didn't win by pulling the other guy down. The idea was to force everyone up.

It wasn't just a camp; it was a basketball bazaar, an emporium where knowledge was bought and sold not with silver but with sweat. Every day, out with the old and in with the new and a guy could make a name for himself too if he was so inclined. Coaches who had gotten a break through the camp and risen in the ranks brought other unknowns: Mike Fratello, Ron Rothstein, Tom McCorry, all high school coaches who in their quiet moments wondered how good they were.

Out on the courts it was business as usual, wall-to-wall talent. Reputations came and went like the wind. Marquee players, accustomed to owning the spotlight, melted in the shared glow. Obscure kids would arrive wide-eyed and looking-for-mother's-skirts and then blow everyone away. It could go either way. Five-Star proved that.

The camp seemed ageless. There was an ebb and flow to the June week that continued into August and through the winter basketball season to the following summer and from one summer to the next. Returning after a year, it became again as if no time were passing. There was no need to renew the intensity, only add to it.

John Thompson could relate to that. That's how he was doing things down at St. Anthony's in Washington, D.C., and how he would someday do things at Georgetown University. In the early seventies, he began bringing his kids to Five-Star, players such as 6'7" Donald Washington, "Superman in shorts," according to Garf, along with Merlin Wilson, Dane Edley, John Smith, and Greg "Big Daddy" Brooks.

He brought more than just big kids to Five-Star. "That really put us in the big time," Garf says. "It meant we were getting the top players, not just from New York and New Jersey and parts of New England, but Washington, D.C. too. I credit John Thompson with a good portion of the early success of the camp. We were very close in those days, despite later misunderstandings over some things that may or may not have happened."

It's difficult sometimes to pinpoint where something went wrong. For Garf and Thompson, it may have been back at Camp Rosemont one afternoon after Thompson gave an impromptu rebounding clinic. Brendan Malone, no slouch himself as the Detroit Pistons would later attest, was showing some campers the ropes. Thompson, an old board man, got interested, rolled up his sleeves, and jumped in. He wasn't upstaging, just adding. "He was doing a fantastic job, sweating like a regular Five-Star worker, so I said something to him like, 'I didn't know you could do that,'" Garf remembers.

"I had just never seen him do it." Garf was trying to compliment him, but Thompson apparently took it wrong, like his intelligence was being insulted. "Thompson was always a big kidder and he said something back like, 'What's the matter, do you think a black guy can't teach?' He didn't say it viciously or anything, and I just laughed and started to kid him back, but after about 30 seconds of stammering I realized he wasn't kidding."

There was a problem with Patrick Ewing too. It developed later when Ewing came from Rindge & Latin High in Massachusetts to Five-Star in the late seventies. Colleges, for good reason, were already drooling over him. Garf could see why. "He ran the floor as well as or better than any center that ever lived and still does, but I thought he needed to work on his inside offensive game. I told him so and advised him to get extra instruction at Station 13."

Station 13 was Marv Kessler's brainstorm. He wanted to give campers something to do after the 12 morning stations besides going back to their bunks or pigging out. He figured 90 minutes of concentrated drilling on a single aspect of the game was just what everyone wanted. Yeah, right.

Garf loved it immediately and told the campers it separated the horses from the old plugs. Different coaches taught at Station 13. When Ewing got to camp, Rick Pitino was working it. Pitino was head coach at Boston University by then and probably wouldn't have minded having Ewing, but anyone was welcome at Station 13. Pitino was still one of Garf's fair-haired boys, though, and it got back to Thompson that he was trying to steer Ewing in his direction.

What was actually said, according to Garf, was something more along the line of, "Pat, you don't have any moves, not one damn offensive move. You're doing everything on athleticism and individual ability, so please go over to that great Boston U coach at Station 13 and learn some back-to-the-basket moves." When it filtered back to Thompson, the part about Pitino and Boston U were mentioned, but there was nothing said about the moves and Station 13.

To make things worse, Thompson was apparently under the impression that Garf telephoned Ewing and encouraged him to attend BU. Garf swore he never did, that he never even had Ewing's number. "The closest I ever came to telling him to go to BU was advising him to go to Station 13," he says. Thompson announced it to the world at an awards banquet in Syracuse anyway, the story goes, and the mess never got closer to being straightened out than that.

The two men shake hands now if they cross paths at a gym, but that's the extent of it. "John Thompson was not only good for the camp, he was also great for *HSBI*," says Garf. "When I was struggling, still getting the report going, he ordered a four-year subscription, the length of his contract. He sent a check for $500, in advance, which kept me out of the red. Despite what happened later, without his St. Anthony's players, I just don't know if Five-Star ever would have gotten as big as it did. You can't hide facts. Facts are facts."

Fortunately for Five-Star, the Washington Express wasn't totally derailed. Frank Williams, the coach at Coolidge High, made sure his kids were a part of things (quietly providing round-trip tickets in many cases), as did Joe Dean Davidson at the other Dunbar High. "Frank Williams became very much a part of the camp and Joe Dean Davidson, who unfortunately passed away in the spring of 1990, was without a doubt a key figure in the scheme of things," Garf says. "When they write the history of the Interhigh League, which at one time was one of the strongest leagues for its size in the country,

Davidson will have to be rated among the top three coaches, especially in terms of developing young players. He sent us kids like Anthony Jones, who later went to UNLV, Ken Matthews, Joe Tweet, John "Be Be" Duren (Indiana Pacers), and Craig Shelton (Atlanta Hawks). Shelton shared the sportsmanship award one year with Kimberly Belton of Columbia Grammar Prep in New York City. Belton and Shelton, I'll never forget them. The D.C. kids strengthened the whole camp."

*　*　*　*　*

Five-Star was rolling. So were some of the coaches. Campers couldn't leave the grounds, but after they were tucked in, their leaders could and did. If it was a Friday night and the Fireside was dead and there was a particularly good floor show at The Concord, that's where they headed. The only problem was they weren't welcome. There was even a fence with a sign reading "Guests Only."

There were ways around anything. In the old days Chuck Daly and Bob Knight used their influence to get guys in, but there were too many fresh young faces. They were on their own. Desperate measures were called for, so they'd pile into their polyester leisure suits and white patent leather belts and shoes and hoof it. One of the leaders of the pack was Mike Fratello, a street-smart guy from Hackensack, New Jersey.

Fratello, later coach of the Atlanta Hawks, and his confederates put some serious moves on The Concord palace guards. "There were four sure-fire ways we used to get in," Fratello remembers. "First was the straight payoff. There was a van that transported guests from the parking lot to the front door and we'd give the driver five bucks to let us lie on the floor.

"If the wrong guy was working that night, we'd use a screen play. One guy would keep the guard busy while the rest of us slithered along the fence. Once we got in we snuck from tree to tree all the way to the entrance.

"The 'Back-Door Play' was when we'd sneak up the fire escape ladder to an opening on the upper floor and then walk nonchalantly down the staircase to the night club.

"The best one was the 'Pick-and-Roll.' We'd choose one guy to get in and he would sit in the back seat of a four-door car next to the right-hand side. The door would be open, but he'd be holding it shut. We'd drive to the gate, stall the guard, and let cars line up behind us. He'd finally tell us to get the hell out of there, but by then we couldn't back up with all the cars behind us so he'd tell us to circle around the security shack. As we made the loop, the guy holding the door would roll out and into some high grass. He'd brush himself off and stroll in as dignified as possible."

If all else failed, they assaulted the fence commando style. "One time a few of us got caught," Fratello says. "There were Ron Rothstein and Hubie Brown and Pitino and some others, so we just said to the security guy, 'Don't you know who we are?' We were nobodies but we made up names of famous coaches like Red Auerbach and Adolph Rupp, guys like that, and I don't know if he believed us or not, but he let us in."

Garf got more than he bargained for in Fratello. The guy was a human dynamo. He picked up the nickname "Alligator Man" from the way he woke kids up and put them through morning calisthenics. They named the Alligator Pit in honor of him too. If a camper committed a sin like talking while a coach was trying to explain something, he got to run up some steep hills while everyone watched. He was usually more respectful after that.

Fratello doled out punishment with the best of them. He didn't put kids down, though, and they learned something from the punishment, so it was natural for them to respond when he asked them to clap and cheer at stations. Fratello wanted them fired up. He'd put them through their paces and then huddle everyone up. Each camper put a hand in the middle and shouted *"Five-Star"* or *"Hustle"* or something similar. Kids started doing it at every station. It could be heard all over the camp.

Five-Star had esprit de corps to go with the intensity. The camp even started to look good. Orange had become the official camp color, and a lot of the kids wore their orange Five-Star T-shirts. Every camper got one and felt different wearing it. As the years passed, newcomers would hold back in the beginning thinking the camp was hokey or uncool, but by the second day, most times, veteran campers made them feel part of it.

"We were all a little crazy, but we had great times," Fratello says, "and guys busted their asses to make the camp great." In return, Garf didn't care how they spent their nights as long as they kept their days for him. Guys could even show up for stations just in the nick of time like Ron Rothstein did one morning, still wearing spats. As long as the job got done right, everything was fine.

Rothstein never had to be told that. A suburban brat from Roosevelt High in Yonkers, New York, he'd become a blue-collar guy. He played point guard for Garf's Nationals in the early sixties and was a counselor at Five-Star while in college. Garf invited him back as a coach despite the fact that he went two seasons without a win at Eastchester High.

He stayed at Eastchester nearly 20 years, then worked as a Knicks scout for Hubie Brown until Chuck Daly hired him to show his Detroit Pistons how to play defense. That was just before they walked off with their first NBA championship in 1989. Rothstein was head coach of the expansion Miami Heat by then. He still comes back to Five-Star to talk about the tough side of the game.

"When I started coaching at Miami, we lost 17 straight games," Rothstein says now. "The first time we played the Los Angeles Lakers, we lost by 47 points. The next time, late in the season, we lost by only 13. That doesn't sound like a big deal, but I ran into Magic Johnson in the hallway afterwards and he told me, 'Coach, you guys have really come along.' Coming from him that meant something. You have to be willing to take failure and pick up and move on in this business. You have to be willing to try again."

Nothing gets accomplished without time and effort. Fratello and Rothstein and their cohorts did a lot more than sneak through the bushes at night. There were a lot of young guys coming up who were serious about doing things right and getting up in the coaching world. A person only had to look down the row of bunks in the coaches' quarters to see them, all bright-eyed and bushy-tailed: Richie Adubato, now head coach of the Dallas Mavericks, and Pitino and the two Brendans, Malone and Suhr, who are assistants with the Detroit Pistons. They were all focused and hopeful.

Forks in the road were come to and choices made together and the Five-Star Connection was fused more tightly. Fratello was just one guy trying to climb the coaching ladder, falling down a rung or two on the way. He had secured an assistant's position at Rhode Island University, but a misunderstanding about his job responsibilities left him out in the cold. That can happen. He was then offered a chance to rebuild the program at James Madison University, which meant diving head first again into the abyss.

"It was a question of taking the gamble at James Madison or going back to Hackensack," Fratello says. "Ron Rothstein and I took a long walk and talked it over and I decided to take the college job. It meant I had to hustle for money in the summertime, but that's the thing that holds a lot of guys back, not wanting to risk the safety and security of their high school situation. I believe it was the right choice for me."

* * * * *

Things don't always work out as planned, for coaches or for players. Those who have been through Five-Star and seen a little of the world return every year to tell campers as much. They talk about Pat Siblia of Bloomfield, New Jersey, who won the Outstanding Player Award in June 1971. "He was a hard-knocking post player who could score like hell in the paint," Garf says. "Great hands. Mean but clean. Unfortunately, he messed up his knee or he'd have been a good one."

Or Walter "Stick-it-in-the Bucket" Luckett from Kolbe High in Bridgeport, Connecticut. He picked up the nickname from *Sports Illustrated*'s Curry Kirkpatrick, a frequent visitor to the camp. "Luckett was on the cover of *SI* but got injured not long after that while playing in college," says Garf.

There were other times when everything fell into place. It wasn't always controllable, but it didn't happen on its own either, like the night Lee Thomas and Phil Sellers put on a show in August 1971.

Thomas was a 6'5" kid from Vailsburg High in Newark, New Jersey. Sellers was on his way to the NBA Detroit Pistons, and Thomas helped him get there. It started in the playoff championships. Thomas got a hand on Sellers' layup at the buzzer to save the game. He had to streak across the court to get it, swatting it away just like he'd been taught at stations, coming across with his inside hand to avoid the foul.

Sellers had all afternoon to think about it, and in the Orange-White Classic (Five-Star's all-star game) that night he had a breakaway. It was all too storybook, but the only thing between him and an easy two was Lee Thomas. No, not twice. Thomas hung with him but Sellers rocked the rim, and the rest of the campers just nodded their heads in reverent silence. Say no more, Mr. Sellers.

Garf had seen the whole thing coming, of course. He never missed a trick. The previous winter he'd taken one of his no-obstacle-is-too-great scouting trips to Canarsie High in Brooklyn to watch Sellers play against another NBA-bound youngster, Lloyd Free. Accompanying him was Dave Pritchett, an assistant at the University of Maryland and one of the best young recruiters in the business. One of the best ever according to Garf.

Pritchett, early in his career, spotted a kid named Brad Davis playing center in high school in Monaca, Pennsylvania. He recruited him as a point guard for Maryland, which is how Davis made it to the NBA. Do that once and word gets around quick. He also got Moses Malone for the Terrapins, but Moses skipped college and went straight to the pros. Pritchett still dreams about Davis and Moses together and trips to the Final Four.

"Pit Stop." That's what Garf called Pritchett. He'd usually roll into town just long enough to look at a few prospects and then roar out again. That's how the two of them got tangled up in the first place. Both out on the road, in some gym, scrutinizing. He could just as easily have been called Nonstop, because he can ramble with the spoken word.

Fate insisted they meet. Pritchett hails from Mullens, West Virginia, and in his day was rated the third-best player in the state. The boy could shoot. Garf would adopt him, southern accent and all, whenever he needed a place to stay on his trips to New York. He'd call and Garf would say, "Sure kid, c'mon over," but he'd no sooner get there than Garf would send him out for a pack of Chesterfields and when he got back he'd have to curl up on the living room floor.

It seemed like he'd just get settled down for the evening when Garf would mention a kid with potential and off they'd go. It was like that constantly, so it wasn't surprising that Pritchett was in town the night Sellers and Free dueled at Canarsie. "Howard was just weird as hell," drawls Pritchett. "He could be volatile one second and humble the next and be any damn thing really. What I'm saying is there was no way to control the man. As an evaluator, though, the guy was brilliant. If he couldn't go see a kid, he'd ask different guys about him. He knew one guy would be sweet as hell on any kid with speed and another guy would be in love with any big, strong kid, so he'd subtract and add a little and put the thing together. If he got to see a kid, he sized him up in about four seconds.

"When I first got into recruiting, I used to talk to kids in the afternoon, but he told me it doesn't count until after eight o'clock at night. There was one time, though, I'll never forget this, Howard and I saw seven tipoffs in one day. I needed to see quite a few kids with only one day to do it, so we started out in Brooklyn around eight in the morning, got to Newark about 9:30, fired out of there in time to get to Rutgers by noon, and made it to Woodrow Wilson High in Camden by three in the afternoon to look at some big kid. We stopped at Trenton before taking in a tournament that evening and rumbled into Trenton Junior College around midnight.

"The coach, Howie Landa, was expecting us, and had his kids scrimmage, and the whole time Howard was puffing on his Chesterfields like a chimney. So we're all done, and on the way home Howard was nodding off. He opens his eyes and sees a string of lights, and says to me, 'Pit Stop, that's the biggest damn ship I've ever seen.' I started laughing and told him, 'Howard, that's not a ship, that's the Long Island Expressway.'

"Anyway, to make a long story short," Pritchett says, "I wanted to watch Sellers and Free with Garf, but neither one of us had a car. So we hooked up with Billy Robinette, this runny-nosed assistant from

Marshall University and the nicest guy in the world. We got there and it was a total sellout. There were tables set up 75 feet from the gym floor blocking people. There was no way to get in, but as it got closer to tipoff time, Howard started to breathe heavily, and his gait got elongated, and his arms started to flail.

"He got this look in his eye like, 'Piss on the masses, there's ball to be played,' and jumped up and ran across the tables, so I immediately bogarted through there too. By the time I got to the gym door, Howard was being smooth as hell, explaining himself to the assistant principal, who just gave in. What made it so damn funny was that on the way there, Robinette had remarked how much Howard seemed like a banker, all quiet sitting in the back seat. The great thing was that Howard helped Free, whom he still calls Lloyd, not World B., get into Guilford College. Howard is a special breed."

The furor, every so often, filtered into Five-Star. Part of the deal for campers was a free bus ride from New York's Port Authority to Rosemont. Once, a bag lady got on board and wouldn't get off. Nobody pressed her for a ticket so she wasn't about to budge. She finally did, somewhere along the line. "We never found out what happened to her, bless her soul," says Garf.

Another time, Garf was watching this kid tear up the NCAA league. He was setting screens brilliantly and back-dooring guys to death. It was unnatural for a kid that age to be that smart, and even stranger for Garf not to know him. "He said his name was Nick Mc-Nickel and that he went to DeWitt Clinton," Garf says. "I was immediately suspicious, because I knew that team and there wasn't one white guy on the varsity.

"I told him I wanted to move him up to the NBA league, but the more I talked to him, the more he culdn't answer even the easiest questions about the DeWitt Clinton players. He finally confessed that he went to Hunter College and was CUNY Freshman of the Year. I should have sent him home, but he looked young, and I was impressed by how badly he wanted to stay. I didn't let him play in the all-star game, and never told a living soul, but later I realized that having him there showed how tough the competition really was. He beat kids cerebrally, but not athletically. We had tough campers."

* * * * *

The imperturbable compliment to all this was Tom McCorry, Five-Star's new head coach. Hubie Brown, rapidly ascending to the NBA, needed to step down. McCorry had worked camp a few years and knew the system, plus he'd grown up in Brooklyn, three blocks from Ebbets Field. Hearing the moans of the Dodger faithful had exposed him to every insult known to man (and umpire) and taught him the value of patience.

Nothing bothered him. He was laid-back, as though in his mind he were forever lying in a hammock in the shade. There was a sense of decency about him too, and compassionate toughness. Campers felt that and were affected. Those things he learned at Regis High School from his old coach, Ed Lata. "I was young and trying to find my way in life, and was going about it all wrong," McCorry says. "Ed Lata set me straight. He showed me a lot of personal attention, and I just try to follow in his footsteps."

Lata occasionally coached at camp too, and on rainy days, when Harry Silverman was occupied, he bused the kids over to Camp Summit. McCorry got his start in coaching under Lata, later making a name for himself at St. Dominic's. He coached 6' 10" Tom Riker, who helped him win a couple of Catholic School League championships before going to South Carolina and the Knicks, and also the fiery Rick Pitino. The top assistant at Wichita State today, McCorry is a fixture at Five-Star. "Twice a year, my car starts up and goes to Honesdale. I figure I might as well be in it," he says.

He is usually found near the low post, showing kids some of the same tried-and-true moves he showed Riker. He shows them how to control the defender using their bodies, how to fight for position with their legs, hips, and forearms. "Use your hands and you get called for the foul," he says. Mental stuff too. "Be calm. The great ones never rush. I never saw Jabbar rush. He didn't need a lot of moves either. He had the drop step and the sky hook, but he was effective because he took advantage of every situation."

Which sheds some light on how McCorry happened to be the chosen one when Moses descended on Five-Star.

SEVEN
Packing Their Bags

"Then the Lord said to Moses, 'Stretch out your hand toward heaven that there may be darkness over the land . . . a darkness to be felt.' So Moses stretched out his hand toward heaven, and there was thick darkness in all the land."

– Exodus 10:21–22

Moses was coming, but first came the floods.

Five-Star, by the summer of '72, had grown beyond anyone's wildest expectations. Dear old Rosemont was sagging with nearly 250 campers a week and more were being turned away. It took some finagling to fit everyone in, and aside from diminishing bed space, the camp was running out of room in its two leagues.

The old standbys, the Pro (NBA) and College (NCAA) divisions, simply weren't big enough, and even after stretching them, a third league, the NIT, had to be added. In the end, the NBA would peak at 12 teams, ideally with nine players per team so the "horse" could still be used. The NCAA would increase to 18 teams and the NIT to 10 or 12, each with 10 players. Every camper still played at least two quarters, that never changed, but where and when they played was refined.

The draft remained a war no matter what the year, although it did take on a certain civility after a while. Tryouts were held the first night, about an hour after everyone had arrived and eaten supper. Tryouts were a very orderly, fair-and-square affair. Kids in each league stood shoulder-to-shoulder, from shortest to tallest, and each was given a number from one to ten or 12 or 18, depending on the number of teams in his league.

Everyone with the same number was on the same team. The teams played one another, playground style, shifting from one court to the next, until everyone had an equal shot to impress. The coaches lined the courts, window shopping. If a coach liked something he saw, he'd yell out, "Who made that shot?" or "Name on that rebound!" and the kid had to say who he was. Notes were jotted down and names remembered. That's how it's still done.

Then there's the draft. Retreating to a back room, coaches make their picks by position: centers first, point guards second, then off-guards and forwards. The order of selection is determined by drawing numbers from a carefully watched hat. Whoever gets the first pick for centers chooses last for a point guard, then it's back and forth for the rest. The goal is to achieve league parity.

The coaches make their picks, lick their wounds, then go off by themselves to take a closer look at who they have. Each team has to be broken down into two units of five; one unit of five plays the first and third quarters, and the second quintet, usually the more advanced players, plays the second and fourth quarters.

Campers find out in the morning where they are and who's with them. They're not always satisfied, but if homesickness or stations don't take their minds off their problems, the need to survive on the courts does. It all happens pretty fast and there isn't much time for self-pity.

Everything had been reduced to a fine science, but it took an act of God to convince Garf once and for all that Five-Star was here to stay. The seventh year of the camp was also the year of the Johnstown Flood. Hurricane Edna, not sparing Harry Silverman's palatial estate, transformed most of Pennsylvania into a swamp that June.

"When we were coming up on the bus from New York, we saw it," Garf recalls. "The rains were washing down the mountains and over the hills and the whole area was inundated with water. It rained every day and there we were with one gym and the girls' gym on the other side of Rose Lake, which had swelled over the shores. Maybe we squeegeed the courts and got in one or two games outside, but that was it for the whole week.

"Coaches couldn't get in and kids literally got there two days late, but they came. That was the one week in the history of the camp where if kids wanted a refund and demanded it and took us to court on what we promised and delivered, they might have won. We couldn't have afforded to pay them, but nobody asked for their money back. The kids loved it."

Stations went on uninterrupted. It took some doing. Garf still has the sketch he and Hubie Brown drew up with arrows and dotted lines, mapping out where everyone should be. There were four sections. Section A was the dining room. Ralph Willard, now the head coach at Western Kentucky of the Sun Belt, did "Moving Without the Ball" in the kitchen, using racks of pots and pans to set screens.

The porches of the four bunks nearest the dining hall were Section B. It was rough dribbling around the loose boards, but everyone managed. The gym was Section C. That was cake. It was slightly more cramped in Section D, in the loft above the stage. Tom McCorry taught rebounding there and nearly got cut to pieces when he snapped a fluorescent light in half. That was stations for the week.

"People ask me all the time, 'When did you know you were good?' We knew we had something special that year," Garf says. "Maybe it was because the kids could see we were there dying and trying and doing our best, giving whatever we could with the facilities we had. I like to think they appreciated our work ethic. Kids can be very understanding. A lot of them wanted to come back."

* * * * *

The King didn't. Frank Marino arrived at Five-Star without fanfare that soaked summer, sloshing through the muck like everyone else. He'd been expecting more. He knew about Garf and the camp and imagined it was like a university with sparkling indoor courts and a spacious campus. "Instead, we were up to our asses in mud and I ruined a new pair of Pumas," he recalls.

Marino had introduced himself to Garf that spring at the Westchester County Civic Center. His hometown, Mount Vernon, New York, was a basketball hotbed with NBA brothers Gus and Ray Williams and later Scooter and Rodney McRae strutting their stuffs. Scouts, including Garf, were a permanent part of the scenery, and Marino wanted to ask a favor of him.

Marino was coaching at Tuckahoe High where he had once been an all-county guard. An average college player at C.W. Post, he was hoping Garf could pull some strings for a friend of his who wanted to play in Europe. They got talking, exchanging opinions on players, and the master was impressed with his insights. Garf produced a contract from his suit jacket and just like that he was part of Five-Star.

It took him awhile to fit in, which wasn't unusual. Raised in comfortable, white suburbia, he was more at ease with people who'd endured the inner city. Most of his high school teammates were black kids and his idol was Eli Strand, a talented black athlete who played pro football with the Green Bay Packers. Marino was never sure where he truly belonged.

He is an enigma at Five-Star today. "After that first week, I made a vow never to step foot in that godforsaken place again," he says. "Garf had asked me to work the August session too, but I made an excuse and then showed up anyway to look at the talent. It felt homey and I started to like feeling like part of the family." There were guys there who walked the walk and talked the talk and could do it.

He doesn't like stations, referring to them as "Much ado about nothing." He prefers the school of hard knocks. It isn't that he thinks stations are a breeze or that he can't teach the game; it's that he feels a kinship with rugged, physical, street-wise players. And there's this little thing about holding a job. He's been at the top and the bottom, working as an assistant at the University of Detroit under Dick Vitale when the team made the NCAA Final 16 in 1985, and also at South Carolina under Bill Foster. The past few years, he's been in and out of the profession.

"Maybe I'm an embarrassment at the camp because I have so much experience and am out of work a lot," Marino says. "I admit I'm strong-willed. A lot of guys want assistants who are subservient and predictable and those are not words used to describe me. I don't fit the image." Still, his ability to read a player is respected in the business and his opinion frequently sought.

His heart belongs to Five-Star. There, simply put, he is "The King." Only Garf and Will Klein have been to more sessions. There had been 96 entering the summer of 1990 and he'd been to 77 of them. He has coached in the camp's NBA finals 13 times and won four titles, tying him with Pat Quigley, the coach of Bishop Loughlin in New York City for the most in camp history. It's a tie he vows to break.

The single most important thing to him is his position of eminence at Five-Star. He knows the inner dealings of the camp and the closets where any skeletons are hidden. He is like a brother to Garf. He is also like a raven perched upon Garf's shoulder: his eyes scour the camp, and he has Garf's ear when others cannot be heard. He can dispute Garf in public and get away with it because deep down he too wants what is best for Five-Star.

It's a side he rarely shows and many are wary of him, aware of his tempestuous side and his influence with Garf. Just as many confide in him. "A lot of guys miss the point on me," The King says. "I say and do things sometimes that appear like emotional outbursts, but there is a distinct method to my madness. Guys would be surprised to find out how loyal and grateful I am when recognized for my ability.

"I go to Five-Star for different reasons than some of the other guys. I have been there so much I can tell what time it is by the activity that is going on. I don't go to advance my career. I go there for what happens. You could never coach this much great talent anywhere else. Anybody can learn to teach and organize, but coaching is another matter.

"Basketball is a game of sudden and constant change. Greatness is having the ability to make those types of adjustments, to be a survivor, to think on your feet and let the game come to you and live within it. Some guys have ego problems with players who can do that kind of thing on their own, but the idea is to let the great player channel his greatness toward uplifting the whole team. A coach has to be able to create things to take advantage of his wonderful gift. Don't stifle it. Enhance it."

There was nothing anyone could do for Itchy and Twitchy's game. They'd returned as counselors and talked Garf into giving them the "Pick-and-Roll" station. Right away the squirmy siblings got things backwards. Twitchy was "Pick" and Itchy was "And Roll," but the kids enjoyed it which meant Garf did too. These guys were an all-day Wriggling Brothers circus.

Garf knew he'd rue the decison, but he let them provide entertainment the last night of camp during the awards ceremony. Garf, though he'll dispute this, has a tendency to let things drag on when he hands out awards. He appreciates it when the campers and coaches do a good job and he likes to thank each and every person. It can take hours.

Itchy and Twitchy decided to liven things up after so much drenched drudgery. Itchy did an imitation of Garf, right down to his Chesterfields and Cagney Twitch. That's what everyone called the shoulder-and-arm flutter Garf did whenever he was super serious or irritated. He would pace and puff and holler and hitch. He still does, sometimes in his Palm Beach pants and citrus sneakers, and the campers tease him ceaselessly when he's like that. Good old Uncle Howie.

Twitchy did Will Klein, all studious and stern with his slightly slouched posture and finger on his nose, concentrating, taking in everything that was being said around him. He even talked like Klein, very slowly, and said things like, "OK, who ordered the jar of Vaseline?" and "Just let me know, who's picking up the kids from the bus station?" It was perfect.

The campers were in stitches, even the usually quiet Midwest kids. They'd started to show up in droves, led by Tom LaGarde of North Carolina University and the NBA Phoenix Suns via Detroit Central Catholic High. He was just the first of coach Bernie Holowicki's players to make the trip east. Many more Michigan, Ohio, Illinois, and Indiana kids were on the way.

* * * * *

The Eastern kids had always come, and there was one in particular Garf would never forget. Sean Mannion, a 6'3" guard from Regis High in Manhattan, went to Five-Star three years and was the kind of kid everyone liked, scrappy and always patting the other guy on the back. During his senior year he died suddenly, for no reason it seemed, while watching his girlfriend play basketball. Garf named the sportsmanship award at Honesdale after him.

All the awards at Five-Star are named after someone near and dear to the camp. The outstanding player in the NBA every week gets the Fred Boyne/Charles Brown award named in honor of Fred Boyne, the camp's first trainer, and Charles Brown, Hubie Brown's dad. There's one for Bob Lapidus too, and not just because he brought Garf and Bob Knight together. He was a regular at camp. The all-star game MVP gets his award.

There are awards for Mr. Hustle (in honor of George "Truck" Robinson of Gordon Tech in Chicago, who stole the original "Truck" Robinson's nickname but could play even without it); the Playoff MVP (John Davis, coach at H.D. Woodson High in Washington, D.C., who was forever paying for kids out of his own pocket); and Mr. Playmaker (for Frank Williams, from Coolidge High in Washington, D.C., a resident coach at Five-Star for 14 years).

There are others, all of them special to Garf. The Most Promising Prospect each session gets the Charles "Doc" Turner Award in honor of another legendary camp trainer. A second Sportsmanship Award immortalizes Keith Moon, who died in the Evansville University team plane crash in the early eighties. The Best Rebounder will always be Arturo Brown of Nazareth High in Brooklyn who died in pre-season practice at Boston University.

The most improved camper gets the Paul Friedman Award. Friedman was a junior at Princeton when he died. The Outstanding Player Award for the Development League calls to mind Kevin

to Garf, cruised in en route to the pros. The East Coast kids, conscious of their turf being tread upon, immediately declared war. Pete Strickland, now an assistant coach at VMI, was one of the generals. "All the Detroit and D.C. kids bunked together, and across the alleyway from them were the New York and Jersey kids," he says.

"The first night words were tossed back and forth and the second night somebody threw a can. The next night three or four cans were tossed, so it was something we started to notice. The fourth night some gravel was thrown. It was getting serious, so a bunch of us went over. There were no lights on and things got testy and a little scary, but nobody threw any punches.

"It was just guys marking out their territories, but what we found out was there was a common denominator at Five-Star. It was the one camp you had to go to, and when you got there you'd better have your game intact. What was unusual was I don't remember any racial incidents. There were big-time food thieves though. Guys had padlocks on their coolers but left their suitcases wide open.

"After going through it," Strickland says, "I felt a step ahead of where I'd been before. It was significant not just in terms of time spent there learning basketball, but in terms of a rite of passage too. I won the Playmaker Award, and out of nowhere Bill Willoughby came over and shook my hand. It gave me chills. 'Poodles,' that's what we called him, was a big-name high school player, and he didn't have to do that. For me it was like acceptance, like 'Damn, maybe I passed the test,' not just as a player but as a Five-Star guy."

It was natural to fall in line. Everybody knew that Garf was ultimately in charge, provided Will Klein agreed. And even when the deities disagreed, everybody knew they would resolve the matter and do what was best. Their commitment was pervasive and anything they couldn't handle got worked out on the courts. Things were in place and in their proper order. It was time for a change.

EIGHT

Rosemont Rolls Past, Whistle Stop in Wheeling

"Everybody loves you right now because you can play that game of basketball, but one day they ain't gonna be there patting you on the back."

– USC coach George Raveling

Garf says it was the funniest thing he ever heard in camp. You had to be there. The second week of camp in the summer of 1974 was another rainy period, and after about three days of it, Ron Rothstein stared into the dank mist and said that Garf must have seen God playing basketball somewhere and given him a three-minus rating. "It was a lie," Garf says. "We had God a four-plus for years. I raised him to a five-plus after that, but it still rained four more days."

It wasn't damp weather that finally made Five-Star leave Rosemont. Not even bad food was the reason. They needed more room. The waiting list was lengthening.

Garf and Will Klein were thinking about heading south or maybe farther west. Midwest kids, especially from the Buckeye and Hoosier states, were starting to hog the beds. And boys from below the Mason-Dixon line had a mind to take on some Yankees. Garf resisted increasing the numbers by too much, knowing that would just crowd things and threaten the camp's chemistry. The only alternative was expansion, to offer more weeks so more kids could come, but that could wait a year or so. All things in their time.

First, the Ohio and Indiana kids had to get settled in, which was harder than it sounded because they couldn't stand still very long. Jim Paxson, a 6'4" guard, was one of the worst offenders. Paxson played at Bishop Alter in Kettering, Ohio, and couldn't outrun molasses in January, but he was always open for easy shots and if he wasn't he'd fake you blind until he was.

"Someday they should write on his tombstone, 'He knew how to play,'" Garf says. "Paxson was not overly quick, but he had a better kind of quickness: mental quickness. He epitomized Bob Knight's philosophy that in basketball, 'Mental is to the physical as four is to one.' Knight would talk about that attitude at Five-Star, captivating a hushed audience.

Paxson knew how to move without the ball. So did his little brother John, who energized Five-Star some time later. The Paxsons survived on savvy. "Both of them could set a man up," says their high school coach, Joe Petrocelli. "They both seemed to know which way the defender was leaning and go the other way."

Petrocelli is a mover too. Garf calls him the "Lewis and Clark of Five-Star," crediting him for opening the door to Ohio. Petrocelli got to the state semifinals in 1975 with Jim Paxson and won it all in 1978 with John. "When it came to crunch time, all they'd do was win the game for you," Petrocelli says. "There was not a whole lot I could do with them. They both worked full time on the game and had that inborn something extra. They moved well and were both ambidextrous, like their dad."

That's what Garf loved most, the link to their father, an ex-pro player with the old St. Louis Hawks and a graduate of the University of Dayton. "The beautiful thing about the Paxsons," Garf says, "is that when they came to camp they came with a bunch of other kids, and all the kids' fathers had gone to Dayton and were legendary players in the fifties and sixties. All the fathers sent their sons to Five-Star and the connection there was awesome."

Blue-blood basketball families—the Paxsons, Bockhorns, Uhls, and Meinekes—all flowing deep in the veins of Five-Star. And the Harris clan too. Doug Harris was Jim Paxson's high school teammate and a virtual unknown. He turned some heads at Five-Star and got heavily recruited afterwards. That's what sustained Garf.

All the Midwestern kids wanted a piece of the city kids, especially that weird dude from Farmingdale, Long Island, 6'9" forward Jim Graziano. He could definitely play and, in fact, was dominating the camp, but nobody could relate to his musical preferences. Garf would wake everyone up with college fight songs or Artie Shaw and his Big Band stuff and Graziano would actually get into it.

"He told me he never realized how swingy it was," Garf says. "Very rarely did kids like the music. Most of the time they played their radios—nowadays their boom boxes—in the dorms and I knew that. It's great music, though, and I wanted them to hear it, so I'd play the best stuff as they were walking to their morning workout or stations. That way they had to listen."

Mike O'Koren was back, filling out and looking more like the pro he was destined to become. Garf was getting attached to him and not because he was the first camper to win the Outstanding Player Award twice. O'Koren not only brought half the kids in Hudson County to Five-Star, he worked liked hell every day, so of course Garf lived and died with him after he went to college.

It was strange with O'Koren though. What happened at Five-Star seemed to be a reflection of things to come in more ways than one. For him there was Hawkeye Whitney. Whitney played for Morgan Wootten at DeMatha, was the only kid in camp who could contain O'Koren. It was the same in the Altantic Coast Conference after O'Koren went to North Carolina and Whitney went to Maryland. In head-to-head battles, Whitney usually prevailed.

It wasn't the first time the future had been subtly revealed. Norm "Bruno" Caldwell, a Jersey kid, arrived one summer with a big reputation. Caldwell could score and pass, but a lot of his passes went off the mark. Some observers figured he was playing over everyone's head, but Garf saw it as a lot of razzle-dazzle and said so in *HSBI*. He rarely downgraded kids in his reports, finding ways to let them down easy, but he blasted Caldwell.

There were reasons. Caldwell left camp early and some things came up missing. Garf tucked it away and whenever a coach inquired about Caldwell, he'd say, yes, the kid had gobs of talent, but his gut feeling was he wouldn't stick around long. One coach took him anyway, and Caldwell didn't last the season. It didn't make Garf feel good, but it was strange the way patterns developed at Five-Star.

It was like that for Sam Bowie too. A superb kid and one of the most significant campers in Five-Star history, he caught a cold and broke a finger at camp and it was odd the way injuries later plagued his college and pro careers. "Five-Star very often turns out to be a mirror," Garf says. "The way a kid is in camp is very often the way he'll be in later life. Leopards seldom change their spots."

* * * * *

Sometimes it's possible to change, and no one appreciated that better than George Raveling. An assistant to Bob Knight in the 1984

Olympics before taking the USC job, he is one of Garf's top five all-time recruiters. He revolutioned the system in the early sixties, working for Villanova. He always had a stack of legal-sized yellow notebooks under his arm, like he owned stock in the company, and they were all packed with notes on players from Anywhere USA.

Raveling knew everybody in the business and introduced Knight to Bob Lapidus, who introduced Knight to Garf, and they all used to hobnob till dawn, which is how this whole Five-Star thing got going. Raveling grew up in Pennsylvania, was an All-American at Villanova, and started lecturing at camp in the early seventies. He came back mostly to tell stories about the importance of keeping things in perspective.

Raveling often talked about "Page Four." The campers would gather around, expecting basketball drills, and he'd say, "Let's go back many years ago to a small town and imagine it is a hot and humid day, somewhat similar to today. We cross a grassy field and come upon a playground and three young girls and a 20-year-old college student.

"This group is going about the task of building an old western army fort out of popsicle sticks. A young boy approaches and he is troubled and confused, struggling to become the person he feels he can be, but he has no direction. He wants to talk and he asks the college student to listen, but that college student says to him, 'Johnny I'd like to, but I have to finish this project. It's urgent. You understand, don't you, son? Could you come back tomorrow?'

"The boy understands and says he will come back tomorrow. The next morning that college student is sitting, sipping a cup of coffee, reading the newspaper, and he turns to page four. I think I'll always remember that it was page four. I was that student and a headline caught my eye that Johnny had committed suicide, and far too many nights in my life I hear a voice asking the Lord to let me please live that day over again.

"There are situations all of us wish we could live over again. If I could talk to Johnny, I would say some of the same things I'm going to share with you today," Raveling would continue. "You all play basketball and many good things have happened in my life that started with a little round leather ball. Basketball gave me a chance to go to college because I could never have afforded it. It has given me an opportunity to travel all over the world and find out what I am capable of doing.

"Everybody loves you right now because you can play that game of basketball, but one day they ain't gonna be there patting you on the back, so you'd better prepare yourself. If you beat Indiana on

Tuesday night, does that make you a better person on Wednesday? If you believe that, you're a fool. I have met very many successful people, and the one thing they have all mastered is the fundamentals of winning in life.

"It all starts with a dream, and for many of you it is basketball. The problem isn't that we dream, it's that we don't dream big enough. Work at making it a reality and then you will want to win at anything you do in life. And be a learner. Wealth is not what we put in the bank, it's what we put in our brains. There's a saying I like: 'Give me fish and I eat today, but teach me to fish and I eat forever.'

"Believe in yourself. The question for every day isn't what so-and-so thinks of you, but what you think of yourself. Right now in this room there is enough intellectual power to solve the world's problems. The problem is we don't believe that and most of us don't believe in ourselves. Surrounded by so much negative stuff in your life, maybe it is hard to believe you have depth and dimension, that you can do great things, but the human mind is very powerful.

"Be a worker. My grandmother always told me that God provides for every bird, but he ain't gonna put food in their nests. It's the same with us. We gotta get out and work for it. Input equals output; if you give 25 percent that's what you get. Also, establish a goal, believe there's a method for success and apply yourself to it."

* * * * *

You couldn't get out of Five-Star without hearing the facts. What you did with them was your choice, of course, and Garf and Will Klein had to face a few of their own. It was time to spread their wings, either that or suffocate. They had already decided to pack their bags for Lake Bryn Mawr, 10 minutes south as the crow flies. Bryn Mawr was actually a little older than Camp Rosemont, but the owners, Herb and Melanie Kutzen, were sinking money into it and keeping it nice.

Built in the early 1920s by the Federman family of Brooklyn, Bryn Mawr was an exclusive girls' camp. The Kutzens like to boast that it was the last of five camps the Federmans put up and by then they'd corrected all their mistakes. They say it is the Five-Star of Federman's camps.

It was still birds and trees outside your window, but it wasn't quite as rustic as Rosemont, and the food, while not exotic cuisine, was supposedly better. It was broken-in for basketball too. Herb Kutzen had coached in Flatbush and had run an instructinal program, Project Basketball, at Bryn Mawr for several years. He didn't mind dropping that so Five-Star could have the place all to itself.

Two weeks weren't enough, however, so before bidding adieu to Harry Silverman, Five-Star, in the summer of 1975, said how-de-do to Wheeling, West Virginia and the campus of Wheeling College. It would be a short stay, only two years, but through no fault of Paul Baker. The head coach at Wheeling, Baker was a one-man maintenance crew. "We wanted a place farther west, and Howard knew him through *HSBI*," says Will Klein, who was only too glad for the help. "Baker did a lot for the camp, putting baskets up on the tennis courts and taking care of everything."

Five-Star quickly outgrew the place. Garf and Will Klein had been hoping for 180 kids the first year, and they got 210. The next year they got 270. It was hot, which was a radical change from Rosemont, and the air conditiong wasn't set up for mid-July. The usual students were gone by then. On rainy days, Will Klein had to beg, borrow, and steal in town for more courts, and busing the kids was a headache. It wasn't that easy to get to either, scrunched in between Pennsylvania and Ohio in the northernmost slim finger of the state. Wheeling wasn't the boonies, but it was a haul no matter which way you came.

The association, nevertheless, was fruitful. Garf, sensitive to social graces, wanted a southerner to run the camp and just happened to have one, Dave Odom, a high school coach from Durham, North Carolina. Odom was kind of green in terms of Five-Star, having been part of things only a year or so, but Garf liked his style: plantation polite and gentlemanly outside, iron-willed underneath, and genuine through and through.

Odom, brought up in Goldsboro, North Carolina, a one-school town, was voted most athletic and cutest in the class of 1960, something he is proud of still. He nearly broke his daddy's heart when he showed no interest in carrying on the family car business, but his mother put in a good word and his father had a kind heart after all and they encouraged his basketball.

Odom was five years old and fidgeting when Al "Sarge" Paley took him under his wing. He was eager to suit up at the local Boys Club, but you had to be eight for that, so Paley let him hang around until he ripened. Odom coaches at Five-Star like he is always trying to pay back his parents and ol' Sarge Paley. The campers feel like what they're doing means something to him.

Garf and Will Klein are like kin to Odom. "To Garf, Wheeling was the deep South," he says, smiling, "but it is almost inexplicable what Five-Star has come to mean to me. If I had known about the scrutiny Five-Star guys put newcomers under, I might never have come here, but Garf gave me responsibility and the freedom to grow and develop. He sets the standard that all of us must live up to. Either that or he'll find a way to end our stay, and that's what coaching is all about.

"I'll never forget my first day of stations. I thought I was well prepared, but after the 20 minutes were up I had gotten only halfway through my plan and I was afraid Garf had noticed. He is the all-seeing eye. The second day I overheard Garf talking to someone, saying, 'Watch this one, he's gonna be a good one' and I thought he was talking about a player. He wasn't. He was talking to Kentucky coach Joe B. Hall about Dave Odom and it gave me a sensation unlike anything I've had since I met my wife.

"Willie Klein has shown me that for every star there has to be a supporting actor. He is very reliable and compassionate, and, like a good basketball player, he knows his role in this camp. Five-Star runs smoothly because of him. He and Garf have frightful arguments and there have been hot dog rolls slung at the dinner table and temper tantrums, but invariably before the meal is over whatever it was gets the OK from one of them."

It was like family. Whatever it was, get it out in the open and then figure out what to do. You might be feeling down because you'd gotten your ass kicked on the court or maybe feeling cocky because you'd done the ass-kicking and either way somebody was there to straighten you out.

"Garf feels campers need him the way a son needs a father, yet he needs them the same way," Odom says. "It's his reason for living and giving. He is as comfortable brushing shoulders with basketball celebrities at the Final Four as he is talking to the most obscure ninth grader from the smallest town in America, and that's the reason Five-Star is successful.

"It's not like we don't have ups and downs. The camp is not perfect. We've had fights and isolated stealing, but we handle every problem on its own merit. There are kids here from every state in the union and from foreign countries, kids who otherwise might not mesh at all, and they occasionally clash. The supervision in camp, with a one-to-six counselor-to-camper ratio, cuts into that drastically though.

"The system has a tendency to weed them out too. The situation is very demanding, and the kids who don't comprehend what's going on here or who don't want to be a part of it will find a way to get out. We can tell early on if they've come to camp for the right reasons. We try not to finalize a camper, but the camp is bigger than any one kid or staffer, and there have been some sent home."

* * * * *

Snags, with few exceptions, could be worked out. Coaches were coming to look at the players already, but to make it more appealing, Garf, Klein, and Chuck Daly became partners in a Five-Star Coaching Seminar that ran concurrently with the camp. It was a long weekend of skull sessions featuring guys like Hubie Brown and Bob Knight and NBA genius-jester Frank Leyden. It wasn't for the kids. It was coaches teaching coaches.

Brown lectured on "Preparing for Special Situations in Coaching," and Knight gave a clinic on "Developing Program Intensity." Daly gave advice on getting a college coaching job, advising guys to include a picture with their résumés so people knew what they looked like, and to always be themselves. If you came on phony anybody who was any good would see right through you. And never forget how you got to the top and who helped you get there. It's a long way down alone.

The coaches got free refreshments and courtside seats, if any were left, at the Orange-White Classic, Five-Star's all-star game, the grand finale of every session. One team always wore orange shirts with white letters and the others wore the opposite and everyone knew the proceedings were as important to Garf as graduation and getting married are to most people. Probably more important. He did the intros and public address and it was Red Barber and the Garden and all that incredible, wonderful-to-watch talent combined.

The Coaching Seminar, patterned after the earlier Adelphi College Clinic, was ahead of its time but the logistics were all wrong. It fizzled out after a year or two, although it is still an after-midnight, one-night-only tradition at Robert Morris College in Coraopolis, Pennsylvania, where Five-Star moved after leaving Wheeling. The essence of it hasn't changed and a kid like Joe Abunasser, who is a team manager for Bob Knight and nothing more than a canteen boy at camp, can sit down with his notebook and listen and learn with some of the best minds in the game.

All the moving around didn't affect the level of competition. Dan Schayes, the NBA son of Syracuse Nats immortal Dolph Schayes, mixed it up inside with Long Island and Washington Bullets bruiser Jeff Ruland and just as pretty as could be were Darnell Valentine and Clyde "The Glide" Austin.

Valentine was the greatest camp guard ever in Garf's opinion until Adrian "Red" Autry in the late eighties. Valentine ran Rick Pitino's presses to perfection on his way to the Chicago Bulls and Cleveland Cavaliers. Clyde the Glide, from Maggie Walker High in

Richmond, Virginia, did his thing with the Harlem Globetrotters for a few years and was Garf's original Human Highlight Film. The second was Dominique Wilkins, the Atlanta Hawks dunkmaster who makes no bones that it was "that dude from Five-Star" who gave him his nickname. It fit 'Nique better anyway.

Jeff Lamp came but very nearly didn't. He would eventually play for Virginia University and the Los Angeles Lakers, but he was in a car accident a month before camp in 1976 and had to get stitches. Garf remembers because he came anyway and the camp trainer, 81-year-old Charles "Doc" Turner patched him up so he could play like nothing was wrong.

"Doc created a bandage that looked like something out of a mummy's tomb," Garf recalls. "I swear it started at Lamp's shoulder and ended at his leg. He was encased from top to bottom in tape. He had to get wrapped like that every day. He was the most expensive child we ever had, but worth every yard."

It was just another day at the office for Doc Turner, a legendary New York City trainer who learned his trade patching people up in the Rucker Summer Basketball League at Holcomb/Rucker Park in Harlem. You could see immortals up close there and Doc took care of their flesh-and-blood parts. Some said he had the gift of God in his little black bag, but his bee pollen would do the trick in a pinch. "He was an old-time guy," Garf says. "He was into healing by touch and pressure points, and I don't know if it worked or not, but psychologically you felt better after you went to see him."

Bee pollen was Doc's panacea and guys laughed it off until he used it on them and it made them feel like new. One time Joe Washington got a Rucker League elbow in the kisser and it was bad, but Doc mixed equal parts of bee juice and gauze pad and Washington went back in, scored about 75 points, and the Los Angeles Lakers eventually drafted him. They probably would have anyway but the stuff was magic.

Doc cured Five-Star's ills for years, passing his gift on to James Ross, then his understudy at Long Island University, before passing away at age 85. Ross, now the head trainer at camp and the assistant athletic director and head trainer for men's basketball at Xavier of Ohio, is simply "The Healer" at Five-Star. A native son of Brooklyn, he acquired the title studying with Doc at LIU and Rucker Park and he does more than throw on a bandage. "Bee pollen is a proven entity," he says.

"You stir it up with warm water to make a poultice and you can use it for anything: sprained ankles, twisted knees, headaches, and they all go away. It has to be the French Riviera bee pollen, sun-dried in comb or tablet."

Usually reserved and unobtrusive, The Healer can get downright pushy if someone is sprawled on the court. Anytime a camper goes down, The Healer is there. He got that way after a kid banged his head leaping for a rebound and had to have his jaw held open with a set of keys so he wouldn't swallow his tongue. All it did was save the kid's life. The Healer learned a lot from Doc, but a lot of it is him too. "Doc was a father figure who always soothed the heart as well as the hurt," The Healer says. "He'd fix the kids up and then sit down and talk with them. This camp is interesting that way. It has the best teachers I've ever met and they get involved in a kid's daily problems, not just hoop. I brought my son to Five-Star just to expose him to what happens here."

* * * * *

Five-Star was healthy and in the prime of its youth and ready to take on the world after the summer of 1976. A second session had been added the second year at Wheeling and the camp was running four weeks at full capacity, nearly 1,000 kids every summer. A decade earlier Garf had scrimped and saved for 61, but campers were standing in line for the hottest ticket in town and there was no guarantee they'd get one.

It was worth the wait. Five-Star had become a summertime monolith and Garf was thoroughly entrenched in the college recruiting network, especially on the East Coast. He was still outside the "Coaching Establishment," but a sparkling performance at camp or a solid rating in *HSBI* made any prospect feel fit as a fiddle. Garf was like a personal basketball physician. With one phone call he could help cure an ailing program or give a kid renewed hope. He was on-duty all hours of the day and night and forever giving free advice. Not everyone appreciated his charitableness, however, a fact that would become painfully apparent in the not-too-distant future.

The Five-Star guys and their work ethic would fit right in at Robert Morris College after leaving West Virginia. It was less than an hour from Pittsburgh, and almost before they unpacked guys were calling the two weeks there Pitt I and Pitt II. Over the years two more sessions would be added, encompassing all of July, and the weather was always hot and tough. But it was nothing compared to kids like John Paxson, Isiah Thomas, Mark Aguirre, Michael Jordan, and others who stuck it out.

The Five-Star gypsies liked Lake Bryn Mawr right away. It was spacious and well kept, yet they could put their feet up and feel at home. The coaches' quarters were cozier and the bunkhouses were closer together, which made keeping track of the campers easier. Even The King approved. He began piling up championships almost immediately and was tempted to set up permanent housekeeping.

It was Rosemont without the sags, although Harry Silverman and the rainy bus trips across Lake Summit would be missed. "The early years were the best for me," says Will Klein, "having to sweep the courts and paint new lines and build up the gym floor every summer. The comraderie was amazing.

"I used to coach at camp in the very beginning and I'll always remember Richie Adubato playing in a game of counselors versus campers. It was a close game and we had the ball. During a time-out, I told Adubato the only thing he had to do was take the inbounds pass and make sure to give it to someone in a blue uniform. The first thing he did was give it to a guy in a silver uniform, and I shook my head and said, 'Adubato, you're uncoachable.' How was I supposed to know he'd coach the Dallas Mavericks someday?

"At first, the camp was just a week away from the evils of society for the kids. I didn't think the kids could learn more in a week than their regular high school coaches could teach them from October to March, three hours a day, six days a week, but the basketball thing 24 hours a day was incredible."

Tradition would be upheld at Lake Bryn Mawr. Today, there is one session the third week in June and another in late August, the granddaddy of Five-Star. The first and oldest week became the seventh and last, the end of a cycle that begins in Radford, Virginia, the second week of June.

PART TWO

Radford

NINE
Radford Bound

"A kid can face reality here."

– Dave Odom at Radford

It's hot.

Jack Stephens is dozing off in the seat of the charter bus taking him from Roanoke Airport to Radford University and his first taste of Five-Star. He's been traveling since nine-thirty in the morning, flying in from Marietta, Georgia, then waiting with everyone else at the terminal for the bus to arrive and take them to Five-Star. It is late afternoon and more campers are asleep in the aisle, standing, thinking they are near the end of a long day, but it is only the beginning.

Looking out the windows, other kids have their eyes open dreamily, as if they are hoping the bus will drop them off in front of their homes, not at some sweat box that is a speck in the Allegheny Mountains. A feeling they hope no one sees is swirling in them, making them want familiarity enough to get off and start walking sometimes and sometimes filling them with an assuredness that coming here was the right thing.

There is something similar about everyone riding. "I came for the competition," says Stephens, a soft-spoken 6'2" senior who didn't get many minutes the past season but figures to start for Marietta High in the winter. Three years in a row the team has gone to the state tournament and for the most part he's watched from the bench, and that's his goal, to start for the varsity. He needs to improve his handle, he figures, and learn how to get open better, but he can do some things all right.

Stephens would learn something unexpected over the next seven days. He came to Five-Star expecting to play in the NBA league with the rest of the rising seniors, kids entering their senior year in high school. The NCAA has rising juniors and the NIT has rising sophomores and younger players. Garf will move a kid up if that's where he belongs, regardless of his age, but sometimes a kid with great expectations gets moved down.

It's all decided at the draft. Tryouts are held, the names are juggled around, and Garf gets input from all the coaches before doing anything, but it's not uncommon for a kid to jump up a league or drop down. It's not done to be cruel, although to a wide-eyed kid it can seem that way. Maybe on his home turf he was the top cat, but Five-Star is a different den and the coaches can spot that at tryouts, which is another reason they have them the first night. Get it over with and give a kid time to adjust if he must.

Stephens got bumped down to the NCAA and there were others, but that didn't make it any easier. It never does. Garf is hip to that. On that first night of camp every week after tryouts are over and while the kids are thinking of nothing but bed, he lets them down gently, without them even knowing. Everyone gathers for attendance in the dining hall, and while he gets the names of everyone present from Will Klein, a routine settles in. The veteran campers have it down pat.

They chatter and get to know the new guys until they see Garf step to the podium in the front of the room. They turn their total attention to him, knowing that if they don't he'll get it anyway and the peach-fuzz rookies, glancing around for guidance, follow suit. It happens that way every week until the newcomers become old-timers and lead.

If there are any stragglers, Garf knows how to rope them. Opening night attendance is the first chance the new kids on the block get to see him in action, and whether it's Radford or anywhere else he's the same. They'll find out they can count on that. Going around the room, one of the kids answers "Yo" when Garf calls his name instead of "Here" or "Yes, sir," or something more along that line. The proceedings stop, and after a few moments any heads that were lowered or turned face forward.

"We don't need all that 'Yo' bullshit," Garf says, and kids who have heard it before crack up because they know he hasn't changed and the rookies are shocked a little and look at him like, 'Who is this guy, anyhow?' Coming from Garf, the profanity sounds different somehow, spontaneous, like your father smashing his thumb with a hammer and blurting it out. It's not degrading, he doesn't say it right at you, it's just the way he talks sometimes and the way some of the coaches talk, and the campers don't have to if they don't want to, they just have to make sure they get the point.

The message is twofold really. First, leave the nonsense back in the dorm or pack your bags. Second, relax, be yourself, and if you don't know how, take it easy, there's time to learn. That's the way it's set up. No one has to put on any airs and no one needs to posture and act tough. Everyone can see through the act anyway and the only people you have to answer to are Garf and Will Klein, your coach, your teammates, and yourself, so it's all out front. Nothing is hidden.

Garf is like that too, wide open, like a breakaway layup, and if you're not ready it seems brutally unfair, but he can be as kind as needed rain too. He knows what's coming, that every kid in camp believes he's the best, so he breaks it to them gently. The way he did it at Radford was to give the kids a trivia question and most of them want to go to sleep, but they played along. "What do Michael Jordan, Isiah Thomas, Albert King, Patrick Ewing, and Dominique Wilkins have in common?" he asks. No one knows. "They all came to Five-Star and none of them were on a championship team.

"The point? What's the point? The point is, were they winners? Yes, they were, because they came here and worked their asses off and made the best of it, which reminds me, I may be the only person in history with two racehorses named after him: Five-Star Camp, who won his first two races, and Five-Star Howie, who broke his maiden in May of 1989 and paid $17.50. Guess how much I had on him. Not a freakin' penny. Nada. A doughnut." It isn't just a dull basketball camp anymore, it's Garf's stage, and it's opening night and he's on and Radford University had better brace itself.

* * * * *

Five-Star came to Radford, Virginia, in 1985, requiring yet more room and something a little more south. Texas, Tennessee, Georgia, Carolina kids and kids from the Virginias got out of school before the northerners and were chomping at the bit to get into camp. There was only so much room, and to remedy the situation, Garf and Will Klein turned to their native rebel son, Dave Odom, to lead them to Dixie, which he did, taking them to the 21st century in the process.

Locals enjoy living in Radford because of the peace and quiet that surrounds their town like thick vines. An hour west of Roanoke, it nearly became the second Pittsburgh in the early 1900s until iron ore that wasn't up to snuff and a nationwide financial scare put an end to that dream. Descendants who still feel the futile exhilaration of those times in their bones will tell you it was a little bit like building the ultimate horse carriage the year before Henry Ford.

The New River, which flows serenely past town and is visible from the gym at Five-Star, belies its name. It is the oldest river in North America, literally older than the hills, staying put as the mountains rose up around it. As senile as it is serene, the New lost its bearings years ago and runs generally north from North Carolina through the Virginia Valley until it merges with the Kanawha River in West Virginia.

The university, until the early 1970s, was a womens' teachers college, a branch of Virginia Polytechnic Institute, and is still mostly women. Campers enjoy the scenery, with scores of summer school students sauntering to class, but keep their distance. There are rules and there is also precious little time for flirting, although boys will be boys and Garf doesn't mind as long as they show respect and remember that whatever they do reflects on everyone else. The campers have heard it all before, but at Five-Star it sinks in.

Maybe it's the food. The chefs know the best way to a young man's heart. "I don't think it was ever as bad as it was reputed to be, but people have to find something negative, so they use the camp food," snarls Garf. "They can't do that at Radford because it's the best food in the country. It's not even debatable, we're talking gourmet. It's laid out for the kids in buffet style and they can take as much as they want as long as they eat what they take."

The kids love Radford, with its hospitality, homestyle cookin', and only two-in-a-room dormitories, so Garf does too, or maybe it's the other way around. "This is *the* campsite in America. This is the year 2000 coming to Five-Star. We have a five-court indoor gym at the Dedmon Center and another gym right next to the outdoor courts we can use if it rains. This is what basketball camps are going to be like in the future."

The present contained Jerry Wainwright, which was plenty good enough. The campers who'd never met the Wake Forest assistant coach were introduced after breakfast the first morning and many found him unforgettable. He is strong and tall with a blacksmith's strength, and he walks around like he could pull your heart out and hand it to you but he has something else in mind for it.

His mother is named Valentine because that's the day she was born, and Wainwright, raised on the south side of Chicago, told the campers, "I broke her heart many times, I'm afraid. I used to do stupid shit like hang off the Ohio Street Bridge, and my mother told me I had no respect for her feelings and that cut deep, even though I pretended it didn't. The thing is I lived my whole young life for other people, doing things that I hoped would impress them and make them like me and I'm ashamed to tell you that."

But he told the campers anyway because he's been around enough to know keeping it trapped inside is worse. He serves different roles at Five-Star, depending on where Garf needs him. At Radford he was the NBA commissioner, third in command with the two other commissioners behind Garf and Will Klein, who are equal, and Dave Odom, the head coach. He does things not covered in the job description.

Sunday morning, Wainwright gathered the kids in the tree-shaded campus square to further indoctrinate them and give them some old-time camp religion. "Take advantage of this opportunity," he said, "so you can say you stuck it out at the hardest basketball camp in the country and got as much from it as you could. Show enthusiasm. Be a positive person and believe in yourself. If any of you know guys in wheelchairs, you should know why it's bullshit to ever get down on yourself if you miss a shot or make a bad pass or something. You don't have to get down on yourself here.

"Be coachable. I had two pretty fair players on a team here one year, Ron Harper and Joe Wolf, who both got scholarships and went to the NBA. There was one game I told the team to let each player touch the ball on offense and only then look for the good shot. Harper, who could shoot the hell out of the ball, launched one right away and came over and said to me, 'I felt it, coach.' I didn't care if he made the shot or not. I asked him how he'd like to feel my foot up his ass and we formed an understanding. College coaches look for coachable players and you should think about that.

"And while you're here don't say shit to the referees." Usually coaches make the calls and the campers know better than to squawk, but at Radford, Fred Barakat, the supervisor of the Atlantic Coast Conference officials, runs a camp for zebras. Top-notch whistle-blowers like the ACC's Dick Paparo and Mickey Crowley serve as instructors and occasionally lecture at camp on rules of the game. The refs are like one of the guys at camp, but bad habits are hard to break so Wainwright said, "Some of these guys might call shit you won't believe, but we're lucky to have them and besides, looking for excuses for your performance is just built-in failure.

"We're guests here, so don't throw your pop cans and junk on the grounds. My mother didn't have a great job and had to pick up stuff like that, so I take that kind of thing real close to heart. There's something else, and heaven knows I'm not arguing against the pleasantries of sex and I'm not saying anything about women, but there are a lot of girls here and something like this could happen anytime in your career: I knew some guys who took a girl into their dorm in college and she hollered rape. Think about it, guys. If a girl is willing to come into your room with you and a bunch of other guys, chances are she's done it before and chances are all kinds of other things are coming in with her. Try to remember why you are here." Man-to-man stuff, in case they hadn't heard it before, and if they had it was a reminder that things can happen, so be aware of it and don't be afraid to speak up if something does happen.

* * * * *

Dave Odom, still the camp's head coach at Radford, preached the same sermon, albeit less brusquely. He had long since left Durham High, working as an assistant at the University of Virginia and Wake Forest before taking over as head coach of the Demon Deacons for the 1989-90 season. The new job placed increased demands on his time, so his future at Five-Star, after 15 summers, was in doubt. Looking out over the proceedings during the afternoon, he reflected and reminisced.

"A kid can face reality here," he said. "As a high school coach I was hesitant to send weak players to Five-Star, but now I know it's best to send them to let them find out the truth early and to help them in other ways. I have never seen a kid leave here worse off than when he came. I've seen hard-core city kids cry during lectures when they thought their hearts were too hard to care, and I've seen kids who thought it was uncool to work hard be the last ones off the court the final night.

"Things like that happen because everything here is done for a reason. There was never a better example of that than my first year as head coach. Garf and I spent a lot of time discussing the operation of camp, and he told me to be sure to rotate the times that NIT teams played their games. Station 13 was held at the same time, and he wanted to give each kid a chance to get there.

"About the third or fourth day he came to me and said, 'See that kid over there in the green shorts? If you had rotated the time slots properly, he'd be at individual instruction today instead of playing a game. Two days in a row he's had games.' I have never forgotten that. And you know, people get on Will Klein about still having the first nickel he ever made at Five-Star, but he's done a lot for people who couldn't play a lick, people who just needed a helping hand, people like Willie Negron.

"Klein had left Columbus High and was the principal at Evander Child's in the Bronx. There was a kid at the school, Willie Negron, who was susceptible to epileptic seizures and starved for family. Whenever he got sick or something happened to him, Klein took care of him and still does. When he started coming to camp, everyone there took a liking to him too. No matter where you looked, he was there—at a game, at stations, or wherever, trying to help. We called him 'Omnipresence.'

"Willie became an assistant coach at the John Jay College of Criminal Justice eventually, but back then, he had a special talent. He might be the greatest New York Mets fan of all time. As a child, he couldn't go to the stadium to watch the games, so he listened to them all the time on the radio. He told Klein he could do play-by-play and imitate crowd noises perfectly.

"They even nicknamed him Howie Cosell at school, because he was always doing make-believe broadcasts. He kept after Klein for years to let him do it at camp, but the time was never right. One night there was just Willie and me at the scorer's table during a game and he got his chance in front of 400 campers. He did the whole bit, right down to the cheering crowd, and got one of the greatest standing ovations in the history of Five-Star. The way he puffed out his chest brought tears to my eyes."

*　*　*　*　*

Odom's eyes and everyone else's were wide open listening to Wainwright again at the night program, although it took a few minutes to convince some of the campers to be bright-eyed. It had been a long day, the first real camp day for the rookies, and everyone wanted some shut-eye. They'd caught the tail end of sunrise and had been at it nearly 16 hours.

Garf, knowing all about idle hands and the devil's work, knows how to keep them busy. First there are morning calisthenics followed by breakfast, and from around nine-thirty until eleven o'clock, stations. Then the games begin. Not every league plays at the same time due to the number of courts, so campers with some free time have a choice until lunch: catch some Z's, work out in the weight room, go to the pool, or listen to a 90-minute lecture, the Morning Mini-Lecture.

Rick Pitino, who is always primed for basketball, came up with the idea for the lecture years earlier after he got tired of watching kids stream back to the bunkhouses at Rosemont after stations.

Garf didn't need much convincing, and now it's part of the tradition. The campers aren't required to go, but Garf exhorts them, telling them it separates the guys who make it from those who don't, just like Station 13, and 50 or 60 kids usually show up the first day. By the end of the week, attendance dwindles to 15 or 20 and Garf makes a mental note of those who persevere in case some college coach asks about the kid someday.

After lunch everyone has 30 minutes off before another lecture and attendance at two o'clock sharp, and don't bother to be late because, well, just don't be. That's when the heavies, the guest lecturers, take the stage. Garf retires to the wings, bowing to Bob Knight or Duke coach Mike Krzyzewski or some of his own guys like Pitino, Fratello, or Hubie Brown, basketball's big-timers. The ball is theirs for an hour-and-change and there'd better be a good reason if they take too long too, because Garf has a schedule to keep. There are more games after the lecture and anyone with free time can lounge or gut out Station 13 or grab a coach for individual help.

Dinner is at six o'clock. No one has to eat, but they have to show up to be counted, and afterwards there are more games. Every team plays twice a day, and if there's an open court the kids can play pick-up games or one-on-one, which they do, constantly. Games run until nine-thirty. The camp runs like clockwork until it rains, and then there's a scramble for about five minutes unless Garf sees it coming, which he always does. The camp merely shifts into Plan "B" when it rains and starts to hum again.

The Night Program, at the end of all that, is Garf's idea of a midnight snack. He still treats the kids to the latest Converse highlight film on opening night and the Orange-White Classic is always played on the last night, but usually there is something educational or another lecturer. On Sunday night it was Wainwright. The kids were dragging, but so was he although it was hard to tell. He spoke with intensity and everything he said was off the cuff and from the heart and he started out saying, "There's nothing tougher than being a man. My dad told me something once I never understood until years later, . . ." and he stopped in midsentence.

Some of the kids were dozing and others were chitter-chattering. His sudden silence caught their attention, but the lack of respect sliced deep. Thinking back to Chicago's south side and someone else's pain, he continued, "I was excited beginning to talk just now because I think about what older guys have told me and I feel like doing this helps me pay them back. I see guys here nodding off and talking and saying to themselves, 'Oh shit, not another hour of this stuff,' and now I'm pissed off.

"You guys do this and and bitching becomes a way of life. When I was in high school my football coach used to make us crawl on a cinder track for a mile in shorts and if I came home bitching my father would tell me, 'If you don't like it, get a job.' He wasn't being a prick, he was just telling me the way it was. My dad made life very simple. He told me, 'Don't associate with assholes.'"

The tension was broken and the kids, even the Rip Van Winkles, were at ease and open to him. "I was the seventh boy in a row in a family of 11 kids. When I was eight years old my father took me aside and told me, 'Jerry, out of all the boys we have, you are the worst looking, you're a little on the ugly side.' I said to him, 'Dad, do you really believe that?' and he said, 'Yeah,' so I said, 'Hey, you know, you're messing with my confidence.'" No one was dozing now.

"I have a beautiful wife now, but she wouldn't go out with me the first few times I asked her," said Wainwright. "I kept asking her and she finally said yes and I guess what happened was she said to herself, 'Maybe if I go out with this asshole he'll leave me alone.' We get along great, but I'll tell you something, a lot of you guys are scared of 'No.' That's why you have horseshit games, you're insecure, afraid to embarrass yourselves by taking a risk. You come here and you're worried about your image. You've got inhibitions, self-imposed guidelines that stop you from reaching your potential. If you don't risk some things, you'll never know what you can accomplish.

"The weakest part of all of us is our minds. Did you ever go to the foul line and say, 'Oh shit, why did they foul me?' You lose your poise. As a sophomore in high school I fumbled a punt that lost the state championship. It was the seniors' last chance and they didn't talk to me for the rest of the year. One of them was my brother. I had a good football career after that, but when I go back to my neighborhood and guys say, 'Hey Jerry, how you doing?' I know as they walk away they're saying, 'That's the asshole who fumbled.'

"They'll always remember me for that, but there's a guy none of you probably ever heard of, Bill Golis, who was my coach at Morton Junior College in Cicero, Illinois. I'll remember him until I die, which is something he doesn't even know. He taught me poise and confidence. He showed me that a person is as good as what he perceives himself to be and that whatever happens, whether it's good news or bad news, tomorrow it's old news. That's why I'm here—guys like him."

Having tucked the campers in, Wainwright trundled across the street to BT's, a clean and dimly lit place where the coaches tip a few and unwind. "I've been at Five-Star 15 years and a coach for 23," he said. "This is a tough business. When I got into it I coached a sixth-grade city league team and made every kid shoot underhand free throws because none of them could reach the basket any other way. We were 0–and–12 but we shot 74 percent from the line. I met with unbelievable criticism. In grad school at Denver I coached a team at Federal Youth Prison and it was tough getting road games, but I learned that the two best places to coach are a prison, because there are no alumni, and an orphanage, because there are no parents.

"I'm kidding. I love parents, of course, I am one—but in this business some guys fail because they are too anxious to get to the next level and haven't made enough decisons, haven't had to deal with things like parents on their asses, so they don't have a real feel for what coaching is all about. Norm Goodman prepared me for how fragile this all is. I was his assistant at Leyden High in Franklin Park, Illinois, in the seventies and in four years he was something like 104–4. The only game he lost was the last one of the year every year.

"Goodman was one of those guys who worked from five in the morning till eleven at night and he is in the Illinois Hall of Fame, but every time he lost he got boxes of negative mail. That made me develop the basic philosophy that in coaching nothing is permanent except change and the key to everything is player development. I had started to learn that fact while coaching football at Montrose High in Montrose, Colorado, before meeting Goodman.

"During a game one of my linebackers was dragged 12 yards by some fullback. He had done everything right, read his key, filled the hole, but then gotten beat competively by a better athlete. I ripped the kid from goalpost to goalpost, calling him gutless, saying all the negative things I thought you were supposed to say. An older assistant coach grabbed me and said there was no way I should be saying that stuff, that the kid had done everything he was supposed to do.

"That made me realize something, and instead of tearing kids down, I began to look for all sorts of tools to make a kid a better player, maybe teach him to fill the hole quicker, increase his strength, or whatever. I seldom talk about winning anymore, because then you have to talk about losing. I talk about sports as a process because you play against a lot of different teams, but you are always playing against yourself."

Wainwright, enmeshed in marital difficulties early in his career, passed up a chance to work under Bob Knight at Indiana. "Growing up, I always had a fear of dying, but I never told anyone until I was a sophomore in college," he says. "Some kid from New Orleans, just talking one day, told me he had the same fear and it was like someone lifting an anvil off me. I used to think talking made me less of a man, and it really wasn't until my first marriage ended that I feel I became a good coach.

"Marriage was the first thing I'd failed at and it tore me up, but for the first time I was able to be honest. Athletes and coaches tend to live behind macho veils, thinking that if they're going to succeed they can't show weakness. Athletes, men and women athletes, end up marrying an image sometimes. That's why I talk to the kids the way I do, to let them know that I'm insecure too, only about different things and that I went through the same things in my development they are going through.

"I love this camp. Garf really cares about the kids and treats every kid the same. He never kisses ass, which means we don't have to either. Kids want guidelines, and I guess I feel I have the right to say things because I was one of the biggest assholes going. Every guy here takes any opportunity to speak to kids very seriously because there have been great sadnesses at Five-Star too, many dreams unfulfilled, kids like Chris Washburn and Lloyd Daniels, and a true Five-Star guy feels motivated to never let that kind of thing happen again."

*   *   *   *   *

When Lloyd Daniels came to Radford in the summer of 1985 along with Five-Star, Garf had him rated as "probably the greatest high school basketball player" he'd ever seen. Daniels went to several high schools, never really finishing before being thrust into college, first San Antonio Junior College and in 1987 the University of Nevada at Las Vegas. He was at UNLV for 30 days when he was arrested for buying crack cocaine from an undercover cop and two years later he was shot in Brooklyn during an $8 crack deal gone bad.

Daniels lived, but his career was a corpse, and in all that time he had never learned to read and write or fend for himself except on a basketball court. "I saw Lloyd Daniels play for the first time one night in New York City, for an outside team called the Gauchos in a post-season game and I nearly fell out of the stands," says Garf. "His talent was unbelievable. It was like I was watching Magic Johnson with a legitimate jump shot. I have rarely been as excited watching a player.

"He'd pull up at the three-point line and stick the 'J,' or he'd dump down to an open man, or he'd come down with a 2-on-1 or 3-on-2 and there was no play to be made, nobody open, and the ball would be out of his hands to a man making a layup and you would say, 'How did he do that? There was nobody free.' He was one of those rare players who made you lean forward in anticipation every time he touched the ball and you waited for something great to happen."

Daniels wasn't a bad kid—things just had a way of getting the best of him. He had a cherub's face, but skinnier, which made him look like Popeye's kid, so at Five-Star they called him Swee' Pea. "We heard he had monumental problems even then. We thought maybe we could counsel him, maybe help him and change him, but it is very tough in a week or two to make up for years of damage," says Garf. "That doesn't mean you stop trying. Just because you can't do it doesn't mean you don't try to get through to someone."

It wasn't like other people inside and outside Five-Star hadn't tried before or wouldn't try again. "When you saw him play, it was like a magic wand over all the problems," says Larry Davis, a Five-Star regular who coached him at Oak Hill Academy, a private school in Mouth-of-Wilson, Virginia, that has had luck with kids like Daniels. "Everyone was willing to give him extra chances. I saw him rip up J.R. Reid at camp. He took him to school."

J.R. Reid, readying himself for North Carolina and the NBA, was one of Garf's fair-haired boys, and of course Garf lived and died with him, which meant nothing when he got out of line one afternoon at camp. "During the two o'clock lecture, Reid and a pal of his were cutting up," says Davis, "and Garf chewed them out. It makes no difference whether you're an All-American or an argyle sock league player, at Five-Star you gotta toe the line."

Daniels believed his opponents should too. At camp, Reid was coached by The King, Frank Marino, and everyone was prepared to abdicate except Swee' Pea. "He took Reid apart and it wasn't even what he did, it was how he did it," says The King. "Daniels had mastered all the fundamental parts of the game by playing a million hard-nosed street games where you gotta get up when they knock you down and keep winning games to hold the court, the kind of kid I love."

Dennis Jackson, nicknamed "The Sandman" at Five-Star, was fond of Daniels too. Jackson, now an assistant at Central Connecticut State University, was with Penn in 1979 when they took their Cinderella ride to the Final Four. "The campers call me The Sandman because I used to get 'em up and put 'em to bed," Jackson says. "I used to sing 'em to sleep and they liked that. I first met Lloyd Daniels at the airport in Roanoke. He was looking out for the other kids, making sure they got on the buses. I was standing near him talking about some other kid from New York and I noticed he was looking at me strange.

"I said to him, 'What's the matter, homeboy, you think you got a good game or something?' and he said, 'Yeah,' so I told him I was from Missouri, the Show Me State, and he had to show me. I wasn't really, but later in the week he happened to walk past a three-point shot contest and entered. The way they were doing it was the shot didn't count if it hit the rim, it had to be all net, so Daniels, who is a righty, went lefty and won. He tracked me down and asked if that showed me."

It was easy to become attached to Swee' Pea's innocence and wizardry and easy to take advantage of it. He was not without fault, but when his problems multiplied and it became known how he'd eluded detection within the system, he became a symbol of all that can go wrong in college basketball. The doctored grades and depth of willingness to accept the deceit, not without precedent, seemed to go beyond the "normal" limits of recruiting trickery. It tore at the fiber of all that was right about the game.

Five-Star took it to heart, although Garf has never waited for the prevailing recruiting winds to set his own course. "Ethics should be taught in the schools from the time the kids are very young," he says. "Not using my influence with kids to steer them to one school over the other is how I have been able to last so long in the business both with *HSBI* and the camp. Over the years I have known practically every coach in basketball and been asked many times to help them get such-and-such a kid.

"I said I couldn't do that, that it wasn't professional. I would tell a coach about a kid, and there have been hundreds of kids I've helped send to college, but I would never try to help a coach get a kid and I have never gotten involved with the recruiting of Division I players. I would get involved only at the end of the year when a kid had nothing, no offers. I would call some people and try to help him out.

"I did get involved with one big-timer, Adrian Dantley, who never even came to Five-Star. Adrian was playing at DeMatha and Morgan Wootten told me he was having a tremendous problem picking a college. Wootten asked me to talk to him. We were at a tournament somewhere, I don't even remember where, and I went into the locker room after the game and sat down with Dantley. I asked him to list his top five schools and I would try to help him with the strengths and weaknesses of each as they might apply to him. He told me his five schools and the fifth one was Notre Dame.

"It was interesting because at the time, the early seventies, Digger Phelps and I were on the outs. We had had a misunderstanding a few years before while he was still an assistant at Penn about some information he had given me on a kid for *HSBI*. I made the kid a two-star instead of a five-star, which he turned out to be. I was embarrassed and told Phelps he had deliberately talked the kid down because he wanted him. We didn't speak to one another for five years. If I was ever going to use my influence in a negative way with a kid, do something unethical, that was my chance.

"I could have wiped Digger Phelps out, but there was something more important than that. Morgan Wootten was a good friend of mine and the reason he'd asked me to help his player was because he knew I was not going to be subjective. I told Dantley the truth, that he should strongly consider the Fighting Irish, because Digger is a great coach and Notre Dame is one of the great institutions in the world. Apparently it wasn't such bad advice, because he went there and has done pretty good in the NBA.

"As an addendum to the story, Digger Phelps and I eventually made up, and a few years later he invited me to be a guest speaker at the team's awards banquet. I toyed with the idea of not doing it. They always had heavy hitters there. The year before, Howard Cosell had been the speaker, and I didn't think I belonged in that league. I did it though, and other than the honor of running Five-Star—whoever allows me to do that and I don't know who it is— speaking at Notre Dame is the biggest honor ever accorded me."

* * * * *

The ground rules of recruiting are set by those who do it and benefit from it: players and parents, coaches and universities, and associated businesses. It becomes whatever the participants want it to become and Garf is not naïve when it comes to Five-Star's part in the process. He welcomes the college coaches and recruiters with open arms when they swarm to camp during the NCAA Live Periods, knowing they are not there for the family feelings.

He is fully aware they are there to check out the merchandise and stock the shelves and he understands the reality. For Five-Star it's a case of the more the merrier. When the campers know the recruiters are there, they are even more intense. Part of the lure of camp has always been the chance to be seen. Kids come for the competition and comraderie, but they know if they do well someone will notice. If not the recruiters, then the men who write and sell privately owned scouting reports. They are not subject to NCAA regulations and can roam the camp freely. Garf welcomes them as long as they know their place and keep their distance.

Recent NCAA regulations cut in half the number of weeks the recruiters and coaches, especially major college coaches, can visit

Five-Star, but it has happened more times than can be remembered that a kid from the sticks or some late-bloomer got a scholarship after being seen at Five-Star. Garf knows there are very few such sleepers anymore and that his camp is no longer the only showcase for top high school talent, but his basic precepts of recruiting, like the fundamentals of the game itself, are timeless.

Beyond deciding on his own that contact between coaches and campers wasn't kosher more than a decade before NCAA coaches created the philosophically similar Live/Dead Period within their own ranks, Garf has his Ten Commandments of Recruiting, written in the mid-seventies, which he still quotes chapter and verse (and tongue-in-cheek where applicable) to recruits or any of the multitudes seeking his sage counsel:

"The First Commandment," he says, "is 'Honor thy father, mother, coach, or keeper, but make thine own decision.' Everyone may want what's best for you, but only you know how you feel in your heart.

"Second, 'Thou shalt know thyself and thy level of play and seek a college one notch below what you think you are and two notches below what your father thinks you are.'

"'Thou shalt not bear false witness about thy grades.' The colleges will find out anyway if they check into it.

"'Thou shalt be realistic about thy grades and seek advice from thy guidance counselor.' It doesn't make sense for a prospect to go to a school if he won't be able to keep up academically.

"'Thou shalt not accept a paid visit without prior commitment of a scholarship unless it is thy dream school.' A prospect has limited paid visits and if he has always wanted to go to a school, his dream school, then that's OK. But a kid should not use a paid visit for a school where he will be used as a backup.

"'Thou shalt speak to both starters and bench-warmers on thy paid and unpaid visits.'

"'Thou shalt seek a college compatible with thy personality and lifestyle.' Some kids are homespun types with a low-key lifestyle and should try to pick a college close to home. Other kids, like street-type kids, might have trouble adjusting to a huge campus where they could get lost in the shuffle easily and might want to think about something smaller.

"'Thou shalt covet a team and coach compatible with thy style of play.'

"'Thou shalt not accept an illegal offer.' The pot of gold comes at the end of the rainbow, not the beginning. Remember the saying: 'If they buy you now, they will sell you later,' which is something I stole from the apostle Marv Kessler.

"'Thou shalt forsake conversions unless transformed by the Reverend Billy Graham.' I believe a kid should play the position he is accustomed to playing, not make a lot of switches. Very few conversions work."

These sound simplistic now, but they are substantially the same as the more complex regulations NCAA officials espouse during their regular visits to Five-Star when they advise the campers and warn about the temptations of recruiting and their consequences. Bob Minnix, the NCAA's Director of Enforcement, is a frequent speaker. "The reason we go to Five-Star and all the other camps is mainly to talk to sophomores and juniors before they get in trouble," he says. "Some listen and some don't."

J.R. Reid listened. Garf likes to think he did anyway, and not just to the NCAA. Five-Star campers are regularly subjected to Garf's diatribes about another recruiting ill, at least in his opinion, the Early Signing. "The intent of the rule has been totally warped," he says. "Mike O'Koren, in the mid-seventies, was one of the first kids to commit to a college early. He announced before his senior year that he was going to North Carolina and was true to his word.

"In 1982 the Early Signing Rule was put in so that a kid who knew where he wanted to go before his final season could get it over with and keep his sanity. That was the intent of the rule, to allow kids to get the recruiters off their backs, not to allow recruiters to start recruiting them six months earlier to help them know where they wanted to go, which is what's happened. The whole process was moved up anywhere from six months to a year, which puts some kids at a tremendous disadvantage.

"First of all, colleges might sign a kid only as a backup in case they don't get the big-time players they're after. Where does that leave that kid if they do sign the big-timer? And unless a kid visits a college after practice starts, which very few are advised to do (although they should be), he doesn't get to see the previous year's recruits. He may have heard about them, but those guys will have had a year's experience by the time he gets to college. Because he hasn't seen them, he can't know what their role might be and how the coach might change the style of play around them. By the time he gets there, it may not be the same as it was when he signed to go. That could make a huge difference in a kid's career.

"Secondly, the coach who recruited him could leave or get fired before he gets there. I agree with Dick Vitale, who is very outspoken about that, saying a kid should be able to transfer without having to sit out a year, but that sort of thing happens often enough that a kid should think about it.

"The Early Signing isn't good for the recruiters. They have to make a $50,000 value judgment on a player a year earlier and put too much emphasis on watching him in outside games or at camps. That should make me happy because more kids come to camp in their sophomore and junior years. I should keep my mouth shut but I can't, because it's not good for the game overall.

"No matter how closely Five-Star or any camp—and we do it the best—simulates high school games, the kids still have only a week to work with an unfamiliar coach and totally new players. It kills the cerebral players, who dominate in a structured situation, and makes the superior athletes look better than they actually are, and it's not the way it should be.

"Some kids might feel like they have to hurry up and sign, so the rich just keep getting richer. The same colleges are in the Top Twenty every year because blue-collar guys, recruiters like Dave Pritchett and Tom 'Alphabet Man' Abatamarco, can't outwork them like they used to in the old days. Guys like that, from smaller colleges, used to work weeks and months to develop a close relationship with a top prospect like Abatamarco did with Jeff Ruland, who was one of the best high school centers in the country.

"Abatamarco beat Kentucky out for Ruland and got him for Iona by wearing tire marks in the Long Island Expressway. He went to almost every one of Ruland's practices. That can't happen anymore because of the Three-Contact Rule. It used to be a sophomore might get a letter of interest from a college. Now, by the time the kid is a freshman or sophomore he is being heavily recruited, and it puts all kinds of ideas in his head at too young an age. A father called me once to ask me what he should do about the letters his son was getting. They started to come in after the boy was seen at Five-Star and he wasn't sure what to do.

"I told him the best thing to do was flush them down the toilet. Sometimes the letters don't mean a damn thing. Somebody should write a message across the top of the page, like the ones on packs of cigarettes: 'Warning, this is not a scholarship!' In the minds of some kids, it is. The best thing is to tell a kid to just keep working hard. This father agreed, but he is one in a thousand. Thinking about having to commit a year early puts pressure on those kids when they are less able to make sound value judgments, and it's getting worse.

"The Early Signing Rule has devastated high school basketball. What happens sometimes, especially with star players, is that their senior season gets put in limbo. They think it has no importance. There have been some who didn't even play. It can make their high school coach a lame duck also. It affects the control he has over the kid and makes it harder to work with him as part of the team. AAU and other outside coaches, in some cases, become more important than the high school coach. Instead of the high school coach being king, he is queen.

"In the old days, the sight of college coaches in the stands used to bring glamour and electricity to small gyms all over the country. That rarely happens anymore, and it's sad. Mainly, though, and I like to think J.R. Reid didn't commit early after he heard me lecture about this, a big-name player, by signing early, vastly reduces the exposure his teammates might get during his senior year.

"I don't know how many times it's happened over the years that coaches go to see one kid and notice another one they didn't even know about. The biggest changes for a young player, in terms of strength and maturity and confidence, often come between his junior and senior year. Those kids don't get seen like they should, and it's a waste and a shame."

Other issues would stick in Garf's craw, such as freshman eligibility and the NCAA's Proposition Triplets, and there would be times he and his coaches would in turn get under the NCAA's skin, but Sunday night after Wainwright had put the camp to bed, there was a more pressing issue. Five-Star had five days of stations left and only four days to do them.

TEN
Freight Car Blues

"Five-Star is his artwork and Garf wants each week of camp to be a masterpiece."

– Duke University coach Mike Krzyzewski

Monday night wasn't easy for Jack Stephens. He was holding his own, he figured, and his team was doing well. He had gotten used to the fact that he wasn't with the big boys in the camp's NBA league, at least he thought he had. Sitting on his bed in the dark, he felt out of sorts. It must have been someone else in his shirt and shorts that day on the court, because whoever it was hadn't hustled. Well, maybe no one had noticed, but this was Five-Star, so of course they had. Whom was he trying to kid? Besides, he knew and knowing he'd done that, well, it wasn't easy.

Something Coach Wainwright had said, that stuff about everything eventually being old news, helped him get through the night. It had been a hard day from the beginning. Virginia, it seemed, was hot every day. Georgia was like that too so he could deal with it, but then Garf went and jacked up the heat even more with double stations. For the first time in Five-Star's history, the campers had stations twice in the same day, once in the morning as usual and then again at night. Not even Hurricane Edna had upset the routine like that and she had been downright unruly.

Garf had his reasons for doing what he did. Some of the college coaches working in camp had mentioned that working eight days at camp was cutting into their personal recruiting time. Five-Star nourished their souls but it didn't put bread on their tables, and with all the new NCAA recruiting regulations, they couldn't just pick and choose when to go look at kids. They had to take care of business when the law allowed and they needed the extra days.

It was tough for the kids too. They had to juggle their schedules around the Live/Dead Periods. There was less time for the coaches to see them, which was a mixed blessing. Recruiters weren't beating down the doors of big-timers day and night, but the reduced exposure meant that borderline scholarship players had to impress someone and do it in a hurry. They were better off sometimes doing that on their own turf with their own AAU teams or with their everyday coach. Garf could understand them wanting to give one less day to Five-Star. It hurt a little, but facts are facts.

It had taken awhile, but Will Klein had finally convinced Garf that cutting back on expenses wouldn't bring about damnation or cheapen the overall result. Five-Star had always been eight days: tryouts the first day, six days of stations and intensity, and then a day to pack up and go home. It was a tradition. It was also two days longer and much more costly than normal summer camp. Klein figured if seven days was good enough for the Man Upstairs, it certainly ought to be good enough for Garf and Five-Star.

Something had to go and it wasn't going to be any games or lectures or, heaven forbid, any stations. The only thing left was the coaches. Most of them were hoarse by the fourth or fifth day anyway. Raising their voices loud enough to be heard at stations with someone else doing the same thing on courts next to and behind them was enough to make almost anyone raspy. Ranting and raving on the sidelines during games took care of the rest.

Going hoarse was like a badge of honor. If a guy didn't sound like Gabby Hayes or The Godfather by the end of the week, he obviously wasn't doing his job. Having double stations would take care of everyone's vocal cords quite nicely, especially with the second set of stations in the evening when the air was cooling off. The coaches practically needed bullhorns to be heard afterwards, but they were always harping about adversity building character.

"They say you can't teach an old dog new tricks, but the kids actually seemed to like it," says Garf. "The night stations were some of the best we ever had because we challenged the kids, and champions, when challenged, rise to the occasion." They had good teachers too. Garf gave the orders, and the coaches carried them out. They may have mumbled under their breath, but they sucked it up and there was no noticeable difference in quality.

It helped that Garf was out there, as usual, overseeing everything.

He leads by example, making sure things are in synch, and every 20 minutes switching everyone with a series of blasts on his orange whistle. It's probably the only one of its kind in the country and was a gift from referee Dick Paparo. Garf used to toot a blue one that he had from his days at Friendship Farm, but he tossed it under a set of bleachers when he got the more color-coordinated one.

Garf is all fire and brimstone whenever stations are in progress, and is seemingly everywhere at once. The only time he stops is to admire someone's work. He can't help himself. Whenever a coach invents something new or finds an innovative way to teach something old, he has to observe it and incorporate it, like a basketball computer.

Ed Schilling is a good one for slowing Garf down or stopping him in his tracks. Garf calls him "Thrilling, Chilling, Ed Schilling," or just plain "Chill" if he doesn't have much time to talk, and if it weren't for the fact that they don't look or act anything alike, except that they are both basketball freaks, you'd swear they were father and son. They are that tight. "Chill inspires me when I'm depressed," says Garf. "He's unbelievable."

It doesn't take much to lose a grip on reality with Chill. A unique mix of Midwestern naïveté and streetball shrewd, he is one of the youngest stationmasters ever, sharing the distinction with Brendan Suhr and Rick Pitino. He was also the youngest varsity coach in the country when he got the job at Western Boone High in 1989, about an hour from where he did most of his growing up in Lebanon, Indiana.

The campers can see he's real enough when he demonstrates his ballhandling mastery at his station, "The Chill Drill," accenting his moves with a head-and-shoulders-above-the-rim dunk that no white dude is supposed to be able to do. When campers find out that the movie *Hoosiers* was filmed almost in his backyard and that the church where angry townspeople tried to get rid of Hickory High coach Norman Dale is in real life only 20 minutes south of him in Boone City, they just can't deal with it.

You couldn't make Chill's life up. No one would believe it. His grandfather, Walter Cross, won the coveted Trestler Award, and just to be eligible his high school team had to be in the state semifinals and he had to maintain nearly an A average in his schoolwork. Another Trestler Award winner was Bobby Plump, the real-life hero of *Hoosiers*.

Chill knew Plump's story by heart before he could tie his shoelaces, and Chill's grandfather played well into his eighties, forever telling him about the old days and ways. Chill's father was a star player and his mother a cheerleader at Butler College, and when Chill was born, there was a picture of him in a crib cradling a basketball on the front page of the Indianapolis *News*.

When his father, a few years later, got into coaching, Chill followed him to practice like a puppy, finding out quickly that it was foolhardy to bounce the ball or goof around while the coach was talking. That went for any coach. His mother promised to take the ball away from him if he ever got in trouble, so naturally he never did, absorbing taunts from his friends that might have made other kids fighting mad.

Chill's best friends were the janitors at his school who didn't mind if he stuck around until ten or eleven at night, and also Rick Mount. As a schoolboy, Mount was featured on the cover of *Sports Illustrated* and was a three-time All-American. In the summertime in Chill's junior and senior years, they would meet at high noon in Lebanon Park for a few hours of one-on-one. They played to 21, full court, best of seven, and then sat under a tree where Mount told stories about playing in the ABA alongside Dr. J. and Moses and "Bad News" Barnes, and Chill soaked it in like sunlight.

Every day, before he set out for the park, Chill did his drills for an hour and half: dribbling, passing to a tossback, shooting free throws, everything from A to Z. It was like his own private stations. Then he did chores around the house. Evenings were reserved for five-on-five with teammates or anyone else who showed up. When school was in session, a typical day started with phone calls to his teammates at 6:45 a.m., on the dot. The gym opened at seven and they played for an hour, and after school there was practice, and later, in his room alone, he dreamed of basketball.

He came to Five-Star as a rising junior in 1982 and was one of those diving, bleeding, get-elbowed-in-the-face-but-stay-in-the-game-anyway Midwest players with that little added something. He won the Mr. Hustle Award and never missed Station 13, which Garf duly noted. He came back the next year toting a pad and pencil to jot down what the coaches said at lectures, which Garf also duly noted. "Whenever things start to go bad for me, I still look at those notebooks," says Chill.

"I am one of Garf's finds and over the past few years I've called him every couple of weeks for his advice or just to see how he's doing. Nobody was interested in me until he started telling colleges about me. Until then I was just another runt from Indiana." A person can never tell how he'll develop. A late bloomer, Chill added six inches and 65 pounds to his then 5'8", 120-pound frame between his junior year and graduation. Iowa and Navy courted him, but he chose Miami of Ohio, two hours from home, where he could contribute right away.

For awhile it was straight out of fantasy land. His freshman year, 1985, he led the Mid-American Conference in assists, mostly feeding roommate Ron Harper. His Redskins lost to Maryland and Len Bias in the NCAA tournament, where he was given the nightmare assignment of guarding Adrian Branch (who has haunted many a dream). He blew his knee out his sophomore year and spent Christmas Eve under the knife. He came back but says, "I went from thinking NBA to losing a step.

"I merely changed my focus. Listening to my dad all those years, it was like coaching was a part of me. I remember as a kid, too, during the season, waking myself up to listen to 'Coaches' Corner' on the radio. Every Saturday morning at nine o'clock my coach, Jim Rosenstihl, 'Rosey' we called him, would talk basketball. He'd talk up some player who had gotten good grades or was doing well. There was no need to talk a kid down. If you weren't doing it the whole town knew, especially the Downtown Coaches. They were the older and wiser men in the community who were always willing to help a coach.

"They would sit in the stands and watch practices and go to every game. Listening to Rosey's show, you could always hear the Downtown Coaches in the background, the muffled sound of their voices and their coffee cups clinking against their saucers. It hasn't changed much, except nowadays it's their sons. I do that radio show now with two other coaches from Boone County. That's one of the reasons I went back—not for the free breakfast, but to keep guys like Rosey alive and to get advice from the Downtown Coaches.

"I turned down an assistant's job at Siena College in upstate New York to stay at Western Boone, because that's where you really learn to coach. All you see driving in is corn, corn, beans, and more corn, and then appearing out of the mist, Western Boone. It's the best, though, because you have to do it all. You have to be the head coach, do the recruiting, do PR work, deal with parents, raise money, everything. I love it because the main thing in Indiana basketball is not X's and O's. It's preparing for the bigger game, life, and learning dedication, getting along with teammates, knowing your job, and being able to do it.

"The coaches who win are the ones who teach work ethic and how to win with character. It fits right in with Garf's camp. The first time I went there as a kid I knew I wanted to be a part of Five-Star. The people were not only great coaches, they were great people. They were the kind of people I wanted to be around. The coaches go there to prove they are good, just like the players, and everybody eats the same horseshit food together and travels a long way to barely break even financially, but you are helping kids and it's like the rest of the world is not a factor."

The Indiana kid brought the campers down to earth with his "Chill Drill." He got their attention with his racial equality slam, and then put some serious moves on them. "We're not out here to try to look fancy," he said. "Every move is made with the intention of beating and going past your defender, and in your mind that's what you should be thinking. You want to try to reach the point where no one takes the ball away from you. Coaches love guys who can handle the basketball and do smart things with it."

The whole drill was nothing more than an outgrowth of what Chill used to do on his own every day in his backyard, but for a little kid's game it was all-encompassing. It improved campers' ballhandling skills, foot speed, and court sense, and got them in better shape all for the price of one admission. For a scrawny cornbelt kid, it was the only way to get somewhere, and if the campers were interested, there was more. A lot of them sought him out for the extra help, and Chill never was too busy.

He wasn't the only coach the kids hunted down, though, and he wasn't the only guy who could make the kids bust their humps. Five-Star was loaded with them: Joe Dunleavy from Hofstra College doing one-on-one moves; Mike Dahlem of Cardinal Gibbons High School in Baltimore at the "Footwork" station; Ron Ganulin out of UNLV with his unique "In-Your-Lane, Out-of-Your-Lane" instruction; and Mark VanBuren of Central Connecticut State, whose father had been one of the original Orin-Sekwa guys. Loyalty knows no generation.

There were lots of others too, like greenhorns Sean Miller and Ed Peterson who were counselors and learning the ropes while still playing at Pittsburgh and Yale, respectively. They helped out at stations and anyplace else Garf needed them. They were low men on the coaching totem pole, but nobody big-timed them. They were all plugged into the Five-Star juice and adding to it in their own way.

*   *   *   *   *

Certain guys could come in off the street, cold, and hook right into it. Duke coach Mike Krzyzewski did that Monday afternoon, zapping up the current a few volts. He didn't know the campers had more stations to go through that night, but it probably wouldn't have mattered. His calling card is defense. First, he had to get introduced, which can take some time. When Krzyzewski first came into prominence with the Blue Devils, hardly anyone could spell his name, much less pronounce it, especially the TV commentators, so he became Coach K.

Garf made it even simpler for the campers, telling them all they had to know about the man were six C's: class, charisma, communication, character, commitment, and running a clean program. They already gave him a standing ovation, Five-Star style, before he'd said a word. At Five-Star, kids let you know they like you not by politely clapping and shouting *"Bravo,"* but by rhythmically pounding their palms together, softly at first while everyone gets into synch, and then slowly letting the crescendo build without saying a word until they are lifted and forced onto their feet.

Krzyzewski wasted little time giving campers good reason to repeat themselves. "People talk about defense like it is a pain in the butt, but my kids love to play defense because they have learned how to like it," he began. "Let me tell you a little story. You fellas here at Radford, I understand, have pretty good food. Let me tell you it wasn't always like that. One year one of my players was a counselor at Honesdale and he told me they had clam chowder almost every day. The only thing was, he could never find any clams and neither could anybody else.

"One night at dinner, way across the room, he heard a kid yelling, 'I found it, I found it. I found the clam,' and that's the job of the defense, fellas, to find the clam, to get down to the nitty-gritty of this game. We've had two Defensive Players of the Year at Duke in the past three years, Tommy Amaker and Billy King, and my kids have gotten a reputation for playing tough defense. When I look at a kid, that's what I look at, his defensive attitude.

"If you're looking for ways to improve as a player, you need to improve your attitude about defense, and to do that, you need to improve your quickness and mental concentration. What we're going to do here today is talk about team defense, which starts with each player playing good individual defense. The first thing is having a good stance, with your butt down and your hands up.

"In team defense you have to remember that you are not alone. It's like the fingers on your hand. They all work together. I need some guys out here to show you what I mean." The guinea pig system hasn't changed at Five-Star—it goes back to the days of Hubie Brown and John Fosterbay. Coaches have learned to stay out of harm's way, but they still call on campers to assist during lectures. They are expected to be serious and intense, and Krzyzewski's volunteers, five on offense and five on defense, were true to form.

"Guys usually wait to see what the offense is going to do and then react to it. In good man-to-man team defense, you do not have to be afraid to get beat. You've got to remember that you are not alone. The guy guarding the man with the ball can play right up on him and pressure the basketball. If you make him turn his back, you've reduced his court vision.

"One of the main things is you've got to be willing to communicate. If you've got the offense setting screens, the guy who sees it developing has to let his teammate know. That helps give everyone confidence and creates an aggressive team attitude because a guy knows someone is there helping him out. It's funny too, kids think there's a hard-and-fast basketball rule. If they get screened they think they have to stop right there, but you can switch your feet and slide through. Don't leave it for the other guy to do your job.

"I can't emphasize enough that the key to the whole thing is communication, talking so that everyone knows what's going on. I'll show you something we do at Duke to help us with that." Krzyzewski quickly lined some campers up for his Talk Drill. Defender #1 backpedaled from the top of the key guarding his man. Defender #2 was supposed to move up from the baseline, keeping an eye on his own man while letting Defender #1 know what was going on behind him.

Krzyzewski added two more defenders, cutting through the lane, and made them all hustle their butts off, trying to show them that if they didn't communicate, things could get messy in a hurry, which they did. In no time, the kids were bumping and smashing into each other in the three-second lane like it was rush-hour gridlock in Manhattan, but they were laughing and learning to play smart defense while enjoying themselves.

Krzyzewski had led them to the clam. "There's nothing tricky about defense," he said. "Every one of you guys can talk and every one of you can concentrate. Develop pride in your defense and learn to enjoy playing it. Work your butts off. Take what you've learned today and put it into your games for the rest of the week." For the remaining four days there was an audible difference in camp, with kids shouting *"Screen left"* and *"Switch"* and other tasty defensive morsels.

Krzyzewski hasn't always had that much impact. He started coming to Five-Star while he was coaching at West Point and now says, "I used to dream about the players I saw, knowing we could never get them." That changed after he took command at Duke, with blue-chippers chomping at the bit to play for him.

"Five-Star is the only camp I lecture at beside my own," he says. "The main reason is my friendship with Howard. I like him a lot. If he never ran the camp again I'd like him and be his friend and want to spend time with him because I think he's a very interesting guy. He takes the time to learn about people and understand them.

"I know how much basketball means to Howard. He and Will Klein don't just run a camp at Five-Star, there's discipline there and a desire to see kids improve. Howard gets a great sense of satisfaction from that and I don't think there's anybody who does it like him. Just the way he announces the games and all the other things, there's a little bit of, I call it schtick, all the really good stuff that kinda adds atmosphere.

"It's a good atmosphere, a great learning atmosphere, and really the way one of those camps should be run, but they just aren't except for his, and the reason for it is that it takes so much time and effort. A lot of people would be satisfied just to run things and walk around and watch a lot of talented kids play basketball, just like a lot of other people might buy a lot of paintings just for show. But Five-Star is his artwork and Garf wants each week of camp to be a masterpiece, so he puts that little bit extra in there.

"Five-Star is an integral part of basketball in the United States. It has its place in the history of the development of the game and continues to have that. Some camps, because they're afraid kids would not come back or whatever, would never get on a kid. Howard would get on a kid if he were ruining the camp, and I like that. The kids learn a lot more because very often everyone else is giving them puff pieces, telling them how good they are. They can get their heads out of joint real easy, and I think Howard puts them back in perspective."

*　*　*　*　*

Not every kid needs a comeuppance.

A group of 15 or so campers, after listening to Krzyzewski and playing their second game of the day, spent the rest of the afternoon in the hot sun studying footwork with Jerry Wainwright. The whole thing was their idea, but Wainwright acted like it was his. He didn't let anybody touch a basketball the whole time, making them work on reverse pivots and drop steps and V-cuts over and over and over.

Anywhere else it might have seemed crazy, but it made perfect sense at that time and in that place. "Use your imaginations," he told them. "Basketball is a journey, not a destination. It's all in your mind." He didn't mean they were insane. That's where it all happened first, upstairs, and once a kid understood that, he was ready for Herb Sendek. Even if he wasn't ready, he got Sendek at 11 o'clock that night.

A parson straight out of seminary couldn't be more sincere than Herb Sendek. During his lectures Sendek tells the campers things like, "When you drink the water, remember who dug the well," and "Study so much and so hard that even angels can do no more." You'd expect them to hide their faces and snicker among themselves, but that's not what happens.

Sendek had no business being at Five-Star because he could just as easily have been sitting with his feet up on some desk in corporate heaven. He went to Penn Hills High in Pittsburgh and was a starting guard on their sectional championship team in 1981, the same year he graduated as valedictorian with a 4.0 average. He had a 3.95 cumulative average at prestigious Carnegie-Mellon University, majoring in industrial management, and he toyed with the idea of becoming a nine-to-fiver before he received his true calling.

He was a Five-Star camper his senior year in high school and a counselor all through college. He now says, "From the outset I made myself something of a pest. For me it was a basketball classroom and an opportunity to learn how to be a coach. I asked a lot of questions and made the commitment never to spend any time in my dorm. Garf never does. He runs the camp, but he's the same guy who takes the squeegee and dries the courts after it rains and the entire staff recognizes that. A fierce loyalty grows here."

Sendek inspires similar allegiances. He was Rick Pitino's assistant at Providence when the Friars went to the NCAA Final Four in 1987 and became his right-hand man again in 1989 when Pitino left the New York Knicks to take the head coaching job at Kentucky. Garf had long since put Sendek's brain to good use at Five-Star.

Just after Sendek started coaching at camp, Garf asked him to put together a lecture dealing with the three R's, knowing full well that the NCAA had a plan to put a straitjacket on recruiting abnormalities. The NCAA's plan, which would become known as Proposition 48, was aimed at student-athletes, specifically incoming freshmen and their academic requirements. Garf wanted his campers to know about it and how it might affect them. Not that he liked the plan or for that matter its still-to-be-born kissin' cousins, the controversial Proposition 42, passed in 1989 amending Proposition 48, and Proposition 26, approved in 1990 as a compromise between the two.

The Proposition Triplets. Garf wasn't opposed to kids having good grades or returning sanity to the recruiting process, he just didn't think the Prop Triplets were the proper way to go about it. The whole problem, in his mind, boiled down to freshmen being allowed to play on the varsity in the first place. "The bottom line is that college presidents are trying to have it both ways," he says. "On one hand they are shouting about academics, and on the other hand they won't vote down freshman eligibility."

Garf, given the options, liked Prop 48 in the beginning. It said that a kid needed a 2.0 average in his core high school courses and at least 700 on his college entrance exams to qualify for a scholarship. If he had one of the two he could be a partial qualifier and still get a scholarship, but not play basketball until he showed significant improvement in the classroom. Playing during his freshman year was out.

"Rumeal Robinson was a camper and a counselor at Five-Star," says Garf, "and before he became famous for his free throw shooting at the University of Michigan, he told me that Prop 48 was the key to making him a good student. If it was good enough for him, it should have been good enough for anyone." It wasn't. Prop 48 was criticized as being unfair to financially strapped and minority students. Critics said it placed too much emphasis on irrelevant, standarized tests.

Prop 42, passed in January of 1989, made things worse. It said that a partial qualifier could no longer receive financial aid. No scholarship, period. It wasn't slated to take effect until August 1990, but during the 1989 season Georgetown University coach John Thompson was the eye in a storm of protest over the new measure. Twice he walked off the court during games to bring attention to his concerns. Prop 42, opponents maintained, was even more unjust and unfair than its predecessor.

In January of 1990 the NCAA passed Prop 26, which maintained Prop 42's academic requirements, but softened the blow by allowing any incoming student-athlete to receive financial aid based on family income. Critics of Prop 48 and Prop 42 were not completely satisfied, but it quieted things down considerably. Whether the storm has passed completely remains to be seen.

"If you did away with freshmen eligibility, you wouldn't need Prop 48 or 42 or 26 for that matter," says Garf. "Prop 48 was OK, but Prop 42 opened a Pandora's Box for alumni and booster clubs to come up with the money for a kid to go to college. That would only make things worse. I had mixed feelings.

"On one hand I agree with Eleanor Holmes Norton, the Washington lawyer who said that it was good because it sent a message to the junior high school and younger kids that they'd better put more time in on the books. At the same time, John Thompson and the others have good points. I sort of agree that the SAT is not necessarily a fair way to evaluate whether a student should go to college.

"But forget all that, freshman eligibility is the worst thing that's happened to major college athletics in history. Some people will argue that money and huge TV packages are worse and that's true somewhat, but freshman eligibility is not just a bad rule, it's an insane rule born of greed and ignorance.

"The greed part is the austerity reasons given for having the rule in the first place. There was supposedly no money for freshman teams, but in the last five years NCAA schools have received $750 million from one network for games. Do you mean to tell me they can't afford to have teams for freshmen like they always did before the big money started rolling in?

"The ignorance was the inability to foresee the devastating results of 'quick fix recruiting.' By a quick fix I mean a no-name, have-not college, by either great recruiting, luck, or outright cheating, getting a kid who is eligible right away and can transform them from a have-not to a have. Overnight, the quick fix tripled the fervor to recruit a great player, and I'm proud to say I predicted this would happen.

"In the last 18 years there have been more scandals, devastation, misery, and more schools given the NCAA's 'Death Penalty' for violations than all the previous years combined. The academic side is even worse. Academically freshman eligibility is all wrong. It insures that a greater number of athletes will fail to graduate because a great player has a better chance of leaving school early. I was under the impression you went to college for an education. Apparently I'm wrong.

"If players were made to compete as freshmen first, they wouldn't go into their varsity careers with an aura of being a superstar. They could ease into it. It used to be a kid became a star maybe by his junior year and he would then finish his final year of college. The way it is now, with the media and fans getting into it, the kid has a huge reputation just coming into college. Everything is speeded up. The maturation process is aborted and it's a shame.

"Academically the key year is the freshman year. Some of these kids are concerned with filling 18,000 seat arenas. There are not many who can handle that kind of pressure. The first year of college is when a kid should be getting acclimated accademically and learning the team system. It's not just basketball either. In football kids are playing before they ever go to a college class. Wouldn't you say that sends the wrong message to young athletes and everyone else in this country? If the kids are going to have to fill arenas before they even attend a class, pay them and make them pros. They are either pros or amateurs.

"It should be done the same way we run the camp," Garf says. "Make a kid pay his dues. Before a kid at Five-Star can have the honor of playing in the number one league against some of the greatest seniors in the country, he has to pay his dues by playing in the Development League, or the NIT, or the NCAA. That's what this country is founded on, earning the right to do something, learning the trade. After someone has done the job and proven they are good enough, there is plenty of time to reap the rewards and get theirs.

"The college athletes should prove they are good students and then they can help fill those arenas. I have spoken out against freshman eligibility since the first minute of the first hour it was passed in 1972. Obviously no one was listening, although now there is a trend toward barring freshmen again. I have to think that within a year or two freshman eligibility will be done away with. We should love freshman eligibility, just like the Early Signing, because they have made the numbers increase at Five-Star. Kids think camp gives them a better chance to be noticed, but it's a mistake coming to camp for that reason. I tell kids that all the time."

So does Herb Sendek. His things are books and basketball, in that order—no matter what the hour. The campers raised their hands en masse when he asked, "How many of you think education is important?" Some dropped their hands, however, when he continued, "How many of you think it is important enough to be an educated person? How many of you have enough courage to be put in the nerd category by being organized and doing something as simple as having a separate, clearly marked notebook for every class?

"There are keys to becoming a better student, a good learner, that all of you can do. It is not always a matter of intelligence. It often comes down to making good decisions. All of you have the ability to walk the extra 500 steps to the library, but there are a lot of temptations along the way to stop you: your buddies, your girlfriends, parties. You will find that as the self-sacrifice increases, as the pain of studying while your friends go out increases, your appreciation for the importance of what you are doing also increases.

"The brutal reality is that the world is competitive. Don't let your friends or the NCAA set your standards for you. It's fine to meet the NCAA's standards, but you should live by Proposition 100: 'Each and every day I will try to become the best person I can be.' You can't wave a magic wand to get a good job and have a pleasant life any more than you can wave a magic wand to become a great shooter or a great passer.

"In addition to being organized and making good decisions, you need to understand how to concentrate. You should try to work in silence and use your work space only for work. Schedule short rest periods away from your work space and avoid daydreaming. In basketball and in life, you need to be able to concentrate in order to adapt to an adverse situation, such as having to listen to me talk. If after listening to me, though, just one of you wants to do what it takes to become more of a real person, I will be satisfied."

Sendek might have thought that he was wasting his time, because some of the first-time campers were having great difficulty paying attention and some were nodding off, close to being asleep. But there were also many whose eyes, like Mike McDowell's, were fixed on Sendek and were beginning to see things differently.

McDowell, from Wilmington, North Carolina, listened intently as Sendek, trying to touch the campers with his words, told a story about the 15th-century German artist Albrecht Dürer and his famous drawing, "Man's Hands Joined in Prayer." Dürer, explained Sendek, was one of 18 children. Both he and the brother closest to him in age wanted to attend the university, but their father could afford to send only one of them.

Nevertheless, they devised a way for both of them to go. Albrecht, the more talented of the two, would go first while his brother worked in the mines to help support the family. When Albrecht was finished, his brother would go and Albrecht would take his turn in the mines. So Albrecht went to college and studied art and returned home prepared to keep his part of the bargain.

But his brother said no, that Albrecht could be a great artist if he continued to study and he should do so. He said his own eyes were too weak anyway and his fingers too gnarled from the mines. Albrecht looked at his brother's hands and was moved. In tribute, he drew them as if in prayer, and they have inspired many by their beauty and simplicity.

There are other versions of the story that say Dürer used his own hands or his mother's as a model, but Sendek said his version of the story was meaningful to him not so much for the historical accuracy, but because it made him think about being a good and real person. Sitting close by, Mike McDowell, young and impressionable and nearly entranced, had his hands unconsciously folded in front of him, fingertips together and pointed upwards as if in prayer.

ELEVEN
We Are, Five-Star

"Shoot, shoot, shoot."

– Five-Star campers to Garf

The campers were dragging on Tuesday morning, which was as good a time as any for the Five-Star cheer. Garf pulls it out of the hat whenever he feels the energy level in camp starting to wane. After double stations and Wainwright all day and Sendek burning the midnight oil and Odom making sure they picked up after themselves morning, noon, and night, he figured the campers needed a break. He turned to Duffy Burns.

It's hokey and everybody knows that, especially the campers who don't want to be part of anything that even resembles family, but the cheer is another one of those unexplainable things that happen at Five-Star. It is vintage Garf, but in truth, in true showman's fashion, he stole the idea. He pickpocketed Digger Phelps.

The Notre Dame coach had often used something similar to get his Fighting Irish fired up. He'd ask them, like the Cheshire Cat asking Alice, except with more spirit, *"Gentlemen, whoooo, are you?"* The players would respond, in unison, *"We are, Notre Dame,"* and Phelps would ask them again and again until they were properly psyched. He showed the campers once and Garf loved it, although there was one thing he wanted to change, of course. "We are, Five-Star" made much more sense. It rhymed.

Garf put Burns in charge of working out the details, and whenever he is in camp, which is often, he teaches the cheer to the rookies. Burns was made for the job. He has boundless enthusiasm and a Dom DeLuise disposition. He is an assistant at Central Connecticut State now, but early in his career he coached at "wahoo" Wapahani High School in Selma, Indiana.

The lesson begins at the morning workout. Burns tells the campers, "Gentlemen, put your hands together," and they respond by clapping once, as a group. He next says, "Ready, Go!" and the campers, in cadence, slap their thighs twice and clap again in cadence.

"Gentlemen, whoooo are you?" pumps Burns, and the campers, 400 strong, shout, *We are,* pausing to slap their thighs twice and clap once, *"Five-Star,"* concluding with two crisp claps, a brief pause, and then three more claps. Five claps for five stars. They practice until the timing and emphasis are just right, like a tight military platoon. It sounds and feels like something General Patton would find commendable, and it sends shivers down Garf's spine.

The campers did the cheer and it woke them up. Usually, camp springs to life as soon as Garf gives a shrill blast on his whistle to get stations rolling. The camp is like a movie set where everyone knows his role. The coaches and campers are like actors milling around, going over their scripts and sipping on coffee until the director yells *"Action"* and suddenly the set is transformed. It's real and unreal at the same time.

However, something unexpected can happen at any time, and that's when the coaches play it by ear and make sure that no matter what, the show must go on. Something like that happens when the kids and the coaches are bushed, which usually occurs around mid-week. The rookies look to the veterans, who in turn look to the coaches, who rely on Garf. There are times no one has anything left to give. That's when respect kicks in. "There will be disputes and sometimes you don't feel up to it," says Garf's antidepressant, The Chill. "It's not all rah-rah, but when the chips are down, that's when you gotta get it together. It's a feeling inside you that you can't let Five-Star down because you know it won't let you down."

The coaches never let up at Five-Star. There is too much of a chance that would be just the moment some kid needs a boost or the whole camp comes to an end. It could happen. Life is full of strange twists. However, some pick-me-ups are built into the program. The Situation Tournament is one such perk. Rick Pitino turned Garf on to the idea after seeing University of Maine coach Bob Brown do it at his own camp one summer, but Pitino probably would have invented it himself somewhere along the line.

Pitino noticed that with so many talented players in camp there were always close games, and it made sense to him to practice the moves to use in pressure situations. Maybe a team would have the ball and be down four points with eight seconds to go. What should they do? Or maybe a team would be ahead by five with 30 seconds. Then what? The best way to find out was to experiment and try different things, give it the old trial and error routine. Garf set up a station where coaches could do just that. Every kid visited each station twice a week, and the first time through the coach would give the kids the situation and show them a way out of it.

The next time through he expected them to remember what he'd shown them and run through it correctly. Then he'd show them something else in case the first method failed. The coaches loved it because it gave them a chance to showcase their genius. The kids loved it because it was exciting and fun. They got into it and it didn't seem like drudgery. Garf liked it because he got to see who showed grace under pressure and who cracked. Things like that were interesting and gave him more insight into a person.

He expanded it into a Special Situations Tournament and on Tuesday night the Dedmon Center Gym was rockin'. It was the perfect midweek night program. The kids could blow off some steam and still be learning, plus there were prizes. Each league had its own elimination tournament, running through 15 or so typical predicaments and some not so typical. There is no end to the weird things that take place as one by one teams fall victim to their own mistakes and then it's SRO at center court for the finals.

Garf plugged in the microphone, making sure somebody else double checked because electronic gadgets aren't one of his strong points. Hearing the PA system crackle always gets his blood moving, and the kids were loose knowing they had the rest of the night off, so the only ones with any regrets were the coaches.

Off in the corners, some of them who didn't make it to the finals were shaking their heads, long after the fact, trying to figure out how their best-laid plans could possibly have gone awry. It was amazing how such infinitesimal things could become so monumental depending on the moment—things like a missed screen among hundreds of screens, or something as insignificant as a nervous teenager bouncing a ball off his foot. At Five-Star it's partly for fun, but back home it could mean his job.

The tournament worked out well for Ben Fisher out of Soddy-Daisy High School in Hamilton County, Tennessee. Back home he was the sixth man for the varsity, and being from the Volunteer State and all, it was natural for him to take the last shot, down by two with scant few seconds left and everybody else looking like they were scared out of their wits. It was a prayer really, because there was somebody right in his face, so he had to shoot it off balance and it clanged off the rim like a horseshoe.

There he was, though, following his shot. The only thing he could do with the ball after he got it was try to tap it out because everyone else was tangled up in the lane, including his own teammates, and there was no way he'd survive in that horde. It was every man for himself.

He tipped it and somehow tracked it down near the top of the key, and all he had left was a Hail Mary three-pointer, but he squared up as best he could and the campers had to rub their eyes at first because it looked like he shot the ball left-handed. Fisher's first shot had been a righty, but the kid is ambidextrous and he found nothing but net and that's how it ended.

Garf loved it and walked over to congratulate them, and they swarmed over him like he was Clifton Webb and they were his Cheaper by the Dozen kids and he hadn't died at the train station after all. It seemed like they were that happy to see him. He was happy for each one of them, and proud like any father would be of a son who showed he could do all right for himself. They encircled him and closed the circle slowly until he got red-faced and promised them all ice cream and told them to get the hell out of there and go to bed.

It wasn't the ice cream that made their night sweet, though, or even their victory. It was Garf and his encouragement and support and approval. That was the main thing, the approval. Not every kid got that outside Five-Star. Even though it was just a camp and it was only a week, it was easy to feel like you were a good boy and that what you did was worthwhile.

"I'm too busy and too nervous to notice if something like that is provided at camp," says Garf, summing the whole thing up in a nutshell. "If it is I'm not aware of it and I've never thought about it. That is much too deep for me. I don't think of myself or the camp in those terms. I just try to present the best possible basketball element that a person can. I spend most of my time trying to give the kids that.

"To me it is a matter of timing, making sure stations and games run on time. It bothers the shit out of me if it's dinnertime and there is still a game going on. That means a kid has to come in late and his hands are dirty and he's tired but he has to eat and sometimes it can't be helped because it rains or whatever. I think about those things constantly. Those are the little things I think about.

"Are the charts up? We hang charts for each league with the results of every game and I think of that, little stupid things like that.

126   FIVE-STAR

Did the commissioners put up the results? If they haven't or if one of them hasn't, I get on his case. A kid is going to walk by, looking, and if I were a kid and no one had put up the results and the standings for my league, but the others were up there, I would think no one cared about my league. Even if he thinks that for a minute, even if they're up 10 minutes later, when that kid walked by they weren't up and I worry about that.

"I want to give them the right games, the right courts with the right dimensions. I don't want any small, dinky courts with shaky baskets and loose rims because cosmetically it's lousy, and it cheapens the games. And I want a net on every rim. I can't stand a ball going through a netless rim. When I was in high school I played on rims like that with my friends in the schoolyards and parks around 86th Street.

"Talking about it, I remember one day Sidney Tannenbaum and Donnie Foreman came by and actually played in front of us for a whole day. They played for NYU and were my heroes and I have no idea why they came that day. They were never there before and they never came back again, but they really showed us how to play. That's what I try to do and that's all I try to do, show the kids how to play the game.

"I don't think about approval or anything else. Actually, if I did think about it, *I'm* the one who wants approval. Maybe it goes back to my father. He was a great man and the unofficial mayor of New York and everybody loved him, but in the house he was very stern and very difficult to go one-on-one with. He was opposed to anything I went for except the woolen business or maybe being a doctor or a lawyer.

"I'm not crying about my childhood, but I have seen fathers backing their kids at Five-Star and it is diametrically opposed to the way my father dealt with me. But I'm not into that psychological stuff. I leave that to others."

* * * * *

It is possible to miss some things at Five-Star, like a quick thunderstorm rolling overhead, which happens frequently at Radford in the summertime. If the campers are outside they can't help but notice as they scramble for cover in the gym, and the courts become too wet to play on safely. But if they are already inside, the rumbling can come and pass and it is as if nothing happened. The air outdoors is cooler perhaps, but in the gym the air is unchanged and like any gym in early June.

That's how it was Wednesday afternoon for the arrival of Mark

Iavaroni. It was a lazy day, which was appropriate because Iavaroni, a 10-year NBA fixture, had been one of Garf's biggest sleepers. When he came to Five-Star as a 6'6" junior, he was rated as a "CNP, cannot play" by most scouts. He was just a big, nice kid playing high school ball on Long Island. "Everybody loves big guys," Garf says, "but Iavaroni was a lanky, gangling colt who tripped over the lines just walking onto the court. He wasn't being recruited, but I liked him. There was something about him, I don't know what.

"We hadn't moved to Radford yet, but the year Mike came to camp—for some reason I've always called him Mike—he went to Honesdale for the June session. He had a bad week. We had some weak guards in camp who didn't know how to feed him the ball. He was booked to come back in August, but his father called and said he wasn't coming. He gave me a reason—I forget what it was, but I didn't buy it. It sounded like a lame excuse to me. I figured the real reason was because Mike knew the killers from the city were going to be there and he didn't want to be embarrassed.

"It bothered me, though, not just that the camp was losing a big kid, but that the camp could chase away a kid like that. It hurt me. A kid doesn't have to come to camp and be an all-star, but at least he can come and improve his game. I offered him a camper-worker and his father said no again, but I kept after him and finally Mike came. All the gangliness came together that week. He started stomping and whomping and made the all-star team, which had nothing to do with politics. He was obviously a late-bloomer, because later he went to the University of Virginia and won a championship ring with the Phildadelphia 76ers."

It wasn't so much what Iavaroni said that Wednesday at Five-Star that made his visit memorable, although he did share his experiences and give the campers a few tips. "Doing well at Five-Star gave me tremendous confidence," he said. "I felt like an underachiever coming in and I remember thinking, 'Do I belong here?' Garf recruited me on potential, which shows that you never know who's watching you and when they are watching. The nice thing about coming here was that even if you messed up, you learned to have inner character.

"I know all you guys are dreaming about playing in the NBA and it is really great. Everyone there is a special player. Dennis Rodman of the Detroit Pistons is one of the smartest rebounders I've ever played against. He's not that big, but when you watch him play, watch his movement off the ball. He keeps his opponents' eyes on him instead of the basketball and he gets incredible position. And all of you have probably heard of John Stockton of the Utah Jazz. He's not big either, but he uses leverage to move guys out, plus he's so damn quick. He got that way growing up because if he didn't move fast his brother kicked the crap out of him on the court. It helps to have somebody who cares looking out for you."

It wasn't what Iavaroni did during his visit either, when he demonstrated how to box out and make the most with whatever you had. It was what happened before he even started his lecture. The thunderstorm had driven everyone indoors and it was getting sticky in the gym. The rain was slow in letting up and Garf was growing testy. He was being his usual worrywart self about the schedule, and he was busing kids around and fretting about some kid maybe slipping on the wet pavement outside. He came into the gym all fussed and fumed and was in no mood to be trifled with. The campers, to his utter dismay, were feeling frisky.

They wanted Garf to shoot. They always want Garf to shoot. It's like watching the Harlem Globetrotters. You never get tired of watching the act. Garf invites it, though, repeating over and over how much he hates the three-point shot. He says it will bring ruination to the game. The shot is so easy to make, he says, that a newborn infant could probably sink nine of ten if somebody propped him up and pointed him in the right direction.

"It's a total joke and to make things worse, the rules-makers don't even know how far it is from the basket. They say it is 19'9", but it's clearly 21 feet. My father always told me the foul line is 15 feet from the hoop and I always believed my father. The three-point line is six feet beyond that. If they are going to louse up a perfectly good game, they should at least get the distance straight. Besides that, it's like a layup to kids these days. It's 10 times easier than scoring a layup in traffic."

The campers can't resist making him prove the point. It's almost inevitable, whenever they are all gathered together, that someone will sound the cry of *"Shoooot"* like some ghost of Itchy and Twitchy until the rest pick up on it and Garf either goes into his schtick or, depending on his mood, tells them in no uncertain terms to knock it off. He was in the latter frame of mind that day, but the campers would not be denied.

Garf was looking resplendent in his Virginia warm-weather wardrobe of light yellow sneakers, green trousers, and dark blue sports shirt. He was always neat and the colors grew on you after a while, but at the moment his finery did not reflect his inner boilings. He was feeling foul. The *"shoooot"* spirits started up and he kept his back to them at first, hoping they'd get the hint. They didn't and kept it up until he turned on them and barked at them to "shut the hell up."

That quieted the place except for one small voice in the back of the gym that after a respectful moment of silence softly renewed the call. Garf, talking feverishly with Dave Odom about rearranging the schedule around the rain and busing kids to and fro, stopped suddenly, shocked, as if he had been thrown into a cold lake. He glared and even Iavaroni, standing amused nearby, expected the worst. Instead, Garf broke, like the sun breaking through black clouds.

The campers knew as soon as they saw the Cagney Twitch. It was as if Garf were saying, "All right, you guys," all gangstery and mean, and rolling his shoulders to show them he meant business. Rolling his shoulders was a sure sign that he was loading his gun. Then his stride got elongated like in the old days and he pointed to his wristwatch as if to say, "We don't have time for this," and he threw up his hands in mock defeat. That was the cue to start the skit and for Odom to become his straight man. It was silent cinema time at Five-Star.

Silent, that is, except for the kids. They were raising the roof with their shrieks of delight. Garf says he's never sure if the kids are making fun of him or not when they do that. Resigning himself to it and relishing the moment, he pointed at his watch once or twice more until the campers started to boo, then he rolled up his sleeves even though he was wearing a short-sleeved shirt. Slowly, he unbuckled his timepiece and handed it to his straight man. Odom was hamming it up royally, kneeling before Garf with his head bowed like a valet accepting the king's jewelry.

Garf rubbed his right shoulder, wincing as if he were in pain until the campers hooted louder and made him produce. He cleared the area, moving everyone behind the three-point line, and readied himself mentally while Odom rolled him a basketball. The campers had by then taken up the chant, "Shoot, shoot, shoot," and it was Rosemont all over again with an added flair. He loosened up, wiggling his hands as if he were air-drying them, then drew a two-handed bead, elbows tucked, ball below his chin, and bombed away. He jumped slightly on the release with his palms finishing outward in a classic follow-through.

"Oh, shit!" He missed. He seldom makes it (although he'll argue that) and with his eyes closed he can tell because the campers let him know with a group groan. "Oooooh, shit," dragged out for effect, is one phrase of communication. It's not exactly what Coach K had in mind, but it gets the point across. "Brick" is another way they let him know, and if he bypasses everything they chant "Air Ball, Air Ball," appropriately prolonging each word along with his agony.

Garf perseveres until he hits one, and after each miss the campers keep him blissfully informed.

In this case he never did connect. He missed 14 in a row and then dribbled in for a layup, but banged that off the bottom of the board and then he hurled the basketball aside. The campers roared with approval anyway, and just to show them he still cared he flipped them the bird in return. It could go on all day as far as the campers were concerned, but Garf had a camp to run. At least everyone knew things were back to normal.

That night Garf surrendered the spotlight to "Crazy George" Schauer, a hocus-pocus ballhandler and a longtime Five-Star attraction. Schauer was a walk-on at the University of Minnesota in the early seventies and, according to Garf, became the star of the pre-game warm-up after his coach, Bill Musselman, got a chance to see him play in a real game. His ability to control a basketball and charm an audience earned him a station at Five-Star and an international reputation.

Schauer has a dribbling drill for every limb on a person's body. Up or down, over or under, it makes no difference to him. His playing days are only a memory, but he entertains at camp complete with rock music, props, and spheres of every size and description, a veritable one-man traveling show. His claim to fame is spinning one or more basketballs while performing feats never before seen, such as feeding ice cream to campers who are only too willing to assist.

Schauer gets as many kids involved in the act as he can, hauling them out of the bleachers for asssorted embarrassments. His first chosen victim that night turned out to be a mistake. Mark Hisle didn't mean to, but he nearly upstaged Crazy George, who thought he had the perfect dupe. Hisle, at first glance, appears to be the shy, quiet type, blond-haired and just ripe for pickin'. He is all that except for the pickin' part.

As a child, the only dribbling Hisle did was with a basketball, that's how long he's been at it. Drawing what little added inspiration he needed from watching Crazy George and others, he worked up an act of his own and started doing it regularly at summer camps and for church groups in and around his hometown of Terre Haute, Indiana. His résumé includes a performance at halftime of an Indiana Pacers/Boston Celtics NBA game and another at a Big Ten all-star game.

A frequent Five-Star attendee, he let Crazy George hoodwink him into getting out on the floor, and no matter what he was asked to do with the basketball, go between his legs or around his back, he did it, no problem. His fellow campers were impressed and he enjoyed their attention. But that is not the reason he performs. His favorite audience is Christian youths his own age and younger. Hisle gets invited in and does his thing, grabbing everyone's attention with his ballhandling talents, and then he cuts straight to the heart of the matter. Mini-sermons, not slick moves, are his forte.

In Hisle's talks he tries to blend spiritual uplifting with personal experiences, such as the image that will stick with him forever of an all-state running back he read about in the newspaper one day and saw the next day with his hands against a car being frisked. "The Lord gives you certain talents that you use for him, not just for yourself," says Hisle, who, despite his beliefs, is not self-righteous about the way things are done at Five-Star.

"Garf's language is kinda crude for me sometimes, but you have to hear everything he says and listen to the good stuff and let the other things just pass you by. Garf is my man. He is basketball. He tells you how things really are." The things no one can tell you, you deal with on your own. Not unlike The Chill and myriads of other Midwest dreamers, Hisle created a personal workout and it was nothing for him to shoot 50 full-court, pull-up jumpers as just part of the overall daily regimen. "I write down in a notebook where I need to improve," he says. "In the summer you get better. In the season, your team gets better.

"You have to know your strengths and weaknesses. Sometimes I struggle at camp. I don't play with confidence and it bothers me. I play better within a set offense and sometimes I'm not sure when to give it up and when to shoot it." Every point guard comes to that crossroads countless times and Hisle usually went with what got him there. Before the week ended, he won a free-throw shooting contest and was named Mr. Stations, which was nothing new for him, but he also discovered that it's necessary to stray from the straight and narrow at times and go with the flow of the game. Basketball sinners are forgiven at Five-Star.

Crazy George got rid of Hisle in a hurry. He had better luck with Adam Fletcher, a 6'0" rising senior from Sanderson High in Raleigh, North Carolina. A fun-loving kid, Fletcher said he came to camp to improve his handle. He knew that if he were going to fulfill his dream of playing in Division I, his handle had to get better, and that was never more obvious than when Crazy George asked him to control a basketball the size of the Goodyear Blimp.

It's not that Fletcher is a fumble-fingers. His teams have a strange habit of winning and he more or less owns the Mr. Hustle Award, having won it three times in three visits to Five-Star. Garf calls him "The Beast," noting that "once he gets in your jock on defense, it's over." He learned to be an animal from his friend Scott Gray, another three-time Mr. Hustle honoree who frequented Five-Star in the late seventies before playing at UNLV. "I've been told Scott was the sickest man who ever came to camp," says Fletcher, with all due respect. "He took 21 charges in a game once and he was always making grunting noises.

"He was the kind of player everyone hates. He was in your face all the time and never let you touch the ball. Scott told me about Five-Star. It felt eerie the first time I came. I didn't know anyone, but I remember how I used to look up to the older guys like Billy Owens. He was great. He'd help you out and if you got thinking you were too good, trying to take him on, he'd say something like, 'Get away, rookie, up here everyone is good.' That let you know where it was at right away.

"Now I try to set an example for the younger guys and give it all I've got all the time. Owens made it to Syracuse and I don't know if I'll make it big. I know I have to work and push myself, but it's possible."

* * * * *

Billy Packer examined the possibilities from a different perspective on Thursday afternoon. The noted CBS television hoop analyst was the two o'clock guest lecturer. Right off the bat he made sure no one had been lulled into a false sense of security during the week. An ex-back-court man at Wake Forest, where he also coached in the 1960s, he showed the campers a scouting report listing the Top 100 juniors in the country, then wadded it up and tossed it disdainfully to the floor.

"Some of you may have your name on that list and it's nice to be there, but there are names not on the list who'll do OK," Packer said. "There are kids not at this camp who right now are working on their games just as hard as you are. I used to 'ice' Garf's early *HSBI* selectees on the court and I wasn't the type of player who got a lot of attention. Just because you came to Five-Star or your name is on some list doesn't mean you'll make it. Get that out of your mind. You have to do it on the court and keep doing it."

Having said that, he made them feel secure again. "Once you've made it to where you want to be in basketball," he said, "there are other things to think about. How will you react to frenzied media people firing questions at you, often inane questions they want answered in a hurry? You've spent years preparing yourself to look smooth on the court but no time getting ready for this.

"Here's your moment, and first impressions matter. There are hundreds, maybe thousands of people listening, and in five short minutes you can make yourself look like a fool, or with a little forethought you can do just fine." Packer was no stranger to either end of the spectrum, having fallen into his broadcasting career much the same way Garf fell into Five-Star. There was no way of knowing it would happen, but when it did he eased into it gracefully, as gracefully as he could, considering he had never seen the inside of a TV truck.

Packer lost his broadcasting virginity in Raleigh, North Carolina, during an North Carolina State/Maryland game. "They needed someone and I was the only guy with big enough jewels to do it without practice," he told the campers. "Putting on a headset for the first time reminded me of putting on a jock strap in the seventh grade. It took awhile, but eventually it began to feel comfortable. Some of you guys may be put on the spot someday during an interview and it's important to know how to handle yourselves."

To illustrate the point, Packer dragged young Anthony Cade up to the podium. Cade wasn't exactly kicking and screaming on the way, at least not so you could see, but he is a reserved 6'9" kid from Oak Hill Academy via Tolentine in the Bronx, and Garf had to volunteer him. Cade has tons of potential and could one day find himself in the limelight. Garf knew that and, in addition, Cade had done something pretty special and Garf wanted to show his appreciation.

Cade first came to Five-Star with a reputation for being lazy. He was lanky and deliberate in his movements and sometimes that gave the impression he was about as enthusiastic as a hound dog in July, but he did brood a lot and didn't seem to want to work hard either. Garf found out later it was partly because he had a lot on his mind and couldn't commit himself totally, but Cade, despite his obvious talents and the fact that he had been a camp all-star in the past, had a way to go to prove himself.

He covered a lot of ground late in the week. He missed Station 13 and of course Garf knew that, which maybe had something to do with what happened afterwards, but Cade sought Garf out and apologized. "That made my summer," says Garf, so he was glad to afford the kid a little extra attention as Packer's experimentee. Cade was nervous and self-conscious and stumbled over his words at first, as any teenager might be until the expert taught him how to relax and compose himself. It was easy, no different than up-faking someone and taking it hard to the hole.

"Practice answering the questions you think people might ask you, everyday things you think you know until you try to explain them," Packer said. "And make eye contact too. You would be surprised how many people asking the questions are just as nervous as you are. Making eye contact will help put you in control of the situation." Cade was talking a blue streak by the end of the interview, and afterwards Packer shared his feelings about Five-Star.

"There are certain high-profile guys in the Basketball Hall of Fame and everybody knows those guys. In the past 25 years, however, I don't think there have been two guys who, through their efforts, have helped more kids get the exposure and the opportunity to elevate their skill level in the world of high school basketball than Howard Garfinkel and Will Klein. I say this with a great deal of admiration for both of them, Howie with his persona and Will with his background persona.

"Howie is not a high-profile guy, a media darling. He's never coached in the NCAA or coached a national championship team, but when you consider the hundreds, maybe thousands of kids that he's helped get into college through the camp and personal recommendations, you have to respect him a great deal. The thing I admire most about Howie is how he's helped people like Rick Pitino, guys you know have first-class organizations that he touched at an earlier age. I heard of Rick Pitino through Garf's scouting service when he was just a high school player.

"Pitino has coached in the Final Four, coached the New York Knicks, and now Kentucky, and 25 years after he got started, he still comes back in the summertime to see Howie. That should be enough said about what all of us think of the great contribution he and his camp have made to the game of basketball."

* * * * *

There was more hoop to be played that afternoon and evening, with playoff games and pickup games and all day, like rain on a shingle roof, there was the soothing sound of basketballs bouncing on smooth macadam courts and young voices filling the air like cooling wind. That night there was the Orange-White Classic at the spacious Dedmon Center, jam-packed with parents waiting to take their changed sons home and campers torn between wanting to go and wanting to stay. Nothing could keep them there though. Everything Five-Star had to do for the moment was done. Almost everything.

Anthony Cade was in the NBA all-star game with Oak Hill Academy teammates Gandhi Jordan, a 6'6" senior, and 6'3" Carlos Cofield, another 1990 graduate. With all that talent packed on one high school team, it was a wonder they ever lost, but then there was that thing Billy Packer had talked about a few hours earlier. A camper had asked him how a team like North Carolina State could upset the Phi Slamma Jamma boys of Houston like they did in the 1983 NCAA finals or how in 1985 a David like Villanova could cut down the Goliath, Georgetown.

Packer had seen and done all the Final Fours the past 16 years and he said, "There's a feeling a bunch of players get about themselves and each other, a little bit of chemistry that grows until they won't be denied." It's not the kind of thing that can be figured out by talking or writing down on paper, and if a person doesn't look for it they won't find it although it's there. Five-Star forces you to search.

Lawrence Mitchell stole the show in the Orange-White Classic. A 6'6" senior from Conway, South Carolina, he scored a Radford all-star game record 42 points, most of them coming on sizzling, howitzer-like slams. Everyone knew that Mitchell, who is also an All-American football player, could play a little, but no one had seen him crush the ball like that, mostly because Garf and Will Klein have a strict "No Dunking" rule at camp. They waive it for the Orange-White Classic, but otherwise showtime is canceled. There are reasons for that.

"It's summertime," says Garf, "and guys are trying to make a reputation for themselves. They might try too hard at camp and guys who can't quite get up there yet could hurt themselves. The injury factor is the first reason. Then you have the chance of guys damaging the rims and upsetting the rhythm of the camp. We're not going to let the rest of the camp sit around because one or two guys can dunk. Finally, when dunking was eliminated in college in 1970, Kareem Abdul-Jabbar said, 'When they took away my dunk, I learned how to shoot the sky hook.' If it's good enough for the greatest center in the history of the game, it's good enough for Five-Star."

* * * * *

Jack Stephens wasn't in the Orange-White Classic, but he did win the Most Improved Player Award and his team won the NCAA league championship. It was ironic in a way because he had all but given up on himself that long-ago Monday night. "It was a moral defeat, but I learned something about myself," he said the last night. With Coach Wainwright's words ringing in his ears and his insides, he put it behind him and even grabbed the game-clinching rebound in the finals.

He learned a little about basketball too, like the Bill Walton move he'd been shown at stations. If he was boxed out on the boards, he was told to do what the Portland Trailblazers' and Boston Celtics' great did on occasion—nudge guys out of the way from behind, pinning his hip on their thighs or knees, keeping his body low and his hands held high to satisfy curious referees. There were a lot of little things like that he hadn't thought of before.

There was a different Walton represented in the NIT all-star game, Walton Middle School of Charlottesville, Virginia, in the form of rising eighth grader Tarik Turner. It must have been something they were feeding them down in the President's State that summer, because the four youngest all-stars were all Virginians: Steve Thompson of Fort Defiance; Damon Bacote of Hampton; Damon Graydon of Franklin, all freshmen; and Turner, a herky-jerky, heady-beyond-his years, 5'8" lefty point guard.

There are no guarantees and Turner knows it, but he has been working toward a professional basketball career since he was knee-high to a grasshopper. When he was three years old and living in California, he hung a tin basket on a palm tree and practiced his "J" with a nerf ball. "I always did the best I could," he says. "When I was five, I set a goal to play in the NBA. My dad said if I meant it he would back me all the way and even then told me to act consistent with my goal in every sense of the word, especially my attitude. If I was going to be a pro I should begin to act like one.

"My dad gets on me if I get lazy and my mother is very strict, but not in a mean way. She told me if I get anything as low as a C in my schoolwork there will be no more basketball. Every day my parents tell my sister Tamyra and me to learn five new words, and to show them that we understand the words we have to use them in a story. My parents let us know that education is the number one priority next to family and friends."

Turner, in time-honored Five-Star fashion, made a pest of himself all week, hanging around Station 13 and getting underfoot elsewhere. "I welcome anything the coaches would like to teach me," he said, and wherever you looked he was there, dribbling a basketball or working on a move or watching and taking every bit of it in. It's the same back in Charlottesville where he does his private routine before heading down to The Barn, a playground near his home where the big boys congregate and the lessons become ingrained.

He was selected Mr. Stations at camp, but the plaque and the rest of his Five-Star regalia, including his Orange-White jersey, were relegated to a bottom drawer when he got home. "I am proud that I did well at camp, but I keep my shirts folded away to make sure I do not get big-headed," Turner said. "I know it is necessary to keep playing hard if I want to make my goal. I would like to be the best point guard ever.

"If I keep practicing and improving, I don't think anyone will be better. I learn from others, but I don't want to be like anyone else. I want to be me. Whenever I play that game, you know, where you pretend you are making the winning basket at the end of the game, I don't like to imitate someone else. I don't pretend I am Michael Jordan or Magic Johnson. If I think anything to myself, like if I were the announcer announcing the game, I think things like: 'Turner has the ball with two seconds left. He turns and puts it up and there's the buzzer and yes, it's good!'"

* * * * *

An emptiness rushed in to replace the fullness on the final day. Many of the campers had already departed, leaving the night before with their families, and Friday morning the rest boarded buses back to Roanoke Airport, staring at the warm hills outside the windows as they rolled past. Time, which had all but stopped, returned, and halfway home Five-Star, except for their sweaty duffle bags, will seem like something they imagined. They will discover that it is much more deeply ingrained.

Many of the coaches had departed, leaving the counselors to close up shop. Jerry Wainwright, running on empty like everyone else, was still running. "Let me tell you why I come back here," he said. "I look at Garf as a pseudo father. I use him as a basketball father and I worry about him too. It's real easy to use the word 'family,' but at Five-Star family has embraced the words 'loyalty' and 'work ethic.' Even when I'm not here I feel I have to be an example of what this camp is all about.

"Garf has great insight into human nature. He comes on strong with the kids but genuinely cares about each and every one of them. He has proven to me that nothing you do matters unless it comes from the heart. Being around him I feel like a part of basketball history. He is basketball Americana. He understands the tenets of the old game and won't let them die. Look at Michael Jordan, what a great player he is. When he came to camp Garf told him that because of his height he needed to improve his jumper. That advice hasn't hurt much.

"There is no harder man to work for than Garf. He is a perfectionist, but I always want the guy in the orange pants and slicked-down hair to say, 'Jerry, you did a good job.' I know if I don't, he won't say it. He has done so much for me and I have one goal in life with Garf. Someday I'd like to be able to do something for him."

Will Klein lingered, as is the custom, to check on loose ends while Garf and The King flew back to New York together. They would all catch their breath for 24 hours before heading to Honesdale and

Lake Bryn Mawr. After eight days there, they would rest two weeks in preparation for a draining month at Pitt, at Robert Morris College in Coraopolis, in the shadow of Pennsylvania's city of steel.

PART THREE

Pitt

TWELVE

Chugging into Coraopolis

"Five-Star is a fraternity that probably will never be equalled."

– John Paxson of the Chicago Bulls

In the year 1803, Jeff Ferree, while deer hunting, was slain and scalped by marauding Indians. That was the last known redskin attack in the vicinity of Coraopolis, Pennsylvania, until Colonel Ray Mullis brought his rampaging basketball tribe to Five-Star.

Coraopolis, 10 miles northwest of Pittsburgh, is a thriving and peaceable enough community today, owing its comfortable existence in part to the establishment of Fort Vance in the mid-1700s along the nearby Ohio River. The fortress, providing safety for settlers against bands of uprooted Delaware and Shawnee Indians, brought a gradual end to the violence—until July of 1989, when the turf wars flared up anew.

Basketball came to Coraopolis in the 1920s when a foresighted resident tacked a bushel basket ring to a breadboard and nailed the contraption to a telephone pole. Neighborhood children, weary of kick-the-can and hide-and-seek, took quickly to the sport, playing games in the street with tennis balls. Creative shots were occasionally called for, especially around Halloween. The poles had rungs at ground level, which provided easy access for pranksters who hung tricycles and other toys from the hoop.

Colonel Mullis would have fit right in with that crowd. Originally from Macon, Georgia, his southern heritage has nothing to do with his prominent rank. He earned that after a memorable night on the town at Five-Star. "It was back when the Ollie North hearings were big news," he says, with more than a hint of magnolia drawl. "Me and a couple of friends of mine, Oliver Purnell, a coach at Radford, and Stan Nance, an assistant at Virginia Commonwealth, were having a drink and decided to go to a classy disco. The only problem was I was dressed up and they were in their coaching gear.

"I told them not to worry, that I'd get them in. I had no idea how, but I pride myself on thinking quickly on my feet. We went and when we got there the guard said I could go in but they couldn't, so I said to him, 'I guess you don't know who I am. Get me your boss.' The boss comes out and says, 'OK, big shot, who are you?' Well, I was just flying by the seat of my pants, but I told him I had been Ollie North's first commanding officer at Quontico Military Base when he was fresh out of the academy.

"I knew North was very popular in the area, so I just gave it a shot. The guy got all nice and friendly and put us at his personal table and we ran up a tab of about $200. I swear, guys still come up to me and tell me they fought with me in Viet Nam. I can't tell the truth now or they'd run me out of town." The Colonel has been known to stretch things a little during a game too, anything to wangle a victory. The "winningest" coach in and around Baltimore, Maryland, with over 500 wins at Cardinal Gibbons High, he's never seen a hopeless situation he didn't like.

Along the sidelines at Pitt, trying to end a 12–0 run against his team, it was easy to overhear him telling his players, "Some of you guys look about as ready to play as my rear end. If you guys would just listen to me, we'd kick the hell out of this team. We're playing like the time that other team ran off 18 points against us and we won by 12. If you're playing a good team, there's not gonna be a time they don't get momentum. Let's don't pour gas on the flames. Let's take our time out there. Work it inside, forget those long jumpers."

It didn't have to make sense all the time, as long as it made the kids stop worrying. "Playing Morgan Wootten once at De Matha, we were down by 18," Mullis explained later. "I told my kids, 'We have 'em right where we want 'em, now let's press 'em to death,' and they believed me. They said, 'You know, coach, we do have a good press,' and they felt confident in themselves. Sometimes it helps to say something so outrageous the kids have to either laugh or believe you. It doesn't always work, but it's your only chance.

"We lost that game by a point, but the bottom line is you don't want kids to get in the habit of making excuses for things, and coaches have a responsibility to teach them that. The game should

Fig. 17 **"THE KING AND HIS COURT":** *Frank Marino (Pelham Pelicans) plays hardball on the coaching lines, and has coached in and won more games than anyone else in camp history. Here, he's flanked by the Lebo clan: Jeff (left), of North Carolina fame, and his father Dave, who put Carlisle (PA) High School on the basketball map.*

Fig. 18 *Bill Donlon (asst. Northwestern), the brains behind those plyometric boxes, apparently has jumped out of the picture.*

Fig. 19 **"FROM PUNXSUTAWNY TO THE PROS":** *After capturing the NBA crown with the Pistons in 1989, Chuck Daly holds an SRO crowd in rapt attention in the Gus Krop Gym at Robert Morris. Fresh from Punxsutawny High School en route to a Duke assistantship, Daly also delivered the first-ever camp lecture in August 1966. The rest, as they say, is history.*

Fig. 20 **EVANGELICAL ZEAL:** *Dave Odom is not praying or signaling a successful three-pointer. He's merely using body language to get his point across in a lecture at Radford.*

Fig's. 21 & 22 **THE TWO FACES OF MARV:** *Portland Trailblazer scout Marv Kessler, at his jocular best in a lecture (left), and all business at Station 13 (below). Kessler invented the Individual Instruction concept at Five-Star 25 years ago.*

Fig. 23 **"THE CHILL" ON THE HILL:** *Ed Schilling (Western Boone H.S.) counsels a team in his traditional postmortem after a game.*

Fig. 24 Some say they play harder here than anywhere else in the country. A picture is worth a thousand words.

Fig. 25 Tiny Archibald teaches shooting technique at Robert Morris College.

Fig. 26 **QUIGLEY TIES "THE KING":** *White-shirted Pat Quigley (Bshp. Loughton H.S.) with the team that copped his fourth NBA title in Honesdale, September 1989. Frank Marino demanded a recount.*

Fig. 27 **JIMMY VEE IN HAPPIER TIMES:** *Jim Valvano, former head coach at N.C. State (center), with counselors Walker Lambiotte (right) and Craig "Noodles" Neal. Soon after Lambiotte transferred to Northwestern, one of his best friends supplied the data for the book* **Personal Fouls,** *highly critical of the Wolfpack program. Neal, who played for Bobby Cremins at Georgia Tech, is carving out a career in the CBA.*

Fig. 28 **THE MIRROR NEVER LIES:** *Or hardly ever. Rumeal Robinson receiving foul shooting tips from Mitch Buonaguro (Fairfield H.S.) in July 1985. Robinson later put this knowledge to good use in the '89 NCAA Finals, when he sank a pair of free throws to beat Seton Hall and give Michigan the championship.*

Fig. 29 Patrick Ewing disposes of some trash at Honesdale in August of 1979.

Fig. 30 Shy and retiring Dick Vitale exhibits rare animation while lecturing at Radford in June 1988. The campers were still applauding when Vitale was halfway back to the Roanoke airport to complete his Piston-Laker radio stint in the NBA Championship Series.

Fig. 31 Coach "K," whose Duke Blue Devils made Final Four appearances four of the five years from 1986–90, lectures on defense in Radford in June of 1989.

be fun for kids too, not drudgery. That's one of the main reasons I come to Five-Star, to stay young. I learn something new here all the time and I admit sometimes I get a little crazy, but I try to teach the kids three things: to work hard, to respect the game, and to have a sense of humor."

Taking the game to new heights of savagery never hurt either, which is what The Colonel did all week at the "Fast Break" station. The station had two separate parts, fast break defense and fast break offense, and was designed to teach campers what to do defending against or running a 3-on-2 break. The first time through each coach taught the fundamentals. The second time around, the campers played it for keeps, sort of. The defense took on the offense, trying to stop them from getting a good shot or making a basket. If the defense stopped the offense from scoring, the defense got a point. If they didn't, the offense got the point. When Garf blew his whistle ending the fray, whoever was behind did 10 pushups.

The Colonel had the defense, showing how the two defenders should take positions, one at the foul line ready to cut off the ball with his teammate in the lane behind him, ready to chase down the first pass. The third defender has to catch up, as if he missed the shot at the other end that set up the break in the first place. "The philosophy is we will not give up a layup," he said. "We take an awful lot of charges at Cardinal Gibbons, and, coming in, teams know that if they go inside, there's gonna be a collision."

James "Bruiser" Flint, an assistant at the University of Massachusetts, was his worthy opponent. He's been called Bruiser ever since he can remember, but he was just cruising for a bruising as far as the Colonel was concerned. Bruiser showed his guys what to do, how the guy in the middle bringing the ball upcourt should try to get it to one of his teammates on the wings. "The guy with the ball has to read the defense," he said. "His job is to spread it out, pull up at the foul line, and hit the open man so he can shoot it in stride, without having to dribble. The ballhandler is the most important guy. If he's out of control, the whole play is." He learned that running the point at St. Joseph's in Philly, but nothing he'd ever done prepared him for The Colonel.

The "Fast Break" station had been invented years before by Mike Fratello, and right away he let it be known there would be no holds barred. He had the offense that first year while Dave Odom, ever the gentleman, was on defense. It was close at the end, so Fratello, ever the competitor, went into his three-man version of the four-corners and Odom went berserk. The Colonel, not beneath such shenanigans, decided to uphold tradition and at the same time relive Pitt's tumultuous Indian past.

It began normally enough. Bruiser had to remind his gazelles that they weren't running a track meet, that they had to time the whole thing and not outrun each other. He had a nice lead halfway through and was sitting pretty, he thought. Waiting in ambush were "Big Chief" Colonel Mullis and his braves. During a time-out, they circled Bruiser and his troops like so many covered wagons, firing flaming-arrow taunts at them.

"Offense sucks, offense sucks," they whooped, curdling the blood of their foes. *"Offense ain't shit, offense ain't shit,"* they stabbed, mercilessly, while their Chief orchestrated the attack, waving his arms like the conductor of the Massacre Symphony until Bruiser, his Five-Star Custer, fell.

Garf saw and heard the whole thing but didn't lift a finger to help. It wasn't the Little Big Horn after all and he knew that Bruiser, still the new kid on the block, would take care of Sitting Bull Mullis on his own terms, which he did. Bruiser borrowed a tune from *The Wizard of Oz*, the ominous chorus the Scarecrow, the Tin Man, and the Lion heard outside the Wicked Witch of the West's castle. He had his kids, like the witch's soldiers, hum it threateningly to the defense until they melted.

There was another reason Garf stayed neutral. He could see that the kids, all of them NBA and NCAA leaguers, were having the time of their lives. They could handle it. They knew it was all in good fun and Garf knew none of them would ever be able to forget how to defend against or run a 3-on-2 break again. Besides, Pitt had a reputation for being a rough-and-tumble place. It's been like that since Five-Star came to Coraopolis.

*   *   *   *   *

In the summer of 1977, having run out of room in Wheeling, West Virginia, Garf and Will Klein struck a deal with Jack Fertig for Pitt. "It was Five-Star luck and timing again," says Garf. "Fertig, at the time, was an assistant coach at Robert Morris College. I knew him through *HSBI*. He was working for the legendary Gus Krop. The college wanted to go Division I and they needed to upgrade their tennis program at the same time. They had six beautiful new macadam courts, eight now, which we could convert for basketball. We also got the gym, named after Coach Krop, and made arrangements to use Moon High School in town in case it rained."

Robert Morris College was ideal in many ways. It had been around for a while and felt lived in, comfy enough for a Division I institution. It was founded in the early 1920s as part of the Pittsburgh School of Accountancy and in 1935 was renamed in honor of Robert Morris, Pennsylvania's delegate to the Constitutional Convention and a major financier of the Revolutionary War. Will Klein liked the pecuniary atmosphere of the place even though he was up to his eyelids in bills and receipts.

He was still doing everything the old-fashioned Orin-Sekwa way, putting the personal touch on every piece of mail coming in or going out. "The real work started after we moved to Pitt," Klein says now, "especially after we went to four weeks. We had always tried to keep the competition levels at each week equal, but at Pitt we got into screening kids even more. It was much more work, but we felt it made the camp better."

It's a painstaking process. Klein does the paperwork, but when applications start to arrive in the spring, he and Garf talk on the phone daily, trying to fit each player into the right slot. "There is a great myth that a kid must be invited to Five-Star or be an all-star," Garf says. "They must be bona fide high school participants, but that is all. We send out brochures every February and we could save ourselves about 15 hours a week if we just accepted kids as they applied, but we want everyone matched up with their peers.

"We don't want 5'4" rising sophomores playing against 6'6" rising seniors, for instance. We can't be perfect without having seen them all play, but we try to assign each camper to the right week. It's expensive. It means extra phone calls and hundreds of letters back and forth to coaches and parents and switching maybe half the kids to more suitable weeks. We know it's doing things the hard way, but it's one of the key reasons we have stayed successful."

Pitt started out with two weeks (called Pitt I and Pitt II), going to three (Pitt III) almost immediately and adding a fourth week (Pitt IV) in the early eighties. Every week they were filled to capacity, peaking at 420 campers. The food was good by Rosemont standards, although not on a par with Radford. Nobody died from it, but the campers rarely fought to get in line.

The dorm rooms were nice, and there were more telephones too. That's where lines could become a problem. Kids were always lined up around the block trying to call home. It's an accepted ritual at Five-Star and nobody listens in, although it would be easy to do so waiting for your turn. Patience and privacy count for something around the phone booths. The nicest thing, as far as the campers were concerned, was that the campus was situated near enough to civilization for an occasional late-night pizza delivery.

It could get hot at Pitt in July, almost as if the nearby steel mills had tunnels running underground releasing steam on the courts, which were down in a small, natural dale. It was pretty country, though, blanketed in purple crown vetch and hilly with open, high hills sweeping toward the higher Alleghenies. You could get away from the heat up there or sit under the huge Norway spruce trees that lined one end of the courts, but the heat was good too. It dried the courts quickly after brief showers rolled in.

Perhaps most important, as far as Garf was concerned, the campus was located less than five minutes from Pittsburgh International Airport, which meant that campers from all over the country could get there easily. It quickly became a true basketball caldron, and kids from the Deep South, the Far West, the West Coast, and even overseas were tossed in the pot with New Englanders and Midwesterners and the usual East Coast contingent. It was perfect for coaches and recruiters too, who could bop in and out effortlessly.

There was plenty to look at. Garf still had *HSBI*, which had become the standard by which all other scouting services were measured. The kids knew what a good rating could mean to their scholarship chances and they showed up in droves, anxious to impress not just the coaches but Garf too. He knew virtually every kid in the continental United States and even some beyond. He was at the height of his influence; a simple phone call to a coach could move a kid from Division III to Division I or vice versa.

The NCAA eventually changed the way Garf conducted business. Spurred by member-coaches wary of his potential for pulling strings, especially for coaches inside Five-Star's tight inner circle, the NCAA would force him to choose between *HSBI* and Five-Star. There were never any specific allegations that Garf did anything wrong. It was mostly a feeling, almost a paranoia, that coaches outside the camp had that Five-Star guys, Garf's Guys, were getting an uneven break.

The feeling festered until the NCAA had to do something, and Garf didn't really help matters in the beginning. "In the '70s and early '80s, I put in a rule that you had to buy *HSBI* or you weren't welcome in the camp," he says. "This was before all the NCAA regulations about Live Periods and Dead Periods, and I wanted to limit the number of coaches coming there. If I had opened the camp to everyone, there would have been 500 coaches there. That's not what the camp is all about.

"Plus, it seemed to me that anyone who came to Five-Star back then should be someone who was recruiting kids primarily from the Midwest and East Coast. If you were recruiting from those regions, then you should have *HSBI*, or otherwise you didn't know who you were watching. I can see now how that might have been misinterpreted, especially by a guy who didn't buy the report. I maight have been wrong, I'm not saying I was 100 percent right, but I have a little self-interest too."

* * * * *

The NCAA disruptions still were a few years off and in the meantime, good ol' boy Dave Pritchett kept coming to camp, whether he was wanted or not. Garf's preoccupation with Five-Star had cut down on their to-hell-and-back scouting trips, but Pritchett still rolled in on a regular basis, sizing up the talent for Davidson College and talking about bygone days with the fellas. Now and then, he got under Garf's skin, which wasn't all that difficult.

"I believe I am the only man banned from the camp twice," Pritchett says, laughing. "I'll never forget this. One of the times was when I was still coaching at Maryland. I had brought Garf a highlight film to show the kids, explaining to him that I needed to take it back with me in a few days. Well, he didn't show it and he didn't show it, and I needed to get the thing back to Maryland and after a while I just took it. The only thing was I couldn't find him to tell him. I found out later that on the last night of camp he showed a film and he didn't notice until it was up on the screen that it was a different film. Then he started steaming.

"You have to understand that Howie can't put a plug in the wall without screwing things up, so he got himself into a frenzy over the whole thing. The projector only works half the time anyway, and he hadn't learned yet to delegate that chore. The next time I showed up, Mitch Buonaguro, who is the head coach at Fairfield University now but was a scared little grad assistant at Boston College then, came running up to me saying, 'Coach Pritchett, I told him what a great man you were and what a great coach you were, but Mr. Garfinkel swore that if you ever came here again he'd get the highway militia to keep you out.'

"We worked that one out but Howie got over it slowly. The next time I got thrown out of there was while I was the head coach at Davidson. Howie had this deal where you couldn't talk to the kids in camp and as I was sitting there on the bleachers one day one of the kids walked past and said 'Hi' or something, so I turned and said something back. That's all we said, and it was the kid who said 'Hi' first, but the only thing Howie saw was my lips moving in the direction of that kid. He was all hyper that week because the place was full of coaches and recruiters, so he said to me, 'Pit Stop, get your ass the hell out of camp.'

"I fought with him a little, but I knew it wasn't going to do any good until he cooled down. I checked into a hotel and tried to come back later and he was still adamant as hell about it, but I just charged right in there anyway and said, 'If I were interested in bumping one of your damn kids, I could recruit the hell out of him after he leaves here.' He just let it go and settled down after that."

The two of them were peas in a pod when it came to evaluating and recruiting, so they never stayed mad long. The relationship, more often than not, was on friendly terms although they never totally stopped butting heads. Sometimes they did it literally. "Garf, in the late seventies, had started to do more of his work for *HSBI* over the phone," Pritchett says. "He would use me once in a while as his eyes where his legs couldn't go. I'd give him the lowdown on a kid and he'd tell me what he knew and it was the kind of thing neither one of us told anyone else because we'd have got our asses kicked if we did, you know, because it was confidential material.

"We couldn't just keep it to ourselves, though, so instead we invented 'Graveyard Talk' or 'Kitchen Talk' or whatever the hell it was we called it. It was a milder version of gossipy stuff that was still pretty damn interesting. Garf added it to *HSBI* and after you got done reading it you knew who was who and what was happening in the world of basketball, the kind of juicy stuff everybody loves. Maybe it set the stage for all these guys in the newspapers now, the columnists. Who the hell knows? Anyway, my point is that Garf and I would talk over the phone all the time and other times we'd get together to talk and there was this one time, I never will forget it, we smacked into each other at Cole Field House down in Maryland.

"I was still with Lefty Driesell and I was out scouting Creighton and Notre Dame for the NCAA tournament that was coming up, but first I had to stop at Cole Field House. Morgan Wootten's DeMatha kids were getting it on with Dunbar High and I just had to be there. We had won the ACC regular season title but we got beat by NC State in the tournament, and I was still running that through my mind and thinking about having to play Digger Phelps and a few other things when Howie came firing up and pounded me in my chest and said something like, 'Pit Stop, you corn-bran, backwoods, son-of-a-bitch, how the hell are you?'

"Well, it was five minutes before tipoff and everyone was down around the floor area and I was pretty fired up myself, scrambling around looking for players and everything else, so all at once I pounded at Garf and grabbed him, kinda playful like, but of course he's no bigger than Barney Fife and he slipped out of my hands onto a canvas dumpster. He cut his nose with his eyeglasses and was bleeding a little bit and he had coffee grounds on his clothes and all of a sudden there were 200 coaches rushing around like mad hares, sprinting across the floor screaming that Pritchett and Garfinkel were having a hell of a fight.

"Howie was laughing, but the rest of those guys didn't even see that. They were worried as hell because he was the Czar of Basketball, at least that's what I called him at the time because of his power. It seemed like every league in the country had somebody working at his camp and half of America wanted to be on his good side, but he didn't give a damn about that kind of thing.

"The other guys didn't know that, and they came over to me and said I couldn't treat a man of his stature like that and I just said, 'The hell I can't.' I knew the whole thing was just a damn joke. Howie still had to get the upper hand though. He called me up later and said I didn't care about him, that he could have been hurt or killed and that I didn't even stick around to find out. But when I explained to him that I had to get out of there and get my scouting done he understood what I was talking about."

*   *   *   *   *

Marv Kessler kept showing up too, though Garf wondered about the wisdom in that sometimes. Kessler had left Martin Van Buren High for Adelphi College, a Division II team in Philadelphia, and he hadn't changed much. He'd show up and do things like teach the campers to yell *"Oy vey"* whenever they took a charge on defense. Most of them had no idea what it meant, but he'd show them how to set their feet and how to roll just right with the impact to avoid injury. The *oy vey* part, he told them, was in there to convince the ref to buy their act. All week at stations and in games they shouted it.

Other times he'd come just to lecture, often at the end of the week, but Garf was tempted to put a stop to that after Kessler told a story about Marshall Williams, one of his players at Adelphi during the 1976 season. Williams was his center and at 6'6" could jump out of the gym. He tended to stand out because the guards were small and the forwards, a Jewish kid named Al Blumin and a Puerto Rican kid, Joe Nava, "couldn't jump two inches between them," says Kessler. "Williams had to get every single rebound."

That was OK by him. "Marshall Williams was a special kid. He came from Bed Stuy, from pure poverty. He didn't know his father. He came from a big family and got other scholarship offers but chose Adelphi so he could stay close to home and help out. It was tough for him but he was a good kid, and if there was anything wrong about him it was that he was too unselfish. He wouldn't shoot.

"A little way into the season we had to play St. Francis of Brooklyn, a team that had a strong center, and I told Marshall that the only way we could win was if he got the guy in foul trouble. I told him he had to shoot, so he did and he scored 35 points and after that he started to get it together. One night, a little while later, we were on the road playing at Long Island and the team was 8-5 and going good and he grabbed a rebound. He made the outlet pass and got to the foul line and collapsed.

"The refs figured he had just lost his wind or something. After about a minute, though, they sent both teams back to the bench and it was just them standing there with Williams, waiting for him to get up and say, 'I'm OK now,' but he wasn't moving. A nurse came out and gave him mouth-to-mouth while I pumped his chest, 5 times, 10 times, 15 times and nothing. The nurse didn't know I was his coach and after a minute or two just looked at me and said matter-of-factly, 'Look, he's dead.'

"Marshall had taken two medications, one for his asthma and one for a bad toothache that had started to bother him just before the game. The combination caused his heart to hyperventribulate, so there we were, out on the road, with Marshall's body lying on the court, all still and motionless, with a blanket over it.

"I just wanted to get out of there. I gathered myself, but I couldn't find my players. One of my guards was wandering out on the highway in his uniform, not caring that it was ten degrees above zero. The other guard was pounding his head on a locker. His head was bleeding.

"After that I wanted to give it up. I told the kids a couple of days later that I didn't have the heart to go on, but I said it was up to them. They had a team meeting and told me they would go on under three conditions: that we start a fund for Marshall's parents, that we fly the flag at half mast for a week, and that we have a minute of silence before every game. They wore black arm bands and dedicated the rest of the season to him.

"It was too late to find a big man to replace Williams and we were hurting for scoring, so we went with a three-guard offense. I didn't expect much, but something happened and there was a transformation of the team. Guys started playing like they'd never played before. The team was half black guys and half white guys, but suddenly there were no more barriers. They were playing for something outside themselves.

"Nava and Blumin start jumping out of the gym and rebounding and we ripped off 13 straight wins. Every time a kid made a good pass or took a charge you could hear them shout Williams' name to each other, 'Marshall, Marshall.' We beat teams we'd never beaten before. We won close games, buzzer games, and ended up 21-5. We got our first NCAA bid in 13 years, but the kids decided not to go. They'd done what they had set out to do.

"The point of telling that to campers," Kessler says, "is that if that happened at Indiana it would have been the story of the century, but also it took a player's death to bring a team to life. A coach would never ask that much of you, so it shows you should really be able to motivate yourself. If a coach plays you out of position sometimes or is using you in a way you think isn't right, what does it all mean?"

College basketball fans and players would ask themselves similar questions in the spring of 1990 when Loyola Marymount University star Hank Gathers, moments after a thunderous dunk in a West Coast Conference tournament game, fell helpless at midcourt and tragically died. Gathers' death got more headlines than Williams' had, but both deaths affected people close to them deeply. It never sits right when a kid's life stops for reasons no one can fathom.

You could hear a feather drop whenever Kessler told his story, which is why he stopped telling it late in the week. Listening, cocky kids got knocked down a peg or two, but there were always one or two others, it seemed, who were so deeply affected that they could barely move a muscle. Len Bias was one, when he was a camper. Emotionally drained, the future Boston Celtic draftee didn't want to play in the Orange-White Classic. Bias would later weave his own sad tale, but there were others who didn't perform up to snuff after Kessler got done, so now if he talks about Marshall Williams, he does so early in the week to give everyone time to recover.

* * * * *

Pitt had been properly initiated. In no time it was bubbling over with talent and that first summer became known simply as the "Year of the Guards." Not even Garf, the self-proclaimed and widely acknowledged King of Guards, could have come up with a more stellar cast than showed up at Five-Star's door.

There were four who stood out: Chicago Bulls-bound John Paxson, the latest in a long line of Bishop Alter dependables; Jimmy Braddock, who had North Carolina written all over him; Detroit Pistons' flit Isiah Thomas, then the main cog in coach Gene Pingatore's wheel at St. Joseph's High in Westchester, Illinois; and Ray McCoy, from Bloom Township, just outside Chicago.

Out of all of them, Ray McCoy was the best. Paxson wasn't and neither was Thomas, at least not at that time in that place. "It was the greatest head-to-head guard competition in the history of camp," says Garf. "They were so close you could barely tell them apart, but McCoy had the better week. Isiah had injured his ankle and was a half-step behind what he could have been, but McCoy, based on what he did in camp, was rated even with or slightly better than Thomas and Paxson."

That was the thing. A kid could come to Five-Star with as many notches on his gun as he wanted, but what he did there was another whole shootin' match. A kid might stare down the barrel of a loaded Isiah Thomas or John Paxson Special once or twice in his entire high school career, but at Five-Star it was one mean hombre after another, every day, and after the dust cleared that week, McCoy was the one left standing.

Not even gunslingers can rest on their laurels long and survive. If they've got a reputation to protect they gotta come out smokin' every time, and McCoy didn't. He had a tendency, when something was bothering him, to stuff himself with food, or maybe he just plain enjoyed eating, but all too often he headed for the icebox and emptied it. There are worse things in life but not for a basketball player, not for a kid who lives and dies on quickness.

Every person has his reasons for doing things and there was never a nicer kid than Ray McCoy, not at Five-Star. He even wrote Garf letters after leaving, thanking him for all he'd done, mentioning "the things you are doing for me I'll never know about," and he'd sign them Raymond "Howard" McCoy, out of admiration and respect. Paxson and Thomas caught and passed him but only because he must have wanted it that way. The boy could play the game.

So could Thomas, who even then had that sparkling personality and disarming smile that disguised his competitiveness well. Even with a sore ankle he was here and gone faster than a lightning bug's glimmer and he knew enough to spend time at Station 13, where he and Kessler worked on, of all things, his quickness. Kessler taught him how to flick his inside hand while on defense to distract the man dribbling the basketball. He should flick his wrist and fingertips, making the dribbler pay more attention to him than the offense and also gradually moving him to the outside.

As a defender he had the guy where he wanted him then and could go for the steal or set up a trap, and Thomas did it to perfection. There was only one thing he did wrong. He kept using his outside hand. "He still does that, but he makes millions of dollars a year, so what's the point," Kessler says now, laughing. "What I remember most about Isiah was his court smarts. In one game his team was losing by one point with about two seconds left and there was a jump ball at the other team's end of the court. He pulled a guy on top of him trying to get a foul, like the guy had pushed him or something. He didn't get the call, but I fell in love with him as a player when I saw that. He was so mentally advanced."

John Paxson was no slouch either. He was another one of coach Joe Petrocelli's thinkers and, like his older brother Jim, did things off the ball that made your head swivel. He was steady, smart, sure-handed, the kind of player a coach would give his eyeteeth to have. He was a good kid, the kind of boy a girl could take home to meet her mother. Coming in as a sophomore he was also unsure of himself. "After my brother came back from camp he talked about it, so most of us in the Dayton area knew about Five-Star and started to flock there," says John, now in his seventh year as a professional.

"I had been told I had talent, but I didn't feel like I was that good a player. So many times, when you're a decent high school player, there's going to be nights when you're just better than everybody else, but going to Five-Star was the first time I got to play against that many really good players day in and day out. You kinda realize at that point what it takes, what you're gonna have to do.

"Everybody assumes that every year I went I was an all-star, but that's not true. It was hard, especially the first year. One thing I learned was to seek out better competition after I got home, the best I could find. At that point I wasn't thinking that someday I might find out I wasn't good enough to play in college or the NBA. I never really worried about if I were going to fail; my whole idea was to keep becoming a better player."

He went to Notre Dame before making the NBA, and the experience gained at Five-Star was a valuable ally. "When you're young, you think you'd like to get a college scholarship to help out your family so they don't have to pay for your education. There is no doubt a camp like Five-Star is worthwhile for that. For one thing, there is so much exposure. I was lucky in that I was able to take advantage of the opportunity to go to a camp that was that good and I think the benefits were tremendous."

It wasn't all sugar and spice. "Everybody dreads the stations by the third or fourth day. They've had enough. Just waking up was bad too sometimes, especially at Robert Morris where you had to get right out of bed and walk up those hills to do calisthenics with the Alligator Man, Mike Fratello. There is no question it pays off, though. You learn so many things. The stations made you think about different phases of the game. The situations were specific, just like they happen in a game."

Paxson has found experience to be the best teacher. "There

have been guys who have come and gone in the NBA who have more talent than I do, but learning about the game itself and how you have to work and what you have to do mentally are the things that have kept me around all these years. It is tough up here. Every year there are new guys coming in who are good athletes and good players. I'm not a superstar in this league, but I play roles and I think I do that pretty well and that's helped keep me around too," he says.

"A lot of guys come from being great college players and can't accept playing a role. They think they'll be a superstar in this league, but that can't happen to everybody. The quicker you assume roles and are willing to be a team member and not worry about your individual stats and things like that, those are the kinds of guys who tend to stick around. I've had every role possible. I've been a starter, some seasons I've come off the bench, other times I've played very little. I've learned that over the long haul if you just stick with good work habits you're going to get your chance.

"In this game you get stereotyped quickly, and I'm basically thought of as a guy who can shoot it and play with some intelligence, so that's what I work on. I'm not the kind of guy who is very fast or athletic. I've never even dunked in a game. I'm 6'2" and I never even tried. Every time I get a breakaway I just lay it in because I know I can make those."

The dream, no matter how difficult to achieve, is worth dreaming. "It's not always exciting playing in this league," says Paxson. "Sometimes when you do something this long, it gets to be a grind, but I think you have to put it in perspective too. It's a great way to make a living, and when you think about all the time and effort you've put into it, it would be silly to give it up. It's still a kick for me and I've played with some pretty good players.

"My first two years, I played alongside George Gervin at San Antonio and I didn't really mind having to give him the ball a little. The last five years I've played alongside Michael Jordan. That can be a problem sometimes because we all stand around and watch him. He can do so many things and he makes it look so effortless. He is one of those special players. I don't know if anybody can come along in the near future to do the things he does."

Five-Star memories linger. "It's amazing when I think back on it now," says Paxson. "I grew up loving the game, and here I am making a living playing basketball. It's a neat thing. Being there with Isiah and Ray at camp was special. They were great players and they made me better. I can remember coming home from camp and wearing my Five-Star T-shirts around the neighborhood. Guys who knew anything about basketball could identify with them. They knew it was *the* camp to go to.

"Five-Star is a fraternity that probably will never be equalled. I went back there a few summers ago to work Station 13 and it's the same. Garf does the same stuff, walking around the way he does and everything, but that's what makes the camp so successful. He had a good formula and he hasn't varied from it. Even that shot of his, he used to shoot it when I was there. He used to miss quite a few back then and we got on him for it, but he took it pretty well. He is a classic. Garf is Five-Star basketball."

Paxson is too. "He was a super camper and a super player even when he wasn't at camp," Garf says. "One night in Cleveland I saw him in an Ohio all-star game. He was tired from having played in the Dapper Dan Classic the night before, but he scored 21 points in two minutes of regulation and one overtime period. I think he did every one-on-one move we ever taught at camp. It was the greatest single performance I ever saw except for Calvin Murphy."

Murphy, had he played at Five-Star, would no doubt have been one of Garf's fair-haired boys. Standing 5'10" out of Norwalk, Connecticut, Murphy was "the greatest high school player, pound-for-pound, inch-for-inch, and shot-for-shot, in history," according to Garf. "He put on a show at a tournament in Harrisburg, Pennsylvania, one weekend that was nothing short of total domination. He shot 54 percent from the field over two games, and in the finals scored 62 points in 29 minutes. All the announcer had to say was, 'Basket by Murphy, this is a recording.'"

There is one other camper Garf doesn't mind mentioning in the same breath with Paxson and Thomas and the rest, even though he wasn't there during the famous Year of the Guards. Gordon Austin came the next year, showing up with a friend and an armload of books. He told Garf that by coming to camp they were missing a few days of school and wanted to keep up their studies.

"Austin was a 5'11" point guard from Linden, New Jersey," Garf says. "Everybody had him rated as a two-star player, if they rated him at all, but when I saw his cerebral floor play, I rated him a four-star. He went to American University and for a while was the leading assist man in the nation. He graduated with honors and became an assistant coach at Penn. He was one of my all-time sleepers."

THIRTEEN
Knight Train

"Loyalty is one of life's intangibles and makes life simple."

– Garf

It was something you could barely hear at first, unless you strained your ears, and even then only in the dead of night. Otherwise you heard nothing. Garf may have sensed it in his bones, but if he did he never said so. The future, if it arrived at all, would arrive on its own. It always had and there were distressing things to deal with in the present. Still, there was change in the air.

Air Jordan was building and getting ready to sweep up from the south. No one knew that, least of all Michael Jordan himself, as the seventies wound down at Pitt. He was busy trying to master the fine art of operating in Zero G's. Garf was preoccupied elsewhere as well and not particularly enthralled with the situation. Disloyalty was rearing its ugly head. That happened from time to time and he did his best to reconcile himself to it, but it would never be that simple.

Sam Perkins had nothing to do with it, although it all started with him. He was never even a camper, but Garf wanted to do right by him anyway. Perkins, to quite a few people, appeared mighty laid-back to someday be an NBA all-star. He'd left Brooklyn and Tilden High for upstate Shaker High, on the outskirts of Albany, and could dominate a game as much as any high school center, but he appeared lackadaisical. Garf knew better than to judge someone on reputation alone and, after taking a long look at him in a pre-season scrimmage his senior year, knew he was a good one.

Later, when that season's McDonald's All-American team had more or less been selected, Garf called his friend Morgan Wootten to tell him a mistake was being made. Perkins' name wasn't even on the list of possibles. Garf said the committee would be the laughingstock of basketball if he were left off. Wootten had no objections but said nothing could be done. There were always 24 players so he couldn't just throw somebody else on, and besides, the ads and announcements were already sketched out. Adding one name would make them lopsided.

To balance things, Garf came up with "Jumping" Joe Ward, a move that will never stop bothering him. Ever. Well, maybe someday if things can be explained. Ward, out of Griffin, Georgia, deserved the bid. That wasn't the problem. On the surface he'd proven himself worthy by coming to camp, making the all-star team, and scoring 25 points in the Orange-White Classic. He also won the Rebounding Award and was a religious and sincere young man.

It was, as newsman Paul Harvey says, "the rest of the story" that was so troubling. To get to Five-Star in the first place, Jumping Joe had called Garf personally. He'd been to another camp earlier in the summer, right in his home state—the BC camp in Milledgeville, Georgia—and had been accused of loafing. He had a bad ankle, which hampered his play, and his camp coach was aware of the injury but later was quoted in a scouting report calling him a "dog."

He wanted to come to Five-Star to settle the matter. Garf made room for him, and suggesting him for the McDonald's team was no fluke, but he still shakes his head in disbelief when he thinks about it. "Sam Perkins made the team only after another player got injured," says Garf. "Unfortunately, Jumping Joe Ward didn't make it, but what is mind-boggling to me is that the next time a great player came along from Griffin, Georgia, a kid named Darrin Hancock, he went to the same camp where Jumping Joe was called a dog.

"It bothered me, so I sought out Jumping Joe and asked him about it. He hemmed and hawed, and wasn't as upset as I thought he should be after he saved his own reputation at Five-Star. At the time, his best friend, James Martin, was the assistant coach at his school, and now head coach. Couldn't something have been said or done? Maybe it wasn't up to them where the other kid went, and Five-Star would go on without him, but the lack of loyalty there, not feeling a sense of loyalty, was unbelievable."

Disloyalty has always been a sore spot for him. "Loyalty is not something you have to do or that is owed. It is one of life's intangibles and makes life simple. I'm loyal to my friends and workers and my campers, and I've come to expect it back. I think anyone would. To me it's just normal, everyday consideration.

"If Five-Star helps a kid or a coach, I would expect him to spread the word, that's all. That's not much. That's why I'll never forget Delray Brooks or his coach at Michigan City Rogers High School in Indiana, Bill Hahn. Delray started coming to Five-Star as a rising freshman. He came four years, did very well here, and later went to Indiana U and Providence. Before his senior year in high school, though, the BC Camp, according to an article in *Sports Illustrated*, offered him one of their "Dollar Specials." Delray could have gone to BC for a buck, but he came to Five-Star.

"There have been many others, thankfully, and I guess one of my problems is that I'm not a politician. I should probably learn to play the game. I should probably not be so adamant and so negative to people who I think are not loyal to me. I should forget about it and continue to deal with them, but I snap. Maybe I'm a lunatic about this, but I'm not a very nice person to people who are disloyal to me."

Thinking that way makes it harder for Garf to come to grips with the next phenomenon of the modern basketball era: no-shows. Kids had always changed their minds about coming to camp and that was to be expected. Things came up, and when they did they'd call or write to let Garf know. It forced him and Will Klein to rummage through their card files to find a replacement, but otherwise there was no harm done.

The no-shows were another whole breed of cat. They'd say they were coming, take a precious spot, and then simply not show up. "It's annoying, but the kids with real chutzpah are the ones who then want their money back," Garf says. "Mainly, the lack of commitment-keeping, the lack of respect, is what drives us up a wall. It's getting worse in the world today. We have stressed keeping commitments since day one, and I feel we have done a good job, but obviously more has to be done."

A kid could have talent coming out of his ears, but without loyalty and respect, he had zilch, all of which made Deryl Cunningham that much more pleasant when he happened along. It was much later, in the late eighties, but Garf will forever link the two together. Cunningham, like Isiah Thomas before him, was one of coach Gene Pingatore's kids. In Garf's book, he more than filled his famous predecessor's shoes. He did well at camp and was good enough to end up at DePaul University. That isn't what set him apart.

"When Deryl got back home to Westchester, Illinois, he did something out of step with the times," Garf says. "He went to the homes of two players from his area to make sure they got to camp during the week best suited to their abilities. It wasn't that he sent them to camp, that isn't what I cared about, it was that he did that for those two players totally on his own. That's a rare person who would do something like that, especially in today's climate. It wouldn't shock me to see him surprise the entire world and be a pro someday. I would love it if he did."

Stranger things have happened.

* * * * *

Saint Peter never came to Pitt, not so anyone noticed anyhow, but Jerry Wainwright got to meet him after leaving there in the summer of 1979 or 1980 or thereabouts. He forgets the exact year sometimes because that's when he died, or at least the radio stations said he did. Quite a few people felt bummed out when they heard it, especially him, but what actually happened was he showed up baffled at the Pearly Gates after a nasty car wreck and the good saint turned him around and sent him home again.

Garf and Five-Star were relieved to hear it was all a big mistake. They weren't ready to name an award after him just yet and they had already nearly lost The King the same way. Driving home to New York from camp in the fog one night, The King's car swerved off the Tappan Zee Bridge. He spent more time underwater than he cared to remember and was laid up for months.

Wainwright managed to stay on terra firma, but in his case that wasn't much better. He was heading home from Pitt about six o'clock in the morning with a carload of kids. Just outside Elkhart, Indiana, on a four-lane highway, a tractor-trailer, trying to pass, clipped him. Wainwright went through the windshield, broke every bone on the the right side of his body, punctured a hole in his heart, and lost a lung in the deal. The kids, mostly from Highland Park, were banged up but all right. The story went over UPI that Wainwright was dead.

"I was in intensive care for 30 days," he says. "The strangest part of the whole thing was that after I got out of there they put me in a room with a guy who had Legionnaires' Disease. I woke up in the middle of the night and the guy was delirious. He ripped out all his plugs and tore aside my bed curtain and said, 'Lucifer, is that you?' The guy's monitor was going wild and all I could think of was that I was in the hospital with every bone in my body broken and I was going to get infected and die of Legionnaires' Disease."

His accident gave him a much deeper appreciation for the frailties of the human body. He was never what you'd call out of shape to begin with, but after the accident he got into physical fitness and eating right more than ever and started telling the campers about weight training and manual resistance training like there was no tomorrow. He'd show them a few basics at stations or during a lecture, then leave it up to them whether they wanted to learn more.

Wainwright would grab their attention by appealing to their vanity. "I had a high school job in an affluent school district once and there used to be fistfights before every practice to see who would be shirts and who would be skins," he'd say. "That's one of the gravy things about being in good shape. It helps your self-image. You look good. It is good for injury prevention, making your muscles stronger around the joints, and it can also enhance your skills, making your legs stronger for jumping and rebounding.

"There are a lot of misconceptions about weight training. There is a belief that it can affect a guy's shot badly. Anybody who tells you that just doesn't want to take the time to learn. At Wake Forest our guys work out three times a week, 45 minutes at a time, and afterwards they take 50 free throws and 100 jumpers. It doesn't take away from their shot; it can add to it. You can very easily develop overall strength without losing flexibility."

"When I started lifting I used to be into weights and numbers, seeing how quickly I could lift the most weight. I ripped myself up doing it that way. Now I'm into progressions. I'll tell you something honestly, a lot of guys throw up during our workouts, but the bottom line is human performance. I always tell you guys that the mind quits before the body does, but it's all tied in together. Your diet matters too. I work out every day and sometimes I hate it, but I feel good afterwards."

Skipping rope, Wainwright says, is perhaps the best overall athletic conditioner. It develops agility, hand-foot coordination, rhythm, and balance. A complete jump-rope program, using a weighted rope, improves your physical condition, increases endurance and stamina, and develops upper-body and leg strength. There are ways to do it right, and for the price of asking Wainwright would show campers how, but it wasn't Wainwright who taught the Air Man how to outleap Isaac Newton.

* * * * *

Michael Jordan breezed into Pitt in the summer of 1980. Outside his hometown of Wilmington, North Carolina, he was a virtual unknown. Dean Smith at UNC knew about him and the Tarheels were already courting him, hoping he would remain a well-kept secret. At Five-Star he was just another kid on the list. Had it been otherwise, all hell might have broken loose at the draft.

The coaches did start to buzz after watching him at tryouts, but the draft was peaceful. "We had heard a little bit about Mike, he was just called Mike back then, but most of us hadn't seen him play," Garf says. "Brendan Malone ended up with him on his team and was so upset he wanted to have Tom Konchalski drawn and quartered. Seeing how Mike turned out, the story is pretty funny today."

Tom Konchalski, who would figure prominently in Garf's future and the future of *HSBI*, was partly responsible for Jordan being at camp. A highly respected evaluator of talent then and now, he got the ball rolling to make him a two-week camper-worker. He remembers it like it happened yesterday.

"One Saturday morning earlier that year I was driving to an all-star game at Kutcher's Sports Academy with Roy Williams," Konchalski says. "Roy, who is now the head coach at Kansas, was a part-time assistant at North Carolina then. He told me this kid, Mike Jordan, had been to their camp at Chapel Hill and they were very interested in him. They hadn't seen him play against great competition, though, and wanted him to go to Five-Star.

"I called Howard and he said based on Roy's recommendation he would be willing to take a chance, so Roy and Jordan's high school coach, Clifton Herring, worked out the details and it was done. Pitt I, in those days, before the Nike camp came along, was the Cadillac of Five-Star camp sessions. All the sessions were great, but the best players made it a point to go that week every summer. We weren't sure if Jordan was quite good enough, so he was signed for Pitt II and Pitt III instead.

"I was the one who drafted him for Brendan Malone's team. Brendan was scheduled to work the camp that week, but his wife had been in a motorbike accident and he had to leave camp for a couple of days. He was going to miss opening night and told me who to pick. He wanted Greg Dreiling as his center and Aubrey Sherrod at the two-guard spot if at all possible. I got the first pick and took Dreiling. When we got to the two-guard spot, though, based on what everyone was saying about Jordan, I picked him over Sherrod.

"When Brendan got to camp the next day, he wasn't very happy. He liked Dreiling, a future NBA player (Indiana Pacers), but he took one look at Jordan's name and asked, 'Who's he?' Sherrod, a fine player from Wichita, Kansas, had played for Brendan before and Brendan knew what he could do. Brendan cursed me up and down the hills of Robert Morris University, but no one, as they say, has looked back since."

Malone had good reason to be upset. He'd been burned twice already. "The previous summer," says Konchalski, knowing time heals all, "Glenn 'Doc' Rivers (Atlanta Hawks) was supposed to come to Pitt as a camper-worker. Brendan had the first pick for off-guards in the draft and took him. Rivers wasn't in camp yet but was due to arrive the next day. The next day came and Rivers was nowhere to be seen. Brendan was frantic, so we made phone calls and Rivers' guardian swore he was on the way. He never showed. Brendan blamed me.

"Later, almost the same thing happened. Brendan had the first pick at point guard and wanted Anthony 'Cosell' Brown, a fine player from Alexander Hamilton High in New York. Everyone called him Cosell because he never stopped chattering. He wasn't there for tryouts, but his grandmother telephoned to say he would just be late. He was playing with an all-star team in Hawaii and they'd been delayed. Brendan said to me, 'Are you sure?' and I told him the bus arrangements were all set, to go ahead and take him. He did and Cosell didn't make it and I got cursed out again."

Looking back, Malone figured getting "stuck" with Jordan just evened the score, and Jordan's lack of notoriety prior to his arrival at camp undoubtedly spared Five-Star a fur-flying fracas. Had the coaches seen ahead of time what Garf witnessed at Jordan's camp debut, the draft would have been a war to end all wars. As it was, Garf nearly burned a hole in his high-tops rushing to spread the word. "Jordan's first game was in the Gus Krop gym," he says. "They threw the ball up for the jump and the teams ran up and down the court three times and I knew. I immediately went to the phone to call a newspaper friend of mine, Dave Krider, who did the pre-season All-American teams for Street and Smith.

"I told him I was watching something I didn't believe, a kid I knew would be one of the great players in the history of the game. The kid had blocked three shots in two plays and was a gazelle, running up and down and jumping and shooting. He was awesome. I asked Krider if Jordan's name was on his list and he said it wasn't. I told him he had to put him 'Top 10,' that he would look like a fool if the kid wasn't there, but he called me back the next day and said there was nothing he could do. It was too late."

Air Jordan had lifted off. He arrived, he would later say, with sweaty palms and a feeling that maybe he didn't belong there. Both he and the rest of the basketball world found out otherwise. It hadn't been Jordan's idea to go to Five-Star in the first place. He thought of himself as nothing more than a country boy from Laney High who had no business sharing the courts with all those All-Americans. He hadn't even made his high school varsity team until his junior year, but his coach noticed something a little extra in him and insisted he go to camp, forced him. Some coaches are like that.

Not everything went picture-perfect for Jordan at camp, which is maybe the only example of a kid's performance failing to mirror his career. He was co-MVP his first week with "Chocolate Thunder II," 6'10" John Flowers from Fort Wayne, Indiana. Flowers didn't destroy backboards like the original Chocolate Thunder, Darryl Dawkins, but his team shattered Jordan's in the playoffs, winning the title and giving him something to tell his grandchildren.

The Air Man was instrumental in his own grounding. His team was down by one late in the game and he had the ball out on the wing. There was no dunking, so he couldn't do one of those make-you-catch-your-breath slams. He was still Mike then and not doing them yet anyway, so he tried to drive the lane. It was on Court Two, center stage, with everyone watching. The most incredible professional basketball player of the late eighties and nineties dribbled the ball off his foot out of bounds and that was that.

It was obvious that he had the whole package, though, and his team's defeat was good in a way. Garf could forevermore tell incoming campers the trivia tidbit about Jordan never capturing a camp championship, and prove once and for all that the Five-Star Mirror has the final word (though Garf would gladly make an exception in Jordan's case if and when the Chicago Bulls win it all).

The Mirror's reflection seemed slightly off with Chris Mullin, the southpaw city slicker sharpshooting his way to St. John's. He was pegged as an all-star even when he came to camp way back then, but he scored only four points in the Orange-White Classic. The Golden State Warriors can show you in black and white that that was a lot of malarkey, but the Mirror was just saying he would have off days too and had to be adaptable.

The Mirror went dark with Len Bias. He was at Pitt III the same week as Michael Jordan. "There aren't any stories to tell about Bias," Garf says. "He was a very good high school player among many others during the weeks he was at Five-Star. He was sort of a sleeper. He made a bigger name for himself and got a lot of All-American attention afterwards and became a great college player, but he was by no means a superstar at camp."

There would be plenty of stories to tell about him later. He left an indelible mark on the game. Some will tell you that there's no better way to get the point across about drugs than to put a commercial on

TV with famous players talking about how to play basketball better. Let three or four guys like Jordan and Bird and Magic do their thing and then have a voice say, "Now, here's a word from Len Bias" and then just flash a picture of a tombstone on the screen.

Len Bias was a true tragedy of the times. The terms "good kid" and "hard worker" might have been invented to describe him. After his summer at Five-Star he went on to play for Maryland and was drafted by the Boston Celtics. The night the Celtics took him he went out celebrating with his friends, the story goes, and decided to try some cocaine. It might have been his first try. It hit him wrong, which happens all the time, every day, although you don't always hear about it, and he died.

Bob Knight had his own method of dealing with the drug issue, which he used unsparingly at Pitt later on. He stopped by to lecture after Bias died and his words were timeless. He talked about the game itself and about what separates some players who make it from others who don't. The campers knew he cared because of the way they felt elevated whenever he spoke, but Knight said, "I don't feel sorry for Len Bias, not in the slightest. He had his own mind and his own body to take care of and just wasn't smart enough to do it.

"Those of you who have been popping pills and smoking dope are doing the same thing Len Bias did. Those are serious bad shots you're taking, boys, serious poor judgments that you're using with your body and mind. Len Bias was better than anybody in here. I've seen you all play and not one of you can touch Len Bias. The only college player I've seen in the past few years as good as Bias was Michael Jordan, and I'm not sure if he was as good as Bias was in college, and Bias is dead.

"He's not sick and he's not hurt, the son-of-a-bitch is dead. He isn't ever gonna play again and you know why he's dead? He's dead because he just wasn't strong enough to take care of himself. Somewhere along the way he wanted to be one of the boys. He wanted to be cool. Well, he was so cool that he's cold right now, colder than hell. That's how cool he was.

"You boys will be in all kinds of situations where there are temptations and all kinds of opportunities to do something detrimental to yourself, and when it comes right down to it there's only one person who can take care of you and that's you, yourself. Your buddy doesn't really give a damn about you, particularly if he's popping pills or smoking dope.

"You know what he wants? He wants you right down where he is because he can't handle the fact that you're tougher than he is. I'll give you a phrase to use the next time somebody offers you some dope: 'Stick it up your ass.' If he asks you a second time, tell him you know where to stick it and you'll be glad to show him. Take care of yourselves, boys." Knight hit on a few more things, but it was tough for the kids to concentrate after that, at least on basketball.

The Mirror was murky with Mark Aguirre. It was wavy, as if it were having trouble coming into focus. Novices assumed it was broken, but that's pretty much the way things turned out. Aguirre was a two-week camper-worker whose reputation as a player was overshadowned only by persistent rumors that he was a pouter. He got to camp late. "Mark showed up in the middle of the third day for whatever reason without telling us," says Garf. "He said, 'Didn't my coach call you and tell you?' but that wasn't good enough for me.

"We knew he was coming and he had been drafted, but by the time he got there we had gone on without him and things were in place. I wasn't going to kick a kid out of the NBA league at that point or give a team an advantage by giving them an extra guy. That wasn't fair, so I told him he would have to wait until there was an injury or something else happened. A whole day went by and he just sat there.

"There are dues you gotta pay at Five-Star and I wasn't about to change things for one kid. Someone got hurt on another team and we made the switch eventually, but Mark got to play in only two regular season games. In the playoffs his team won when he sank a jumper from the wing at Moon High School in town on a rainy day. I thought he might just split for the second week, but he stayed and won the Outstanding Player Award."

Aguirre could play; there was never much doubt about that, even though his teams didn't always do well. He helped thrust DePaul and coach Ray Meyer back into the spotlight after many years out of it and later established himself as a high-scoring but moody star with the NBA Dallas Mavericks. It wasn't until he paid his dues again with the Detroit Pistons that he shined. A Five-Star guy, Chuck Daly, was in charge of the Pistons when they acquired Aguirre midway through their 1988-89 championship season.

There were some tense moments with the Pistons before everything settled into place. "When Mark first showed up," Daly recalls, "we put Dennis Rodman on him during practice and he couldn't get his shot off. He couldn't get it off against Rick Mahorn either, a nasty player who likes to hit you even if you happen to be his teammate. Mark just held up his hands and said, 'I've got no gripes' and started to understand what we were all about and what we were all about was team. That's what guys like Isiah and Bird and Magic understand. Team."

*   *   *   *   *

By the mid-eighties Pitt had grown to four sessions and Pitt II had become a monster. It seemed like all the basketball behemoths were on the prowl the second or third week in July, looking for prey. The NCAA's evolving Live/Dead Period regulations had little to do with it at first, although they would affect things more significantly in the near future, limiting the days coaches and recruiters could visit the camp. Pitt II would then reign supreme, but for the time being, the big-timers were making reservations for early July.

The more immediate factors at play were competition from rival camps and the AAU's rise in popularity and importance, both of which unalterably changed Five-Star's future. Garf and Will Klein's success had spawned similar camps that challenged their preeminence: Bill Croneauer's BC Camp; the Eastern Invitational in Trenton, New Jersey; Metro Index; Prep Stars; and others, including the Nike-sponsored all-star camp at Princeton University.

The level of talent was seldom if ever comparable to Five-Star overall, except at Nike, but the new camps were often closer to home for kids and especially appealing on a regional basis. Players who in the past had gone to Five-Star for two or more weeks began going for just one week, and Pitt II, with its mounting reputation, became their first choice. Attendance did not drop off, but the talent level, though it never became weak, did slack off somewhat during sessions running head to head with the upstart camps.

Garf knew they were there but seldom looked back. "As far as camps go, we are and always have been only in competition with Five-Star," he says. "We compete with ourselves to make every session better than the last. We are the best teaching camp in the country and to me that's what basketball camp should be about—teaching. In my mind the other camps are absolutely no threat. We've got them buried. It's no contest and hopefully it will stay that way. I don't consider Nike a threat either because it's not a true basketball camp, it's an academic camp.

"There's room for Nike and we are not in competition with them. They have always cooperated with their camp dates, not conflicting too much with ours, and they help kids get to Five-Star after they are done there. Why shouldn't a kid go there? He gets free tuition to a camp that can help him academically, a plane ticket, and garments. We know we are not going to get the strongest players during the

Nike week and it, along with the new NCAA rules, hurt Pitt I but eventually made Pitt II our best week for talent."

The AAU teams and tournaments made a dent that couldn't be ignored. "Our biggest competition is the AAU and I can understand that," says Garf. "A lot of the kids were brought up basketball-wise by their AAU coaches and they feel bound to them more than even their high school coach. They feel they owe them tremendous loyalty. Some kids prefer working with a set team too, which is fine. They should do that. It only causes us pain and woe when the AAU dates come out late and kids who have signed with us have to make all kinds of switches. We can live with that."

More than anything else, it was timing and availability that made Pitt II fit for neither man nor beast. Steve Hale of Tulsa, Five-Star's first player from the state of Oklahoma, lumbered in and no sooner arrived than North Carolina scout Ed Fogler noticed him. "Fogler was always at camp and was one of the few guys who used stations for recruiting," says Garf. "More guys should do that because you really get to see how a kid reacts to discipline, but they don't. Fogler saw how Hale worked and he went wild over him."

Ron Harper, beating a steady path to Miami of Ohio and the NBA, arrived as no particular threat to anyone and earned some respect. "He came with no reputation but was maybe the biggest sleeper in the history of the camp," says Garf. Harper had no trouble keeping awake with alarm clock Jerry Wainwright jangling in his ears, wisely staying one step ahead of and two jump shots behind Wainwright's well-intentioned foot.

The King wrapped up his third NBA title in 1981, despite the intimidating presence of two future Louisville Cardinals, Billy Thompson and Milt Wagner. The place was crawling with lesser-known beasts, and a few of them combined forces to knock Thompson off in the semifinals, opening the door for The King. He'd wait a few summers to get his fourth, but with kids like James Blackmon filling the void, he could wait.

Blackmon was from Marion, Indiana. "You can't be taught to play as good as he played," The King says. "James was on my team, and I sort of adopted him for the week. He provided one of the most dramatic moments ever for me. We were in the quarterfinals of the playoffs, down by a point with the clock running out. During a time out, I was going over a play with the team and James told me to just get him the ball and he'd score. He did, shooting from just over the halfcourt line, and we won.

"In the semifinals, there was a similar situation and he penetrated, had the good shot but passed off. The guy missed and we lost. I told him, 'James, you weren't put on this earth to let someone else decide it.' He went to Kentucky, where things just never panned out. He was a shocking bust. Maybe it was the wrong school for him, his personality or playing style, but whatever, that was one of those great sadnesses that sometimes happens with kids you get close to who come through Five-Star."

Through it all, the Five-Star connection remained intact. It was an ever-tightening, binding thing. "The interworkings of the camp probably helped Johnny Newman make it in the pros," says Garf. "One week at Pitt, Rick Pitino had Station 13. On the last day it was about 105 degrees and it had been like that all week. Only eight guys showed up, but Pitino was intense as usual, and drilled them for an hour and 20 minutes.

"At the end, only three guys were left, and Johnny Newman was one of them. He had sweat pouring off him, and he was ready for more. Pitino recruited the hell out of him for Boston University, but he went to Richmond. Years later, when Pitino was coaching the Knicks, General Manager Al Bianchi brought him a list of players they could obtain, and Newman's name was on it. He took Newman."

* * * * *

Pitt III, immediately following its predatory predecessor, was not exactly a walk in the park. Garf and the gang started to call it "Baltimore Week" because that's when Bob "Sugar" Wade, then coaching at Dunbar High, could be counted on to bring his Chesapeake Bay boys like Reggie Williams (Spurs), Reggie Lewis (Celtics), David Wingate (76ers), Tim Dawson, Mike Brown, "Boobie" James, and the Dozier twins, Perry and Terry (who won back-to-back Sportsmanship Awards) north to Five-Star.

The pipeline continued even after Wade took over at the University of Maryland, with coach Pete Pompey bringing youngsters such as 6'6" forward Dante Bright and Michael Lloyd, a 6'1" guard. They were both all-stars. "They were what you'd call precocious children when they arrived, but after their first week they both returned and worked in the canteen to pay their way. It was very enjoyable watching them develop responsible attitudes and mature right in front of our eyes," Garf says.

Garf appreciated the loyalty, which might explain why Wade, who started the whole thing, was one of the few guys who could prove him wrong and get away with it. "I loved Bob Wade's kids. They were great campers and players. In the early eighties, though, he wanted to take one of them, Tyrone "Muggsy" Bogues, as his first guard in the draft. I said he should try to go for the best player. Bogues, after all, was only 5'3", a nice little player, I figured, but I told him there were probably much better guards in camp. I didn't want him to screw up the competitive balance by taking his own players.

"I was always a stickler about that. Wade picked him anyway, but I was vehement and vetoed it. Wade was an ex-pro football player and kinda tough too and he glared at me and we had a big argument and he won. As a postscript, had I won, it would have been one of my few mistakes on guards. Bogues led the team to an undefeated championship and I ate humble pie. He got the Outstanding Player Award and played with Wake Forest and is still in the pros, so Wade was right and I don't mind admitting it."

Some mistakes are not so easily rectifiable. Chris Washburn, according to Garf, was probably the greatest rising sophomore in camp history. He was the first tenth grader to skip the Development League and go straight to the NBA League. Even there, he dominated. "Chris came to Pitt III and part of the reason he jumped directly into the NBA was because he was in summer school during Pitt I, when we held the Development League," says Garf, "but he was an exceptional player too."

At Five-Star he was coached by The King, who had them all in his day. "Washburn was the easiest kid in the world to work with," he says. "He was a charmer, and a little flaky even back then. Sadly, someone was always willing to overlook his faults to let him play." The indulgence cost him dearly. Washburn was shuttled through high school and then North Carolina State on his road to the pros. There, his private shortcomings and substance abuse habits caught up to him. By his early twenties, his priceless talent had eroded and his career was washed up.

The waste was preventable. Tom McCorry, on a recruiting trip between visits to Five-Star around that time, spotted Washburn playing in a Boston summer league. The kid was set to begin classes in the fall but was apparently living with a girl and partying in Beantown. "All the other freshmen were taking orientation classes at the time," McCorry says now. "It was the ultimate selfishness on the part of those who let him slip through. If along the line someone had made him do what he was supposed to do, that kid might not have ended up the way he did."

*   *   *   *   *

By the time Danny Ferry got to Pitt, in the summer of 1983, the camp's role in the basketball world was changing with the times.

The days of relying on Five-Star solely for exposure were coming to an end. Since its inception and through the years of unanticipated burgeoning, the camp had stressed competition and teaching, although the lectures and stations for many campers were the vegetables they had to force down before getting to dessert, getting exposure.

Kids went to Five-Star in no small part to be seen, to catch the eye of scholarship-waving coaches and scouts. In the early years the camp was considered a paradise in the dismal reality of recruiting. All any coach or bird dog needed was a way to get there, and without having to flush the sandlots and playgrounds of Everywhere, USA, he got a front-row view of the finest talent in the country.

In the beginning it was a mutually beneficial, almost symbiotic relationship, and Garf's place in the scheme of things was secure. It was very simple—he knew everything there was to know about the players and more, and through *HSBI* was in touch with virtually everyone in the coaching community. It was an unquestioned fact that his word carried weight in the scholarship process. Like Caesar, the wiggle of his thumb, up or down, brought results, albeit less dire ones.

Garf's influence inevitably lessened as recruiting practices became more sophisticated and scouting networks more widespread. However, his influence was never as absolute as some people feared and believed. If asked, he could surely point a borderline player in the right direction or turn some coach on to just the kind of kid he was looking for, but the bona fide blue-chippers, the ones some colleges would sell their dorm mothers for, Garf left alone. He sat back and watched the spectacle unfold like everyone else.

Nevertheless, the NCAA saw fit to step in and change the way he did business. Separately, the NCAA-member coaches had decided to crack down on recruiting abuses within their ranks. There were too many Chris Washburn-type stories to ignore and still sleep at night. Cleaning out their own backyards seemed like as good a time as any to finally do something about the mounting criticism of Garf and Garf's Guys, his so-called Five-Star mafiosi.

That was all coming to a boil when Danny Ferry brought his considerable talents to Pitt in the summer of his senior year, but nothing could have been further from his mind. Even if he were aware of Garf's problems, there were more pressing personal matters to consider, such as being stared at by a couple of hundred college coaches and avoiding a real, live, head-for-the-root-cellars tornado.

As it turned out, Ferry actually had to endure two tempests that week. The first one was easy. The tornado winds shaking the

Quaker State didn't hit Five-Star directly but did knock the power out in Coraopolis and the surrounding area. "It was the first time the Orange-White Classic was not played," says Garf. "There had to be at least 200 coaches and recruiters there that night, but we couldn't see two feet in front of us. We were tempted to shine car lights down from the hills onto the courts and I think we could have pulled it off. We could have lit that court up like it was daylight, but God forbid if anyone got hurt. Ferry was pissed off because he wanted to play in the game so badly."

It had been a rough few days for young Danny Ferry, starting with cyclone coach John Calipari. "Ferry was a super player, but Calipari, head man at the University of Massachusetts and one of our resident coaches, was known for going nose-to-nose with campers if he thought it was necessary. Ferry did something Calipari didn't like and he got into it with him, which I was used to by then. I almost had a heart attack, though, when I peeked over at someone listening in outside the fence. Standing there with his ears cocked was Ferry's father, Bob Ferry, the general manager of the Washington Bullets.

"Calipari didn't know about this and there he was counseling Bob's son rather aggressively and I was dying. I walked over to Bob Ferry to get a feel for how pissed off he was and he said, 'Who is that coach? That's the best thing I ever saw. My kid needed that. The coach is 100 percent right.' Now you kow why Danny Ferry was such a superstar at Duke and why I think we haven't heard the last of him yet. His father could have easily said he didn't send his kid to camp to be abused like that and pulled him out of there. A lot of fathers might have."

Had there been a spotlight big enough to illuminate the darkened courts, plenty of campers could have shared it with Ferry. Garf, like a doting basketball grandfather, just happens to have pictures of a few stored in his mental billfold. Rumeal Robinson, who would be heard from at Michigan a few years hence, was there. A rising junior, he was high scorer for the week, voted the best defender, and named Mr. Stations in his league.

Garf had to remember that the Mirror images are reversed when it came to reading Robinson. He was a camper for three years and came back as a counselor while in college before and after clinching the 1989 NCAA championship for the Wolverines with a pair of pressure free throws. Only Garf knew what was in store when Robinson, after upsetting J.R. Reid in the camp semifinals, was whistled for an offensive foul in the finals that cost his team the game.

Before Robinson was through with Five-Star, Garf would have to come up with a new accolade for him, the prestigious 30-for-30 Award. In his camp career he had that many chances to go to Station 13 and took advantage of every one. Only three other kids have done that in 25 years. He was the first and the rest were all yet to be heard from.

The Looking Glass seemed to be tipsy with Kevin Walls of Camden, New Jersey. He scored only four points in the Orange-White Classic and the thing must have been cracked because he was a consensus All-American his senior year, averaging 44 points per game. But he went to Louisville and shortly thereafter had to transfer to a lower level NAIA school to get his shot off, which Garf still says was one of the greatest shocks in basketball history. Walls was a super player, but only the cream of the crop went to Five-Star and the Mirror never lies.

There were many others, and Garf remembers all their names and what they could or couldn't do with a basketball. If he didn't remember, The King did, or Tom Konchalaski, who slowly was becoming more and more a part of the family. It was a close-knit bunch, and you had to be a part of it to understand. Those who weren't, didn't.

*　*　*　*　*

It came to be known as "The Garfinkel Rule," which made perfect sense to Garf because he was the only one affected by it. The NCAA, in the 1983–84 season, passed new legislation that prohibited Division I coaches from working (coaching or lecturing) at a basketball camp established or run by an individual providing recruiting or scouting services. Garf, with Five-Star and *HSBI*, was the only one the rule applied to. Once again he was in a class by himself.

It was a dubious distinction. "This was a left-handed way for them to make me get rid of my college coaches," he says. "It was pinpointed. It was like saying a black-haired Jewish guy who lives on 55th Street in Manhattan can't have college coaches in his camp. One thing had nothing to do with the other. There was no connection between running a camp and running a scouting service, not the way I did it. I am a professional and I didn't use the camp for anything underhanded. They were telling me I either had to dump the college guys or get rid of *HSBI*. To me, there was no logic in it."

NCAA-member coaches employed a different rationale. They had been saying right along that so-and-so was running such-and-such a camp like an exclusive country club. They had to beat the bushes for prospects, while Garf's Guys supposedly got to sit back and relax at Five-Star and let the prospects come to them. Family, schmamily. It was a smooth operation and it was high time something was done about it.

"The problem was potential abuses more than anything else," says Bob Minnix, the NCAA's Director of Enforcement. "It was kind of a paranoia. Recruiters are a strange breed of cat. My job is to see to it that NCAA rules are administered, but it has been my perception over the years that recruiters, in many instances, need something to complain about. Nobody likes to give the other guy the slightest upper hand.

"I have been to all the camps in my 15 years with the NCAA, not just Five-Star, but Nike and BC and even Blue-Star, the girls' camp. They have all given me free access to the camp and the kids and there has never been a problem with that. I have seen it first-hand, talked to the kids and the coaches and seen it with my own eyes. If there was ever a problem and someone could in fact show me the problem, then it would be time to take care of that problem. But going on the word of recruiters and coaches who maybe didn't get a kid for whatever reason isn't the way to do it."

Nevertheless, the NCAA-member coaches ruled that Garf should make a choice and it was up to Minnix and the rest of his enforcement team to carry out their wishes. "So I was faced with big-decision time," says Garf. "Give up what in essence was my life's work or give up the guys that I love, coaches who were important to the camp. It took me about a minute and a half. I was making $40,000 off *HSBI* and I needed it to put a roof over my head, but I would starve before I would fire my coaches, my guys. I couldn't be that disloyal."

He sold *HSBI* lock, stock, and barrel. "The NCAA didn't feel too bad about it because he sold it to his right-hand man," says Minnix, but Garf was none too pleased. He didn't mind selling it to his close friend and partner Tom Konchalski as long as he had to do it anyway; the hard part was having to unload it at all. "It annoyed me because even though those same coaches had made me successful by buying *HSBI*, to me they were taking this thing too far," he says.

"What annoyed me even more was the fact that none of the guys they were worried about were college coaches when we hired them. We never hired a college coach in the history of the camp. We did hire Five-Star people, guys who were great high school coaches and became great assistant coaches or head coaches in college and the pros, but all the college coaches who have worked at Five-Star have been Five-Star graduates. They are family members. All these guys have paid their dues.

"I didn't have a gripe with the NCAA. They are just the cops, like the guy with a billy club walking his beat. The NCAA people I have talked to love the camp. The college athletic directors and presidents pass the rules, and all the NCAA does is enforce them. We've got to have rules though. Without them there would be chaos. I have no problem with that. But the AD's and presidents just don't know any better, I guess. They have no conception what *HSBI* is or what Five-Star is, what it's all about.

"They think the camp is a meat market where kids are being proselytized. To even think that it is better to take guys like Mc-Corry, Odom, Wainwright, Rey, and all the Five-Star coaches away from the high school kids is ludicrous. The things they tell them are the things they should hear once an hour, 24 hours a day. If that happened we might not have so many problems with drugs and alcohol. We probably wouldn't have betting scandals and things like wildings in the parks and streets.

"When I sold *HSBI* I gave up 20 years of my life. I had put time and effort into making it the best service in the country. I also had to give up tremendous revenue, which I have not been able to garner again. I flat out lost between $40,000 and $50,000 a year."

Selling his scouting service didn't stop the caterwauling. "It is typical of the way people perceive things that very few believed I actually sold *HSBI*," says Garf. "They believed that I would do what they would do, unethically pretend to sell the report and still be involved with it.

"Howard Garfinkel was not brought up that way. Tom Konchalski didn't even have to buy *HSBI*. He knew I was dead in the water, and if he hadn't bought it I probably would have had to fire the coaches and keep it because I had to pay my bills. But if I said I sold it to a guy, I sold it to the guy. I have never written a line or written up or evaluated one player for him. I have given him ideas maybe five times and he may have used them or not, I don't know.

"It shocked the basketball world that I made the decision I did. Many people never thought I would do it, but in one way it gave me great pleasure. I was getting weary anyway, and the way I was going it was good he took it over. I knew he would do a job at least as good as me and as it turned out he has improved *HSBI*. It is the best scouting service in the country, and if anyone doesn't buy it they are a fool."

The NCAA coaches accomplished in one fell swoop what Garf's father had been unable to do after years of wrangling. The controversy didn't end there, however. The focus was merely shifted more sharply onto Garf's Guys. It made no sense to those outside the inner circle that coaches would keep going back to Five-Star for nothing. Garf and Will Klein were paying them peanuts to work like slaves for a week out in the sticks or in some suburban sweatbox and nobody was buying that BS about family and loyalty. There had to be something else in it for them.

The NCAA coaches would continue to press the issue, coming down harder on Garf and in greater force entering the nineties, nearly eliminating his hiring options altogether. The recruiting advantages they perceived Garf's Guys as getting would grate against their self-imposed Live/Dead Period limitations, creating additional friction. At the time, though, Five-Star was secure, and from that moment on *HSBI* was in safe hands.

*   *   *   *   *

Tom Konchalski, for many reasons, would have felt right at home at Orin-Sekwa, up in Ichabod Crane country. He is lanky with long, thin fingers like old Ichabod himself and is slightly stooped from bending to shake so many hands. Garf says he is "the most polite man you will ever meet. He hates nobody. He could find good points about Stalin and Hitler." It's not that he's blind to evil. His eyes, in fact, are among the most trusted in the business.

Konchalski, too, is a basketball aficionado. He grew up in Queens in the forties and followed his boyhood idol, Connie Hawkins, from boys club to boys club and playground to playground. "Hawkins was Julius Irving years before Julius came along," says Konchalski. "I will always remember his tremendous hands. He did things one-handed with a basketball that most guys couldn't do with two hands. When I was about 13 years old, in junior high school, my brother and I traveled around the city watching him play.

"I never talked to him, of course, and years later I was introduced to him and he was genuinely embarrassed by all that idol stuff I told him about." When Hawkins later got caught up in the collegiate betting scandal of 1961, Konchalski never lost faith. "In the spring of his senior year Hawkins met Jack Molinas, a lawyer who had been thrown out of the NBA for betting on his own team," he says.

"Molinas supposedly used Hawkins and a friend of his to meet and influence players. In return, it was said, Molinas would take them out to eat and give them a little spending money. Hawkins was very naïve, and when the story broke I knew he was a victim. He was banned from playing in the NBA but he later brought a lawsuit against the league. The NBA knew it would lose millions, so they settled out of court for annuity payments."

So Konchalski, on top of everything else, proved he was fiercely loyal, and like water seeking its own found Garf and Five-Star. He and Garf actually started out as cross-court rivals. In the early sixties, Konchalski got to know Mike Tynberg, and whenever Tynberg's Gems played Garf's Nationals, Konchalski would get if-looks-could-kill glares from Garf on the opposite sideline. "I thought Tom was giving him information on my players," Garf says now, laughing.

Konchalski started visiting the camp in the seventies and became known as "Tom Tennessee" after he started going there more regularly. An unofficial scout for Tennessee and Holy Cross, he often showed up with Stu Aberdeen, an assistant coach for the Volunteers. As the summers passed he and Garf ran into each other more frequently on the scouting trail and started to hit it off a little better. In time Garf learned to trust him and use his expertise at camp, most notably at the draft.

Konchalski liked the way things were done at Five-Star. He made it a point to go there, helping out if needed when he was finished bird-dogging. It got into his blood. Garf hired him to do a station, and with his height he was a natural at teaching back-to-the-basket moves. As the camp expanded he created the Development League, better consolidating the younger talent, and for six years served as the league's commissioner.

When Garf changed the emphasis of *HSBI* from the written word to a telephone service in the mid-seventies, he relied on Konchalski to be his legs and help with the paperwork. They were a good team and eventually became partners, so when the NCAA forced Garf to drop his pride and joy, Konchalski was there to catch it. Under his care, *HSBI* has remained the leader in an ever-widening field.

Konchalski only has to meet a person once to remember him for the rest of eternity. Even kids he meets for the first time he looks at long and hard as if he's seen them before but can't place where or when. It'll come to him finally, after he introduces himself and exchanges pleasantries, that the kid bears a striking resemblance to someone he watched play in the past. Invariably it turns out they both came from the same school or town or the kid is the son of someone he scouted 20 years ago. It happens often enough that Rod Sterling ought to come back and look into it.

His memory for names and faces is the stuff of legend. "I swear this is a true story," Garf says. "One winter I was picking out photographs to use for the camp brochure. There was a nice shot with seven or eight kids in it and I wanted to identify them. Tom was helping me and it took him about two seconds to rattle off all the names. Then we noticed another kid, just his elbow really, down in the corner. Tom had to think about it for 30 seconds or so, but he came up with the name."

His courteousness is the stuff of legend too. "Tom Konchalski is so straight and so saintly that it's amazing," Garf says. "There was a kid at Five-Star a few years ago from Canada named Barry Bekkadam. He was a good player who came to a couple of sessions and ended up going to Maryland. Konchalski put him in *HSBI* and there was a joke going around camp that when he wrote him up he couldn't bring himself to use foul language and called the kid Barry Bekkadarn."

Konchalski has no official connection to Five-Star, but the camp is undisguisedly dear to his heart. He rarely misses a session, striding the sidelines like some basketball scrivener keeping his files up to date and straight, and he peers up from his notes only to observe a play or greet any number of friends and associates. "I was always a terrible ballplayer so doing *HSBI* is my revenge on the game," Konchalski says.

"Personally, I have always enjoyed basketball more at the high school and college levels because the kids play for the love of the game. It is innocent and beautiful to watch. Garf has always had a love of the game. His legacy on this earth is Five-Star, and over the past 25 years it has been one of the most influential developments in the history of the game. The camp is one reason there have been significant improvements in the way the game is played. I would go there even if I weren't doing *HSBI*.

"Professionally speaking, I believe that camps like Five-Star and the others have become too important. Garf is correct when he says that a kid's senior year should be his most important. Professionalism is seeping down into all the lower levels and too much emphasis is being placed on a kid's summer performance. The reality is that if you want to attract attention, you'd better be healthy in the month of July."

Konchalski did not change the way *HSBI* rated a player. He refined it but adopted Garf's original format of five stars with applicable pluses and minuses. And, like Garf, he bases his judgments on a young player's potential. "Whatever registers in my mind's eye when I see him play, given a kid's size and skills, is what I use to determine the level I feel he can play at," Konchalski says.

"I look at a kid's physical ability, things like quickness and strength, as well as defensive and offensive skills. I take into account his attitude, his commitment and work habits, and his intensity. The more I know about a player the better, but there are always intangibles too. You can't cut open a kid's chest."

You didn't have to with Sean Elliott, who came to Pitt from Arizona in the summer of 1984 with a brace on his knee bigger than the Grand Canyon. A rising junior, he was not well known outside his home state and Garf needed convincing from a friend of Elliott's, Jerry Holmes, to take him. When he arrived strapped down tighter than a pack mule, Garf thought maybe a mistake had been made. Then he shone the Mirror toward him.

"It was the largest brace I had ever seen," Garf says. "I swear it covered half his body and all of his leg. He was a great kid and you could see he had talent. He could shoot but he was skinny, and with that brace I thought maybe he wouldn't make it. It turns out he had been injured but was wearing it mainly as a security blanket. He won the NCAA League Outstanding Player Award and came back for a second year as a camper-worker. He killed everyone both weeks. He was a dominating bitch."

The mistakes came later. Elliott missed half his senior season with injuries and was left high and dry by the McDonald's All-American committee. Garf knew they were in error and got them to make the kid an honorary 25th selectee based on promise and potential. "He did not have a huge reputation, but I knew that 20 years down the road we'd have looked bad if he wasn't there. For going out on a limb, which is what some people thought we did, it wasn't a bad risk. The Mirror was right again."

Shortly before the game Elliott was leaning on his kitchen window at home when the glass broke, severely slicing his left wrist. The McDonald's Classic was out.

In a missive to Garf Eliott wrote, "At the end of the summer, I promised I would write you a letter thanking you for being so kind to me at your Five-Star Basketball Camp. At first I was very skeptical about you, but this soon changed after I saw how you treated me and everybody at your camp. I saw lots of concern. I saw that you were not concerned with making a nickel here or there but to let the kids have a good time and to offer lots of knowledge and maturity. You were more than I expected.

"But this letter is not only to thank you but to disappoint you. After spending two weeks in a splint, the doctors decided it was best for me not to play in the 1985 McDonald's game. For this I am greatly disappointed. This was a once-in-a-lifetime chance and I cannot tell you, rather there are no words to express how I feel. I feel I have let you down as well as my family, school, and the staff at [Arizona] University." The San Antonio Spurs forgave Elliott four years later, making him the number three pick in the NBA draft.

You had to know how to look at it and fiddle with the thing, but the Mirror never missed. The same couldn't be said for Tommy Lasorda. The Los Angeles Dodgers' manager showed up unexpectedly at Pitt I in the summer of 1985 and gave an impromptu lecture that they're still buzzing about. He could see all right, which he proved with a World Championship three years later. He just couldn't shoot.

The Dodgers were in town playing the Pittsburgh Pirates. Lasorda's first baseman, Sid Bream (who has since moved to the Bucs), wanted to say hello to his younger brother who was a camper that week. They were escorted by then NC State coach Jim Valvano, who knew the way well. Valvano was a friend of Lasorda's and also a one-time Dodger batboy (an honorary position Garf would give his eyeteeth to hold, even for one game).

Garf made them feel welcome despite the fact that they irritated him no end, arriving at the end of stations and momentarily wreaking havoc on his schedule. Besides, he was feeling chipper. It was one of the best weeks for talent ever, with kids like Rex Chapman (all-star game MVP and later the Miami Heat), Steve Bardo, and Kendall Gill (who went on to form perhaps the best backcourt in the nation at Illinois), Fess Irvin (James Madison), Scott Williams (North Carolina), Tom Greis (Villanova), Carlton Screen (Providence), and Rumeal Robinson in the crowd.

Garf convinced Lasorda to speak and during the intro was his usual spontaneous self, telling the campers, "As we bleed Five-Star orange, he bleeds Dodger blue." This was Pitt and the Dodger skipper wasn't getting out of there without a test. The campers gave him a nice ovation and then implored him to *shooooot.* Garf had to explain what they meant and it took him seven tries, even more when they made him repeat the act at the end of his talk, but the place was hopping and he didn't miss again.

"I never knew anything like this existed and I am tremendously impressed," Lasorda said. "You should be congratulated for coming here knowing you came to improve your skills. As a player, it is important to play the game hard and to play to the best of your ability. But with the God-given talents you have, the main thing you should remember is not to fail yourself in the area of getting an education.

"You are outstanding basketball players and winning is very important in competition, but I believe this as much as I am living, that if God had planned for me to be a high school baseball coach, I would try to impress upon my players the importance of getting an education. That is more important than winning games at your level.

"If I were a college baseball coach, my objective would be to impress on my players the importance of preparing themselves for a way of life. When you get out into the world, if you are not totally prepared, you will fall by the wayside."

To everything there is a season. "As the manager of a major league baseball team, though," Lasorda said, "I have to forget those other two philosophies. The Dodgers have got to win. If we don't, we're in trouble. I get fired. To show you how badly I want to win, I'll tell you a story.

"A couple of years ago we were playing in Cincinnati. I got up on Sunday morning and went to church and guess who came in and sat right next to me, John McNamara, the manager of the Reds. All we did was look at each other. I knew why he was in church and he knew why I was there.

"At the conclusion of mass we walked out the center aisle together and as we approached the main door he whispered, 'Wait for me outside, I'll be right there.' I said OK but thought it was strange. Why would he want to meet me outside? I didn't walk outside. I watched him and he went to the right side of the church and knelt down and lit a candle.

"So I went down the left side of the church, very quietly, waited up in front by the altar, and when he left I walked up the right side and blew his candle out. I knew one thing, he was not lighting that candle for a dead relative. He was hoping he could win and all through the game that day, I yelled from the dugout, 'Hey, Mac, it ain't gonna work. I blew it out.' We clobbered 'em that day 13–2, so you can see you gotta give it your best at all times and you gotta win."

Not bad for a rookie.

FOURTEEN
Picking Up Steam at Pitt

"Playing this game, the mental is to the physical as four is to one, boys, and that's what the hell is gonna separate you as you go along."

– Bob Knight at Pitt

Alonzo Mourning and Billy Owens were like ships in the night, continually passing each other without realizing it. They weren't doing it deliberately and it was fated they would collide fairly regularly in the Big East, but they never came to Five-Star together. "It was just as well because I didn't have to try to figure out who was better," says Garf.

The eighties were beginning to wind down at Pitt, but Mourning, Owens, and another less-heralded but equally talented player, Christian Laettner out of The Nichols School in Buffalo, New York, were just getting wound up. They would be the leaders of the college pack in the nineties and potential professional superstars heading into the 21st century.

They weren't the only ones leaving their marks: Sam Bowie of Lebanon, Pennsylvania; Dominique Wilkins, and other future NBA players such as Reggie Williams, Johnny Dawkins, and Mark Jackson were all forming a lasting impression. They were at Honesdale, though, at cool and windy Lake Bryn Mawr, far removed from the grunt and grime of Pitt.

You could flip a coin to see who got Alonzo Mourning or Billy Owens when they were in high school and not worry about losing the toss. It always came down to heads or tails trying to decide who was the best and who was second. It was done mostly for argument's sake because Mourning at 6'10" and Owens at 6'9" wouldn't even play the same position at Georgetown and Syracuse respectively, so how could anyone really judge? People did, though, and Garf was glad he was spared the dilemma.

Mourning came to Five-Star from Indian River High in Chesapeake, Virginia. He must have practiced blocking shots along the way because after he got there no one could get one off against him inside the paint, and it seemed like he was still standing there, like an immovable Sequoia, long after the game ended. Those endless arms of his haunted a person's dreams. If he didn't get a piece of the ball he made you alter your shot so much it almost came straight back down.

He arrived with Boo Williams, an ex-college player running the Boo Williams Summer League in Tidewater, Virginia. Williams had already helped produce J.R. Reid and was hopeful Mourning would turn out to be as good a player or better. "Alonzo's high school coach, Bill Lassiter, sent him to camp not for exposure or competition," says Williams. "My summer league provided plenty of that. He sent him for the stations and for the opportunity to meet people."

Mourning was warmly welcomed, but Williams got a rude reception. "I coached in the NBA league, and in my first game The King had me down by 50 points and kept his press on the whole game. That was his idea of an initiation. We became friends, though, and used to stay up half the night arguing about who the best players were in camp. The King is a great guy, but the truth has never been told about how uncanny it is that he always seems to end up with the first pick in the draft."

The King will swear on a Bible it's just dumb luck, but he had a rare miss with Mourning, nursing a broken heart until he realized that Walt Williams was there to take care of him. The King lost in the finals with Duke-bound Laettner at Pitt I in 1987, but at Pitt II he won it all when he and Williams had a private, after-hours skull session. They figured out that the only way to beat Mourning was to draw him outside. He was impenetrable at close range but not as effective when he had to bend down in a defensive stance.

If Williams could hit from outside, Mourning would have to come out on him. He couldn't just sic the guards on him and sit back in a zone. Everything at Five-Star was man-to-man. Zone defenses had been taboo since before anyone could remember. Bishop Alter coach Joe Petrocelli talked Garf into trying zones one year and the day they were supposed to do it, it poured pitchforks. Petrocelli's roommate, Seth Greenberg, an associate coach at Long Beach State now and a 20-year Five-Star staffer, saw the deluge and said, "I guess this proves God is a man-to-man guy," and shortly thereafter the experiment was called off.

The only problem with The King's scheme was that Williams had to stick the "J," which Williams, headed for the Maryland Terrapins, did. He buried his first two shots and Mourning went out after him, opening the lane like the Red Sea. The King's kids filled it faster than fleeing Israelites, and he had his fourth title. It was probably his sweetest.

Garf knew about Mourning coming in. He had heard he was better than J.R. Reid, which he didn't want to hear. Mourning was only a freshman and Reid was older and still one of Garf's fair-haired fellows. You had to do something extraordinary to top that, which Mourning did. Garf watched him play a few games and then raved about him to his friend Billy Packer. "When Billy came to camp I told him Mourning was the greatest center since Jabbar because he had a jump-shooting game to go with his inside strength," Garf says. "He said to me, 'There you go again with your Greatest Player Ever stuff. You've always got a latest greatest.' He wasn't that interested, but a couple of years later Packer was doing an Olympic game and talked about having seen Mourning play. He was in shock, saying stuff like, 'We knew the kid could play, but we didn't know he could shoot the jumper.' I said to myself, 'Billy, why didn't you believe when I told you Alonzo could do it all?'"

Billy Owens quietly dominated Pitt I and Pitt III for three summers. He did the same thing over four winters in his home state of Pennsylvania, leading Carlisle High to four straight Class AAAA state championships. He shared Most Valuable Player honors with Mourning in the McDonald's All-Star Game his senior year but did things very differently. He was all over the court. He was 6'9" and could knock your shot into next week, but he could handle the rock like a runty guard too.

Owens was also blessed with a soft touch. He was deadly from 15 feet and could nail the three like it was made for him. Mostly what he did was make everyone around him better, like a Magic or a Bird. He started coming to Five-Star as a rising sophomore and every July "uplifted every one of his teammates," Garf says. Owens influenced the entire game, all 10 players, elevating even his opponents to new levels. There was a constant ebb and flow from him to everyone else and then back to him again. The camp vibrated.

Life was good with Owens. It was funny at the time, even though Garf and the coach involved eventually had a parting of the ways, but Charlie Moore of Lake Clifton, Baltimore, knew how to use Owens' talents to their utmost. "Moore had a play and I remember it like it was yesterday," Garf says. "He'd yell out '44 Reverse,' and the team would make three or four passes with Owens taking a 24-footer at the end of it. This was on an outdoor court, but he'd make the shot almost always, and Moore would throw his hands in the air and shout, 'Lord, it's a simple game.'"

*   *   *   *   *

Garf seldom gave anyone the axe. Except for guys like Dave Pritchett and Buddy Gardler, whom he hired, fired, and rehired almost every week, coaches were safe as long as they did their stations right, stuck with the program, and didn't mess with a camper's head. Pritchett and Gardler were innocent on all three counts. Firing Pritchett was pure fun and Gardler's only sin was being able to shoot. Garf knew Gardler could make mincemeat out of his two-handed set shot, and he had to suffer for it somehow.

Gardler is a 20-year man at Five-Star. He played under a couple of good ones, Jack Ramsey and Jack McKinney at St. Joe's in Philadelphia (later the coaches of the Portland Trailblazers and Los Angles Lakers, respectively), ripping the nets with his lefty jumper. Presently the coach at Cardinal O'Hara High in Springfield, Pennsylvania, Gardler's lost a step or two but can teach a kid to shoot the pill like nobody's business. Garf loves his style but they just seem to get on each other's nerves.

It's a good bet Gardler and Garf will tangle whenever they have to share the same turf, but they always see eye to eye when the subject is shooting a basketball. That's about the only place where Garf grudgingly but graciously gives ground. "We've gotten into it once or twice over the years, but who wouldn't after 20 years?" Gardler says. "Garf does a great job with the camp, and I go back whenever I can to renew old friendships."

Gardler can flat out shoot the rock. "The more hours you spend practicing, the more a seed grows that makes you believe you can make the shot," he says. "It's kind of like Pac Man. Some kids practice for hours and can get a million points and others do it only sometimes, and have trouble getting ten thousand. Becoming a good shooter comes down to spending time on it and concentrating.

"Concentration is the most important thing. You can't worry about the defense being on you and the score, or what your girlfriend is going to do after the game. If you really like playing the game, though, it is the easiest thing to learn. You just have to put in the time and love it and be a little bit of a fanatic. A lot of kids think that to shoot well you have to go out for a half hour a day, but it takes lots of practice, intense practice, to be good.

"Half of shooting is mental. So many kids do everything right physically but don't believe they can shoot. On the other hand, some do the basics all wrong but believe they can make it, like Walter Berry. When he played for St. John's, and even in the pros, his shot looked awkward but after a while it became instinct. The physical aspects are important too, starting with a player's feet. Players should spot up and get their feet underneath the shot. Quicker players have a tendency to float on their shot.

"The hand position is the same as it is for the pass or dribble: fingers spread and palms off the ball. The index finger of the shooting hand is in the middle of the ball, and the thumb of the guide hand forms a T with the thumb of the shooting hand. And think about what you are sighting on. No one is bionic to be able to focus on the front or back of the rim. Try to see the whole basket. Prove it sometime by shooting at a dead rim with no net or backboard. It'll go in, so try and see the whole basket.

"The follow-through is where most shooters make their mistakes," Gardler says. "They tend to rush it. The way to think about it is to imagine someone standing behind you watching you shoot. They should be able to see your wrist enter the basket. There's a great way to practice the follow-through and the whole shot.

"While you're sitting watching TV maybe, pretend you are shooting. What you want to do, maybe two or three hundred times a night, is to take your shot, getting the wrist snap and the elbow lock and the back spin. You want to control the air six feet above your head. The more hours you put in, the more confident you will feel in your shooting. If someone asks you the strong part of your game and you don't say shooting, you don't believe you are a good shooter."

* * * * *

The mental and physical in basketball are inseparably intertwined, although they can be studied separately. Bob Knight needed no one to tell him that when he lectured at Pitt at the tail end of the 1980s. The Hoosier coach never stopped coming back to Five-Star. It is the only camp he speaks at except for his own and he had no trouble telling the campers why.

"This camp is the absolute best camp for competitive basketball anywhere in the United States," Knight said. "I mean not closely the best, but by far the best. Howard Garfinkel has a better concern for you kids, and I don't care if it's one of you who's capable of playing at North Carolina or Kent or Indiana or the Division III level, he has an interest in all of you and a concern in seeing that all of you have a chance to play."

It was hot at Pitt and crowded in the lecture hall as Knight spoke, but listening to him, it was as if he were talking to each camper individually, touching each one inwardly. It was Bob Knight with his ferocious reputation, but he seemed gentle and caring, like somebody's kindly granddaddy, and everyone listening soaked in the wisdom of his years.

He told the campers that over the years thousands of kids had come to Five-Star, and of those, only 126 had played in the NBA. His NBA facts and figures weren't meant to discourage. "Think about that a minute," Knight said. "That means a couple of you in here will have a chance to do so.

"A lot of you will have the chance to play Division I basketball and there will be some of you who should have the chance to play NBA basketball who won't get there because you'll succumb to something: laziness, drugs, lack of attention. All of a sudden you'll be 30 years old and you'll wonder what the hell happened to you.

"Some of you right in this room, if we brought you back 10 years from now, it would be just that, 'What the hell happened to me? If I were only 18 again. If I could only start this thing again.'

"And there'll be some of you who don't make it as college players for the exact same reason, and you should make it. You've got the world by the balls right now at 17 or 18. You haven't been out on your own. You haven't had to go out and compete with other people just like you guys, so you're the kingpin in your town, your community, your district, your state, anything.

"Hey, the woods is full of those guys, boys, and I want to talk to you a little bit about what separates you from other guys just like you all over the country. Why will some of you go on and get a chance to play college or even pro basketball and some of you, with the same ability, not have that chance?

"One thing that we take for granted in this country is education. I have a kid working for me from Columbia, South America. Less than 20 percent of the kids there will be able to get a high school education. Think about that. Take advantage of what the hell you've got academically, boys."

First things first, in life and in the game. "I don't think basketball is a game of shots and great plays," Knight said. "There are great plays made in games, but you win because you play the game well.

You don't win because you block shots or dunk shots or hit three-point plays, you win because you understand how to play and that involves anticipating what's happening in the game.

"I want you to keep this in mind. Playing this game, the mental is to the physical as four is to one, boys, and that's what the hell is gonna separate you as you go along. A kid who doesn't throw the ball away and a kid who doesn't take bad shots is a pretty damn good player. Given average skills and average athletic ability, he knows what he can do with it. You can learn to play basketball and it goes way beyond the physical skills. Don't worry about what kind of a shooter you are, what size you are, how quick you are. You know you can't teach yourself to grow or to be a hell of a lot stronger or quicker, but you can teach yourself to be a lot better basketball player.

"You can have a concept of how to play the game. Very few that play the game have it. I'll use two words for you: *look* and *see*. Everybody looks but not everyone sees. There are players who look and don't see a thing, and there's a hell of a difference, boys.

"There are only so many things that can happen in this game. It's an easy game to figure out while you're playing. I can anticipate and then recognize the situation and react to it. Most true basketball players are reactors, but guys like Magic Johnson anticipate. He's the best player in the world at bringing the ball up the floor. If Magic needs to dribble four times, he does. If he only needs to dribble it twice, that's what he does because when he gets it he knows where everybody is.

"Larry Bird is the best passer I've ever seen without the dribble. He catches it and gets rid of it because when he catches it he already knows where people are. That's not because he has any better vision than anybody else, it's because he uses it. Your eyes are the best thing you have to use in this game."

The rules apply to everyone. "Michael Jordan is the best athlete I've ever seen play basketball," Knight continued. "In my mind there's nobody else close. There are a lot of athletes as good as Michael but none of 'em think like he does. When we had Michael on the Olympic team, if he wasn't playing particularly well I'd go over and take him by the arm and I'd squeeze his arm a little bit, I wouldn't just pat him on the arm, and I'd say 'Michael, you're too damn good to play like this' and Michael would just nod his head and say 'You're right' and that's all you had to do to tell him.

"Some guys who are outstanding athletes who can't understand what a bad shot is, think any shot they get is a good one. If you don't understand shot selection, you're going to have a hard time playing at some point in your career. That's why out of thousands only 126 have played in the NBA.

"We're talking about something here that is going to be very difficult to attain, no matter what. What I'm interested in you having is a chance to play college basketball, and then you just see what the hell happens. To be able to play that way, you've got to be able to put the game together in your mind in a way that you're getting the most out of what the hell it is that you have.

"Offensive basketball, boys, is playing without the ball. If you come down and change your position every time down the court, if you make a move as soon as you see the defensive man, you become tough to play against. If you wait for the ball and think you're gonna play with the ball, the woods is full of guys like that.

"Watching the games here in camp I get the feeling sometimes we ought to build an island for you guards, put all of you on an island over here and play with the forwards and the centers because you guards do more to screw up basketball than referees do. It isn't even close.

"The thing you gotta understand is that when you were the guy who set the tempo for everything, how many of you in a halfcourt situation brought the ball down and took a shot? Think about that. Why? I dribble because I want the other four guys involved. If you bring it down you have to get rid of it and you can get it back and shoot it or get it back and penetrate, but I don't want four guys standing while the guard is dribbling.

"Give it up. You guards would be amazed at what all happens to you when everybody on your team knows that you're gonna first of all give the ball up and that you're gonna take the good shot after you get the ball back out. Think a little bit, guards. You want guys to help you a little bit, to pick up a guy that's loose on defense or somebody rebounding for you? It all starts with you.

"How many of you think about the players on your team, who the best shooters are, and you work like hell to set those people up? Or how many of you come down and just make a pass because you've exhausted every move known to man and haven't yet gotten a shot? How many forwards think the guards dribble too damn much? How many of you get open and you don't get the ball? You've got centers and forwards who are working like hell to get open. They've got to rebound. They're playing the physical part of basketball and a guard has got to help those guys."

Shifting the focus, Knight said, "Defense can be played by anybody. The problem with this game is everybody thinks about scoring a bucket. When I played guard for Ohio State I was playing once in a game at Madison Square Garden against St. John's. I remember making a diving shot and getting fouled before the shot. I made the basket but it was disallowed. I remember going to the free throw line with a one-and-one thinking, 'Christ, I got the bucket taken away.'

"I happened to make the one-and-ones, but I didn't think that was nearly as good as making a bucket and that's how we think as players, but the free throw did a hell of a lot more. It got somebody a little closer to foul trouble. It gave us a break and gave us two points. If you understand how to play basketball you understand that. As a guard, you don't have to dribble down and shoot it. Come down. Get it inside. Make a move. Get it back.

"If I'm playing defense and the ball is on the other side of the floor, I know he's not gonna hurt me over here where I am. Chances are you're gonna do one of two things: You're gonna try to move toward the ball or you're gonna wait until the ball comes back to you. I wanna think about where the ball is and I wanna think about trying to stop the ball. Now if my man comes to the ball, then I can get involved with my man, but what can I do playing defense away from the ball? I can be in position to help stop the ball. I can anticipate the drive to the bucket and then somebody else has to help out where I was.

"One year there were nine guards taken in the first round of the NBA draft," Knight said, "and only one, Isiah Thomas, was an outstanding physical player. The rest of them were damn smart, good basketball players and that's where you'll all be separated eventually. You have to think the game through. You pick up a guy at midcourt, you channel him to his left because he doesn't go to the left very well, or the right. You don't let him penetrate. You're after him all the time."

Leaving the guards to lick their wounds for the moment, Knight continued: "Forwards, be hard to guard on offense. You're playing down inside, you've got to really work hard to get open. You've got to play off the defensive man on offense. If he goes high, you go low. If he turns one way, you go the other way. Too many guys just stand around and wait for the ball to come to them.

"That's the primary thought most people have on offense, either the ball just comes to me or I go at the ball. The idea on offense is to move to get open and then the ball has to find you. Average athletes can be very difficult to guard because they move extremely well. They are constantly on the move. They are in and out, up and down, and that's the type that's going to be a hell of a player, boys.

"Forwards, on defense, make it tough for the first pass to be made. You're down, you're alert, and then you're getting back down the floor on offense. A kid who gets down the floor on defense stops the break just by busting his butt to get there and probably stops two buckets. By running the court on offense, he's gonna pick up two buckets a game and get fouled and that's another two points and now that's the kind of basketball player who can play.

"Playing in the post, if the guy is guarding you high, take him a little higher. Keep him there. Get a position, get the ball down low going to the baseline. Don't just stand there and let somebody bring the ball to you. Think a little bit. Don't just go out there and play, boys. Try to come out here and think a play ahead of what the hell you're doing.

"It all starts with understanding yourself. Learn your strengths and weaknesses and play away from your weaknesses and toward your strengths. Some of you are not very good perimeter shooters. Don't take perimeter shots. Some of you don't drive with the ball really well. Don't drive. Give it up and play without it. Some of you are overmatched with quickness on defense. Instead of playing somebody quicker and letting him get past you, play position and learn to give him a little room.

"It's a very simple thing, just paying attention to the abilities you've got. Work hard when you're working. How many of you, when you really work out, really work hard? I could take you right now and you might say, 'Jesus, I've never worked like that before.' And how many of you, when you work out, work hard on your shooting? You should all have your hands up on that one.

"And when you shoot a basketball, how many of you say to yourself, 'All right, I've got the court set up into six shot areas'? That's about what there are, boys: two at the top of the key, two at the side of the key, and two at the baseline, and then you've got a seventh which is a driving or posting area. You don't just go out and shoot and dribble a basketball and think that's gonna help you any. You've got to have an organized approach to what you're doing, and when you're working out by yourself you have to demand something of yourself.

"How many of you, when you're working on handling the basketball, work on handling it in such a way that nobody can take it away from you? How many of you have ever worked hard at dribbling two basketballs at the same time? Why don't all of you take two basketballs in the driveway and work until you can control both of them? If you can handle a basketball under pressure and not lose it, you become a tremendous asset to my team. That's how you learn to play, to develop the physical part of the game, which is secondary in importance to the mental."

* * * * *

Nothing earth-shattering has come along to change Knight's basic philosophy of the game since his lecture at Pitt. The mental still overrides the physical, as four does one. "From a purely coaching standpoint, that's exactly what you're looking for, is a kid who can adjust to what you want done and who isn't locked into how he thinks he has to play," Knight says now.

"In other words, 'My game.' I have a tough time with kids who have to play 'My game.' I want 'em playing mine, not theirs, and the best kids are gonna be those kids who just say, 'OK, here I am, use me however you can.'"

Nor has time lessened his fondness for the camp. "Five-Star has been a really good part of the total picture of basketball," Knight says. "It definitely has a place in the basketball community, primarily because of the way Howie has run it. Will Klein is a compliment to Howard's personality. He's an easygoing guy who does all the bookwork and then all the organizational things that Howard would have in total chaos if it were left to him. So, they compliment each other very well.

"If I didn't think Howard did a good job, I wouldn't screw around with the camp. Howard isn't only concerned about the kid who's the best player. He's concerned about the kid who's a good kid, and he has really helped a lot of them go on to school, to have really good experiences playing college basketball. Not just at the level Indiana plays. Those kids don't need a lot of help, but the other kids do, and he's set up a situation where those kids get a lot of exposure.

"He makes sure that they're coached by coaches who work like hell with the kids. They don't let a kid control a team. They don't let a team be simply a guard-oriented team as so many of these summer teams can be. I think a kid who goes to Howie's camp is really going to get an awfully good opportunity to show what it is he can do as a player at whatever level he's gonna be effective.

"The other thing Howie's done is work really hard to help guys he thinks are deserving in coaching. He's worked hard to make people aware of them, to put them in situations where they might have a chance to go on in coaching.

"He's just done a really good job with people. He's worked hard on behalf of people and because of that I've been willing to do things that he's asked me to do. I just have really enjoyed the relationship that I've had with Howard because I have really appreciated what Howard has tried to do for both kids and coaches and I think he has probably done about as much for both as anybody could have done."

FIFTEEN
Riding First Class

"I'm hitchin' and twitchin', bleedin' from the eyes. My lungs are evaporating."

— Pete Gillen on coaching courtside

Colonel Mullis was giggling like a schoolboy. He couldn't help himself. It wasn't his flank attack at the "Fast Break" station that had him tickled, it was a kid from Bill Raftery's Broadcast School. Raftery brought 30 or so budding Red Barbers to The Pitt in the summer of 1989, turning them loose with their wires and notebooks and tape machines. One of them had The Colonel cornered.

"We're coming to you live from the prestigious Five-Star Basketball Camp," the kid was hollering into his mike, firing questions faster than anyone could answer them except The Colonel, who was keeping right up and loving every minute.

The kid's audience was imaginary, but that was the whole idea, to give him and his young colleagues a chance to get their feet wet behind the mike without drowning. All week they did play-by-play and color commentary at games, grabbing campers and coaches afterwards for on-the-spot interviews. Every morning they'd listen to themselves on tape, get input from Raftery, then start in again. It was the first time anything like that had been done at Five-Star, but after a day or two it was like they had always been there.

Garf and Will Klein agreed to the school because they liked the idea and because Garf and Raftery went back a long way. Garf and "The Scout," Larry Pearlstein, first eyeballed Raftery in the mid-sixties when he was playing at St. Cecelia's in Kearney, New Jersey. He was a step slow but could shoot. Pearlstein was scouting him for Maryland.

Raftery eventually went to LaSalle, where injuries led to a checkered career and compelled him to join the coaching ranks. Over the years, on his rise to the head coaching post at Seton Hall, he and Garf bumped into each other fairly regularly and they stayed in touch after Raftery retired from the business to go into broadcasting. With a good word from Pearlstein, Raftery landed a job as color man for the New Jersey Nets and within a few years became the voice of the upstart Big East Conference.

"I used to read Howard's *HSBI* report just for the language sometimes," he says. "He was a great evaluater of talent, but just the way he wrote the kids up was great. He was very creative. At Five-Star, he has become one of those characters who is very charming, and at the same time, you know he is never going to BS you about anything."

Raftery lectured at Five-Star before devising the broadcasting school plan with his partner, Nordy Holder. "We thought it would be a unique thing," Garf says. "No money was made the first year, but they'll be back. It adds more color and flavor to the camp." There was always room for innovation. Coaches and lecturers were allowed, even encouraged, to use their imaginations. As long as they got their message across, a little flair was fine.

*   *   *   *   *

Stations are where Five-Star's originality flourishes. The same old fundamentals are taught year after year, but each time it is like a seamstress adding another stitch to a never-ending basketball quilt. "This is like a fair," Garf said, looking out over the proceedings at Pitt on Saturday morning, the second day of camp. "It's like a World's Fair where you go from one unbelievable exhibition to another. Don't even ask me how I got all these great coaches."

It has been a slow, thread-by-thread progression, but from the hills surrounding the courts, looking down, the spectacle unfolds anew each season. The intensity is the same at Radford and Honesdale, but at Pitt each station is a blacktop patchwork pattern blending into the next and the next. Around the edges, like embroidery, the campers' families and other interested onlookers sit on the grass or stand along the fences and watch, keeping a respectful distance. Visitors are always welcome and are visibly astounded at what comes to life in front of them.

It starts after breakfast on the way to stations. Campers ascend one hill from the dining hall, then descend another to the courts. At Radford and Honesdale they come from all directions, from their bunks or dorm rooms, but at Pitt they form one long, orange line which can be heard before it is seen. Campers at Pitt traditionally lace their room keys to their sneakers. As they walk the key chains clinking against the metal eyelets make them sound like hundreds of chirping spring peepers, soft at first then louder as they get nearer to the courts. The Five-Star rite of summer.

Then the teaching begins. The coaches' voices overlap and from a distance it sounds like disconnected noises, except for the patter of basketballs and the scuffling of the campers' feet. Up close there is order and sense. Everything is planned. Garf and his "invent guys" see to it that stations are laid out properly: not too many similar lessons back-to-back and never three or four back-breakers in a row.

The coaches' personalities are considered as well. They'll all get on a kid if necessary, but some guys are low-key while others are fired up and Garf tries to juggle them around. It's not always possible, but that's the plan. There are well-established exceptions to the rule, such as Buddy Gardler getting one special court whenever he's in camp and guys with seniority working center stage, but it has little or nothing to do with ego ruffling. Garf wants them near the bleachers so he can sit and watch.

Garf would pay to see Pete Gillen, but for 18 years has gotten Uecker seats for free. He needn't sit so close. Gillen could work anywhere and, with his powerful set of lungs, come through loud and clear. He grew up in the Brooklyn Bay Ridge area, near the Verrazano Bridge, and is used to making himself heard. His friends call him "Stereo" and razz him about being the only guy in camp who never needs a microphone. "When I hear Gillen's voice, I know the camp is going," Garf says. He has to listen fast. The Irish redhead, despite his Pavarotti-like vocal chords, is usually the first one to go hoarse.

Gillen never holds back. It's the only way he knows how to get by. He was an all-city point guard at Brooklyn Prep and a walk-on at Fairfield College before earning a scholarship his final two seasons. A blue-collar, tin-hat kind of guy, he says he got to be head coach at Xavier of Ohio University by "scratching and knocking the rock." That's how his Musketeers won four Midwestern Conference titles from 1986 to 1989 and made it to the Sweet Sixteen in the 1990 NCAA Tournament.

Gillen started out like a lot of guys. His first coaching job was the junior high team at Holy Names. He was at Brooklyn Prep three years until it closed and he packed his bags for Nazareth High. He was still a high school coach when he came to Five-Star, scaring off the wildlife at Camp Rosemont with his yowls.

Gillen is a Catholic High School Athletic Association Hall of Famer today, along with Bob Cremins and others. "It was just as hard beating coaches like Jack Curran (Archbishop Molloy), Ray Nash (Bishop Ford), and Pat Quigley (Bishop Loughlin) as it is trying to beat Denny Crum and Louisville," he says. He paid his dues before getting the head coaching job at Xavier. He was an assistant at Hawaii with Rick Pitino, worked under Rollie Massimino at Villanova, and recruited for Digger Phelps at Notre Dame from 1980 to 1985, getting lucky with the likes of David Rivers and Tim Kempton.

He's had some help along the way. "I come back to Five-Star because without Garf I wouldn't be in college coaching," Gillen says. "He put in a good word for me at Hawaii and his camp is really where a lot of guys learned the ropes. He organizes a camp that has most of the best players in the country, and he's the best in the world at what he does. How many people can you say that about?"

The redhead does all right for himself. His voice will forever echo at Five-Star, and over the years he's become a bit of a pundit, at least to grateful followers and fans of Xavier basketball. He has his own book of quotable quotes, *A World According to Pete Gillen*, which consoles and inspires the Musketeer multitudes in times of loss.

Some of his sayings are borrowed: "When nothing seems to help, I go to look at a stonecutter hammering away at his rock perhaps a hundred times without as much as a crack showing. Yet at the hundred and first blow it will split in two, and I know it was not that blow that did it, but all that had gone before." He picked that up from Jacob Riis, a noted American writer and pioneer in the development of city playgrounds in the early 1900s.

He learned the rest at the hardwood school of hard knocks. After a comeback win in the waning seconds one season, Gillen told everyone within earshot, "We were in the grave. We were encased in mahogany, but we came back." And explaining what it was like to win a league championship one season he said, "Guys were going berserk. It was unreal. They were going crazy, high-fives, low-fives, and I saw new fives I never even knew were available."

Gillen can't help but be himself. The rock pile follows him everywhere. "We aren't a big-name Division I program," he says. "We don't get the Robert Redfords. We get guys with scars and warts and nicks. We have to be a chuck-and-duck, press-and-run team.

At Xavier the keys to winning are free throw shooting and rebounding." At Five-Star Gillen's lot in life is crashing the boards, and to find him one need look no farther than the paint.

Gillen got geometrical at his rebounding station. "Great rebounders go for every rebound," he said. "Timing and position, not size, are the most important aspects. Bill Laimbeer of the Detroit Pistons and Moses Malone can't jump two inches, but they are among the leading rebounders in the NBA every year. Mental preparation is a key too. You should anticipate and know when a teammate is going to shoot and expect every shot to be a miss.

"To be a great offensive rebounder, you have to know the angles. On a shot from the corner, for instance, 80 percent of the time a missed shot bounces off the rim to the other corner or back to the shooter. On a shot from a 45-degree angle, it bounces 45 degrees the other way or back to the shooter 70 percent of the time."

While the non-mathematical campers looked for assistance from their Einstein friends, Gillen continued: "On a shot from the middle, the ball will carom into the lane 80 percent of the time. A high, arching shot will come off the rim high and arching, and a long shot, like a three-pointer, will very often set up a long rebound." It's not guesswork, he says, and if you think about it before a game, your productivity and stats will rise along with your playing time.

Putting the laws of physics to good use is one thing; getting position is another. Defenders want the ball too and most of the time stand between an offensive rebounder and the basket. There are ways around them though. "You can fake right or left and go the other way, stepping across your body," Gillen said. "There is the 'Spin and Pin.' When you see the shot go up, step right at the defender. Put one leg right in his crotch and spin with the other, pinning the defender with your inside hand as you turn.

"If the defender boxes you out, step across your body right next to him. That gives each of you at least a 50-50 chance. If you are near the baseline, go behind the board and screen out your man. Keep pressure on him down low."

The offense has to chip away while the defense has it easy. "You only have to work for two seconds on the defensive boards," said Gillen. "That's how long the ball is in the air on a shot. In that time, don't just turn and watch for the basketball. That gives your man time to go around you. On the release, go right at him, put a leg in his crotch, and block him out. Or use a reverse turn. Go right at your man, face him, and whichever way he goes, you turn with him. Make sure to get a leg in his crotch and block out."

There are more ways to skin a cat and the redhead hasn't learned them all, but he knows what he knows. "The thing that is great about life is that there are lots of ways to do things. The goal is to give each guy a thought or an idea to become a better player and maybe something you say will filter through and make him a better person too. All you can do is keep on knockin' the rock."

*   *   *   *   *

There are other guys Garf would buy tickets to see but instead he brings them to Five-Star. Tom McConnell, an assistant at Dayton, is one. He is the old Five-Star and the next generation combined. "This Five-Star thing is very real," McConnell said, "and it starts with Garf. Professionally, I feel like I could probably never repay what I've taken from here. Good players will always be found, but a lot of coaches might go unnoticed if it weren't for Five-Star. I never leave here at the end of the week without at least one new concept to make me a better coach. With all these great players you get an opportunity to experiment with new ideas. The peer pressure is amazing, not just for the players but also the coaches."

When McConnell works he huffs and puffs like a steel city steam engine and his eyes and jaw are ever-set to the task. He graduated from South Hills Catholic High in Pittsburgh, inheriting the city's work ethic and taking it with him to Butler College. He helped lead the team to the junior college finals in 1980 and transferred to Division I Davidson. Before leaving Butler he had a talk with his coach, Tom Beckett.

It was more like a short chat. It was a sunny day in May, and they were in the coach's office looking over a Davidson schedule. One of their biggest games was going to be against Notre Dame and John Paxson. "Beckett was a great motivator," McConnell said. "He said to me, 'I can't believe you're sitting here. What do you think Paxson is doing right now?' That really hit home.

"I sent away for a picture of Paxson. I started taking a basketball with me wherever I went and when I would go through my workouts, I would imagine playing against Paxson. There were times I couldn't sleep. I would wake up thinking about him, turn on the outside lights, and hit the blacktop. I was really pumped when we finally got to play Notre Dame. One of the first times I got the ball bringing it up court I couldn't believe it, Paxson was on me. I laughed inside and told everyone to clear out. I had done this hundreds of times.

"I met John a few years later and told him about the picture and everything and we laughed about it. Notre Dame won the game and I held my own, but the point is it wasn't just Paxson, it could have been any opponent. I wasn't the player he was, but I walked off the court knowing inside that I had done the best with what I was given. You can't control the hand dealt to you, but you can control yourself becoming the best you can. You measure success by what you do, not by what the guy next to you does."

The guy behind you can be a factor sometimes and McConnell got out the pads teaching "Back-to-the-Basket Offensive Moves." He quickly got the attention of the shorter kids, telling them, "You perimeter players are probably tuning me out, thinking you'll never post-up underneath, but positioning and angles should be understood by everyone.

"Only two people can stop a great post man: he himself, by not understanding positioning; and his teammate, by not understanding how to get him the ball. The first thing we'll talk about is the stance. Post men, let the man with the basketball see you. How can he get you the ball if you move across the lane sideways with your arms down by your sides? Even if he passes it to you, you'll probably miss it. Get a good stance and let him know you want the basketball.

"Split the mark. Find the second hash mark on the free throw lane and split that mark. Now you know where you are, and when you turn to the basket, you have a good angle to use the backboard. If the defender won't let you have that spot, there are alternatives, but if you get it, establish a wide base with your feet. Dig your rear end into the defender's thighs or knees. That makes it awfully tough for him to move and now you can control the action. Get your hands up like a football goalpost. Give the man with the basketball a good target."

McConnell demonstrated and then told the kids to run through it, no holds barred. He gave the defense a break, letting them wear billowy pads, like those used on football tackling dummies, but some serious thumping took place just the same. "If the defense is guarding you on the side, beat him to a spot with your feet and get above him," McConnell said. "If you are being fronted, jam your knee up his butt and turn your back to the defense. Now you're in good position to receive the basketball and do things with it.

"After you catch the ball, keep your goalposts, with your hands by your chin and your arms out. If you use your dribble for no reason, you've lost it. Save that dribble for when you need it. Now it's nostril time. You don't need 800 moves to score. Get right in your defender's face. There are only four ways he can guard you: left, right, front, and back, and there are ways to score on each one.

"He can't take everything away from you. First is the jumper. Show a target, catch the ball, chin it, and locate your man. Fake to the middle, turn to the outside, and pop the 'J.' Don't fade on that jump shot. We want to get fouled. And don't fear getting blocked. It's no insult.

"If he's guarding you inside, ask for the ball, catch it, chin it, and locate. Show baseline and if he takes the fake, pivot to the inside and shoot.

"Now I've turned him twice. Two great moves. Next we'll use the power move with no dribble with your man behind you. Split the mark. Give a target, catch the ball, chin it, and locate. Show middle and turn to the baseline. Use a drop step, turn under, and move with power to the basket off both feet. If you want to go inside, it's the same. Catch it, chin it, and show baseline. Go to the middle off both feet. It's a power move.

"Now we're ready to play. We've got all the moves we need. The next thing is to add a shot fake. Show a target, catch it, chin it, and seal your man, using your body, not your arms. Show baseline, dribble in, one hard dribble so the guards don't strip you, and fake. Stay on your feet. As he's coming down, you go up. If it doesn't work, establish a pivot foot and seal him to the outside. Use your body, not your arms.

"Remember, the defense can't take everything away from you. If they take the baseline, go to the top. If they take away the wings, go baseline. Guards and post men have to work together, understanding positioning and timing. And big guys, don't be afraid to kick the ball back out once in a while. If you're double-teamed or can't get off a shot, pass it back outside for a shot. You'd be surprised what that does for a team."

* * * * *

Meanwhile, the guards were getting what-for at Jim Hoy's ballhandling station. He calls it his "Ballhandling Smorgasbord" and serves up dribbling drills like spare ribs, sweet and down to the bare bone and any way you want 'em except tender. The special education teacher and basketball coach at Freedom High School in Pittsburgh, he's like a junior Dave Pritchett, all drawl and twang and wilder than a hoot owl. He got the campers loose in a hurry.

"Ballhandling is work," Hoy told them. "Let me have someone out here who thinks he can do an around-the-waist drill." A kid stepped forward and did it. "Good. Now, son, I want you to circle the ball around your waist, down to your knees, around your ankles, back up to your knees, your waist, and then around your head five times without stopping." The kid started and Hoy interrupted him.

"Are you the slow kid I heard about in camp?" he said with mock sarcasm. "No? Oh, my mistake. Son, that is terribly slow. I take this seriously and if you don't I'm gonna let you hear about it." The kid concentrated harder after that and handled the ball more cleanly. That was the whole idea. Hoy ran them through more drills than they knew existed: Figure eights, dribbling the ball in between and around their legs; Panthers, dribbling between their legs sideways as they scissor step back and forth; and the Nutcracker.

"It's not named after the ballet," Hoy said as the campers spread their legs and bounced the ball, hard, between them, backwards, catching it behind their back. "Just be smarter than the ball and don't let it hit you. Will this drill make you quicker? Yes. Will it teach you to concentrate? Yes. Hey, you, over there in the yellow bermudas. Nice shorts."

Between humorous insults and smiles, Hoy served it up southern style. "You're all all-stars at your schools and you aren't used to hearing this, but let me tell you, you're god-awful ballhandlers. There are a million little things you can do to gain an edge. When you get home, you better make sure you drag your lazy butts out of bed and do this stuff. Before you even eat breakfast, get out in the driveway and start practicing."

Setting up four chairs in a straight line, he continued: "There's no reason you can't do something like this at home. These are First Team, All-Conference chairs, and before we're through they will have more steals than any player in Division I. I want you to dribble around these chairs, keeping your eyes on me at the far end. You point guards have to look up at all times to read the defense and also to get plays from the coach and call them out. And you big guys never know when you may need to take the ball upcourt or dribble out after a rebound. Pay attention.

"I want you to start at the first chair with a fake. Come to a jump stop on both feet so either one can be your pivot foot. Hit the ball on your knee to draw the defender and then do a crossover step around him. Do a stutter step around the second chair and add one little thing. Look inside and then go outside. Do a spin move at the third chair, keeping it fast and low. Stay tight on the spin. Remember, anytime you do a move, the ball is vulnerable. Keep it below the seat of the chair. Last, go behind your back, going off your front foot. Why the front foot? Because you can push off with it and the next step protects the basketball.

"While you are doing this, keep your eyes on me. As I hold up fingers, shout out how many I have up. If you don't see or if you dribble into a chair, you do 10 pushups. If you were all like Michael Jordan with his athletic skills, maybe you wouldn't have to worry so much about ballhandling, but you are all just regular nerds and I happen to know Mr. Jordan works his tail off so you'd all better too."

Within moments, basketballs were ricocheting off chair legs like bullets off boulders and kids were hitting the ground, not for protection but for pushups. Hoy was rootin' and tootin' and the kids were smiling while finding out where they stood. There was more to this game than met the eye. "In November," Hoy said, "these chairs are going to be living, breathing opponents. If you don't do this stuff now, hard, you'll be sitting on the bench. That's not what your parents paid for when they sent you here. Have fun but work hard."

*   *   *   *   *

The campers seemed to pass through a time warp going from Hoy to Jamie Ciampaglio at the "Art of Free Throw Shooting" station. It was slow-motion personified, which is exactly what he wanted. The first player recruited by P.J. Carlesimo when he was at Wagner College, Ciampaglio was ranked fourth in the nation in charity tosses in 1981, shooting 91 percent. An ex-camper, he worked under Rick Pitino at BU before heading south to the University of Texas.

"Slow down, relax," he told the campers, and as he spoke their eyes drifted, which was his whole point. He was putting them to sleep deliberately. "I shouldn't have to tell you the importance of free throw shooting," Ciampaglio said. "In the 1989 NCAA championship game, Gerald Green of Seton Hall had a one-and-one with a minute left. He missed. With less than 10 seconds left, Rumeal Robinson went to the line, made his, and Michigan won. A lot of other things happened during the course of the game, but one guy missed and one guy didn't and it meant a national title.

"The key to shooting a foul shot is concentration. If you just slow down and concentrate, your free throw shooting percentage will increase. Keep in mind that you should do the same thing every time. Get a routine. I don't care if you stick your tongue out like Michael Jordan or get low like Bill Bradley used to do at Princeton, but never deviate from your routine. If you don't have a routine, get one. While you're at camp, find one and do it.

"I always take a deep breath before starting my routine, but whatever you do, after you're relaxed, get your feet set and comfortably spread. Line your right shoulder up with the middle of the basket. If your outdoor courts back home don't have foul lines, look close where the foul line would normally be. Every court in America has a tiny hole lined up directly with the middle of the rim. It is there to line things up correctly and you can use that as a guide.

"When you get the ball, let it set comfortably in your hands, fingers spread wide with just the pads of your fingers touching the ball. Tuck your elbow so it is directly under the ball. You want balance. Once it's set, stop. Relax. Concentrate. Fix your eyes on the rim and imagine the ball going in. Bend your knees. Anytime your shot is short, it comes from your legs. Fatigue and not practicing are the major reasons you don't bend your knees.

"Don't shoot flat-footed," Ciampaglio said. "Go up on your toes and your shot will be over the rim. Most of the time you won't be getting the rebound. Be ready if it comes but after you release the ball, hold your hands out and watch the ball go through the basket. Your middle finger should be pointing toward the floor and you should keep your eyes on the rim. Complete the shot. End it.

"In a game or while you're practicing, if you make the shot, stay on the line. You should only break the line when you miss to get reset. We never let guys slap hands at Texas. When Chris Mullin was at St. John's, guys like Walter Berry would walk over and slap his hand after he made a shot, but if you noticed, Mullin never took his eyes off the rim."

* * * * *

Garf couldn't have done better if he made it up, putting Evan Pickman on "The Screening Game" station. An East Coast scout for the Los Angeles Clippers, Pickman is a tenured health and physical education professor at the College of Staten Island and the head basketball man at Kutcher's Sports Academy in Monticello, Clair Bee's old summer stomping grounds. "This is the best camp for basketball I've ever seen," Pickman said.

"The first time I came here I hurt my ankle. I got hooked up with electrodes and was OK after five days, but I lost money. I flew in and anded up spending $100 on food. My wife asked me why I killed myself like that for $225 a week, but Five-Star is where you learn at the highest level in the field. They teach more than X's and O's. They teach kids about life."

Pickman's job was to show the campers how to set screens and use them intelligently. A small man with a big voice and a bit of Broadway flair, he said, "You'd better watch and listen today because it will be noticeable if you don't. Coaches expect you to know things at the higher levels and it will show up in the the games you play here too if you don't. There are a lot of great athletes who will never play in college or the pros because they can't think and they can't remember things they've been told."

Pickman split the campers into separate groups of offense and defense to begin his station and right off the bat one group got off to a bad start, walking to their places. "It really pisses me off when you guys don't even know how to hustle for drills by now," he said. "This is what Five-Star is all about, breaking bad habits." That got the lead out and they were all ears after that, but that would change too before he was finished.

Pickman approached the subject from two levels, explaining the fundamentals so the kids setting the screens and the kids having to read them could understand him perfectly. "Why do we set picks? We want the defense to think. That's when they start making mistakes. The easiest job in basketball is guarding the man with the ball. It doesn't take any brains. All you need is heart. All you need to do is say to yourself, 'I don't give a shit what this guy does, there's no way he's beating me.' If you get beat five straight times, maybe you should think about taking up tennis.

"The second easiest job is denying your man the basketball. It takes no mind at all. It's all attitude, so what we want to do is make the defense think, force them to make mental errors. That's how we get good shots. To do that, we have to be in control. To set a pick, the most important thing is timing. Time the screen so the man using it can read it and time his movements accordingly.

"Find the defensive man first and get a good stance. Do it like you mean it." Pickman demonstrated and said, "Look at my legs, gentlemen. This is the stance you want. Stand firm with your knees bent. Keep your hands close to your body or it's a foul. If you are coming from behind, give the guy one step. If you are on the side, peripherally, you can go right up next to him.

"The hard part is using the screen. A lot of guys are too anxious. They don't have enough patience to let the screen develop and then they whine to the coach that the screens don't work. It's because they're moving too soon. The first thing you do, when you see the screen coming, is move your defender away from it. Fake away from the screen and make it a real fake. No disco moves. No dancing out there. Then, run your man into it. Brush your teammate on the way past. Did you ever see Vinnie Johnson of the Detroit Pistons use a screen? That's how to use a screen.

"Now we've got the defense thinking and making mistakes. What do they do? Do both defenders follow the guy coming off the screen? If that happens, then the screener is open. And you guys making the pass, don't make a weak pass, especially you big guys. Maybe in high school you're never out on top, but there are a lot of 6'8" guys playing guard in the NBA.

"The key to the whole thing is to communicate, gentlemen, and I don't mean just with words. This is a new level. Everybody can talk and hear, but the Division I way, the big-time way, is communicating with your eyes. Look. See the whole floor."

*　*　*　*　*

The campers at the NCAA league "Rebounding, Blocking Out, and Pitching Out" station were keeping their eyes open too, anything to make sure Christian Laettner didn't get a piece of them. Laettner, getting ready for his sophomore season at Duke, was back as a counselor, assisting Paul Pryma and making life miserable under the boards.

Pryma, the head coach at St. Ignatius High in Chicago, started out telling the kids to be nice, then told them to get nasty. "While we're working here and when you go back to your high schools, work like hell. Do everything hard. Be active under the boards. Active people are happy people and happy people feel confident. Once you're confident, good things start to happen. We're here to talk about rebounding and the outlet pass and I want you to be active when you work. This is where it counts. Practice doesn't make perfect. Practice makes permanence."

Pryma tried to go on but couldn't. One kid, Curtis Chenault, a 6'2" swingman from Princeton High in Cincinnati, was goofing around. He was probably just tired and it was innocent play and he was paying attention, but Pryma didn't appreciate it. He had already given the kid one or two warning stares but then abruptly laid it on him. "There's something you gotta understand, Curtis. You gotta pick and choose the times to screw around.

"I've seen you work hard so I know you can do it, but you piss me off messing around and you'll piss other guys off too." Pryma let it go at that and Chenault was cool about it. He didn't mind that the coach had gotten on him a little. "I had it coming," Chenault said later. "I knew I shouldn't have been doing it. When I get put down like that or pushed by a coach, it makes me work harder."

Pryma didn't miss a beat. "You've all been told that rebounding is 90 percent desire, so the next thing you want to think about when getting defensive rebounds is your stance," he said. "You want your feet wider than your shoulders and your back straight. Your head should be in the middle of your stance with your chin up. Have your hands up by your head and be active. When you get the rebound, use your elbows to carve a space. If you move the ball around and use your elbows to carve a space, even when nobody is on you, the ref is less likely to call it a foul.

"There are four concepts in defensive rebounding. The first thing is to communicate. When you see a shot go up, yell 'Shot.' Basketball is great in that it forces you to share. Don't be afraid to talk to your teammates. Next is contact. After the shot is up, step right at your man. If you do that and get your foot right in his jock, he'll stop. If he steps at you, let him. Then you can turn and box him out. As soon as you do, go into your stance.

"Find the ball by focusing on the area you think it will be in and remember to stay active. Use your arms to feel what the offensive man is doing. The last thing is to get the ball. When you do, keep it high. Bring it to your head, around your chin, and carve a space. Refs will protect your head if you keep the ball high but not your arms if you bring it low." What Pryma was teaching was no different than Gillen or any of the others, but having Laettner there allowed him to add a new dimension.

"A quarter of a second," Pryma said. "That's the difference between a layup and an uncontested layup at our end of the floor. A quarter of a second. The key to a good fast break is the outlet pass, and the way to make the rebounder a quarter of a second faster is to have him spin on the way down. He should get ready to release that outlet pass on the way down to the floor. In order to do that his teammate has to yell 'Outlet' to let him know where he is.

"What we're going to do is break up into teams and work on that with Christian. He's the offensive man and I'm going to put the ball off the glass. I want his defender to grab the rebound and make the outlet pass with Christian all over his ass. I want the defense yelling 'Shot,' and I want the guys on the wings yelling 'Outlet.' If somebody doesn't do their job, everybody does 10 quick ones."

Pryma didn't mention that Laettner was going to be an animal. He was up and down the spine of unsuspecting Maurice Sheard of Natick, Massachusetts, clawing and scratching him from behind like it was the NCAA finals and Duke was down by one. Sheard came down with it anyway, but his teammates hadn't done their parts so everyone had to hit the pavement for pushups. Then Laettner made his first mistake. He taunted Jeff Gruber, a 5'10" junior, give or take an inch, from St. Joe's in South Bend, Indiana.

Gruber did everything right, boxing out the big Blue Devil and yelling "Shot," but Laettner just reached right over him like someone 6'11" should. He started to rag the kid good-naturedly, telling him he "looked sweet, like a wimp" going up for the ball. Gruber asked to go at him again and tore into Laettner like a bobcat, but he still got beat. It was just something he had to do.

After stations were over Gruber admitted that he'd been pretty nervous checking in the first night, seeing all the tall guys shadowing over him and his basketball future. That had something to do with him taking on Laettner. But he was also head-to-toe court burns. "If I went back home without them I'd be embarrassed," he said, smiling warmly. His eyes darted to the side as he talked, which for him was strange. He was usually direct, totally centered, almost meditative at stations, but he was restless. Off to his left, the Morning Mini-Lecture was in progress and he wanted to be there. Will Rey was giving a clinic on the three-point shot.

* * * * *

Will Rey is like a watch repairman. He takes the game of basketball apart, shows a kid what makes it tick, then puts it back together again, better. He is well-prepared and orderly. His Morning Mini-Lectures are always concise and usually SRO. Kids know a good thing when they see it. The head coach at Loyola of Chicago, Rey served his apprenticeship on the schoolboy circuit in the Windy City, his hometown, and at Evansville College from 1985 to 1989 under Jim Crews.

Rey has been tinkering with things at Five-Star for 10 years. He is head coach and substitute straight man for Garf's three-point exhibition in the absence of Dave Odom or Tom McCorry and camp chauffeur at Pitt, a position of prominence. He motors Garf up and down the hillsides in the company golf cart, sparing himself the added legwork in the process. "It is a special feeling to come back here every year," Rey says. "Garf makes you feel like the camp couldn't run without you." It would, but without Will Rey it wouldn't be as precise.

When Jeff Gruber finally made it over to his workshop, Rey was deep into the gears and gizmos of the three-point shot. It was only 11 o'clock in the morning but already hovering around 90 degrees and humid. Typical Pitt weather. "I know it's hot and you may think I'm spending too much time on details," Rey was saying, "but let me quote Tom Heinsohn to show you why I do this. You all know Heinsohn as the colorman for NBA games on TV, but he used to play for the great Boston Celtics teams in the Bill Russell and Bob Cousy era.

"Heinsohn said that Larry Bird is such a great player because he is a master of the half-inch. That is the difference between making and not making a play. That little edge. Against good defensive teams, you are only going to have a split second to get your shot off and you have to be ready when the chance comes.

"The addition of the three-point shot to the game has created three distinct shooting ranges: the inside, power game from underneath the basket to the foul line; the mid-range game from 12 feet out to the three-point line and the three-point zone. To be effective from the three-point zone, a player or team must be able to score from the mid-range area consistently. That opens both inside and outside scoring opportunities.

"To get that half-inch edge you need, you first have to 'shape up.' What I mean is get ready to shoot before you receive the basketball. Look for the three-point line without the ball. Position yourself on the court one-and-a-half to two feet behind the line. If you are a right-handed shooter, your plant foot, your left foot, should be forward and pointed directly at the basket. Your right foot should be back.

"Don't run behind the line, slide, to save time and space. And keep the proper distance from the line. It would be a shame to have your toe on the line on the shot. Keep your shoulders in front of your feet and your tail end down. Time your movements to the pass. The key is to have your hands ready. Give your teammate a good target for the pass. Let him see your palm. Catch the pass with your shooting hand behind the ball. Don't catch it with your hands together. That chews up time to get ready and besides, the two-hand set shot is obsolete."

Glancing sheepishly over his shoulder to make certain Garf hadn't heard that last remark, Rey continued: "Shape up. Don't wait until you receive the ball to get set. Catch the ball on your right foot and step forward on the left immediately into your shot. Now that you can get your shot off quickly, you should understand how to accomplish it within a team concept. You should be able to recognize what to do based on what the defense gives you.

"One thing you can do is penetrate and pitch. Against a zone, the ballhandler splits the seam. Make sure you keep your ass down low when you do and protect the basketball. As the man penetrates, his teammate creates distance from him, shaping up behind the three-point line. If the defense converges on the ballhandler, he turns his back to the basket and makes a sharp, snap pass back to the three-point shooter. It has to be done in synch. Everything is saving time and space in basketball. If the three-point shooter has a shot, the ballhandler should yell 'Shot' and then turn and look for the rebound.

"You post men should be able to recognize situations too, especially if the basketball is fed into you down low and you are double-teamed. Kick the ball back out. The three-point shooters can help with that situation. After the pass inside, they should read the head turn of the defender doubling down on the post man. Slide over to his blind side so he doesn't know where you are and shape up. If you see the defender doubling down, yell 'Double.' And post men, if you see the double team, dish it back out and yell 'Shot.'

Rey made the concepts as clear as crystal but there was also reality to consider. Observing the goings-on from underneath the basket was Brian Hopgood of Millwood High in Oklahoma City, Oklahoma. A good-natured kid and a hard worker, he'd seen a lot in a short time and knew he wouldn't be shooting many threes, not unless he wanted to find his 6'10" butt on the bench. He listened respectfully as Rey talked about big guys like him taking a beating and then dishing it back out to the gnats for unmolested "J's."

Contemplating his war wounds, Hopgood mumbled, "If I get it low, I'm puttin' it up." He was thinking out loud more than anything and not second-guessing Rey when he also muttered, "Anybody coming in to double-team me is going to get an elbow." It was a convincing argument, one he voiced eloquently all week, earning a spot in the Orange-White Classic. He found the little guys when he had to.

Every morning and for millions of combined minutes the stations breath life into Five-Star. But they are not something that can merely be observed and understood. They must be absorbed, like a fine and pure basketball dust that sinks in slowly only with sweat and patience. They are an ever-changing, ever-becoming thing Garf would gladly stand in line to see.

SIXTEEN
Garf's Gang Rules the Rails

*"The new thing in us, the added thing, has entered
into our heart, has gone into its inmost chamber and
is not even there any more—is already in our blood."*

– Rainer Maria Rilke

"Yo, Howie, Yo, Howie, Yo, Howie."

The campers weren't being rude. They were singing, trying to
cheer Garf up. He was tense and getting tenser by the minute. Pitt
II falls within one of the NCAA's Live Periods and the coaches and
recruiters had descended on Five-Star. They were coming out of the
woodwork like roundball roaches.

It was Sunday morning. Some of the campers had already been
to church. Garf and Will Klein always invite a priest in when the
Day of Rest falls in the middle of a camp session. It goes back to
the days of Jack Donahue's Friendship Farm. Donahue was a
devout Catholic and used to bring in Father Slough from the local
parish to say mass. Garf thought it was a nice touch and even attended when he could. At Five-Star, everyone is welcome, and unless there's a dire emergency, no other activities take place during
services.

It is a sacred time but not without its moments of levity. Garf
likes his sermons brief and to the point. He doesn't want someone
hogging the pulpit. For a while at Pitt he had a padre who was particularly good and fast. He would have made a nice little point guard

for the Vatican five. One year Garf introduced him as "the top priest in Pittsburgh," and the campers, no disrespect intended, howled.

Court Two, where the campers assemble every morning before stations for announcements, was no place for a man of the cloth Sunday morning. Garf was uptight. He had already called The King every name in the book and was looking for someone else on whom to vent his wrath. Anyone foolish enough to pass within earshot would do, and even the sleepiest campers could sense his mounting fury. He never hides it well. If someone isn't sticking with the program, he's going to let them know about it. Young and old alike quickly learn to recognize the symptoms.

So everyone was toeing the line, but with the coaches there it was impossible to escape unscathed. The King did all he could, scanning the sidelines to make sure he got everyone's name and college affiliation so Garf could introduce them. He did it every morning and afternoon, keeping track of the numbers which rose into the hundreds as the Orange-White Classic approached, and even though he read them off quickly, it was like each one was accompanied by a drum roll and cymbal crash.

He was stretched tighter than taut wire and ready to snap, and the campers were trying to loosen him up. The veterans got it going. Only they would dare. A handful of them in the back of the bleachers started out quietly, singing "Yo, Howie, Yo, Howie," clapping rhythmically before each "Yo." It had a rap beat, patterned after the musical group MC Hammer's rap chant, "Go, Hammer." Garf waved his hand at them to stop, but that just made them worse.

They kept it up and the rest picked up the slack and with 400 of them rocking back and forth in their seats and getting stronger, no matter how much Garf snarled, something had to give. They wanted him to shoot, but he was too keyed up for that. He'd have been out there all night. Instead, he danced. It was short and sweet, nothing more than a pit-a-pat with a nice little Cagney Stroll to finish up, but it was dancing. It would never replace the Moonwalk, but it got Garf back in the swing of things.

* * * * *

Recruiting knows no Sabbath. Garf understands what having swarms of recruiters in camp does for business, but he is not completely happy when the place is thick with them. In the Orin-Sekwa and Camp Rosemont era it was fun having a few of the boys over for a look-see and a nightcap. It was still examining the merchandise, but it was different somehow. It seemed more innocent and not at all sordid. Guys stayed all week and pitched in at stations.

Everybody knew everybody and it wasn't a crime to help a guy find a good player and possibly help save his job.

Now, heaven forbid if Garf forgets to introduce someone. The campers couldn't have missed seeing the recruiters if they tried. They stand out like beacons in their short-sleeved sportshirts with their school insignias emblazoned over their hearts. None of them even says "boo" to the kids, which is what the rules stipulate, but the silence only adds to the tension, making the air feel heavy, like a prison yard. Still, there is a lot of private conversing and finger pointing and that's what was at the bottom of the whole recruiting problem.

That's what got everybody's blood stirred up. Not the recruiting process itself. A guy does what he has to do. It's the paranoia thing rearing its ugly head or maybe it isn't, depending on which side of the fence you're on. Most of the recruiters can visit Five-Star for only two or three weeks a summer and when they do it's like they're mimes. A privileged few of their colleagues, on the other hand, could work the camp seven weeks if Garf felt like hiring them and chatter away like magpies the whole time.

That was bad enough, but what really irked everyone was having to watch Garf's Guys chew the rag with blue-chippers while they had to stand there like mummies. Less than 10 feet away Garf's Guys were rubbing elbows and having the time of their lives with the same hot prospects they'd give their right hands to have. Theoretically, Garf's Guys could take a kid aside to demonstrate a move and put the moves on them instead. Even if everything was being done aboveboard, it didn't seem right to anyone confined to the sidelines, and if you asked them it was downright suspicious.

*   *   *   *   *

It is not a pretty sight seeing grown men grovel in the presence of teenagers. Five-Star did not create the spectacle. It goes on elsewhere, incessantly, and it has for years, but the fact remains: It is not attractive. It is what college basketball recruiting becomes. There are a few who wear it well. Some dress it up better than others, and ideally it gives a lot of kids a chance to make something of themselves, but the process, seen from the outside, is nothing to write home about.

For years, some coaches and recruiters claimed that Garf's Guys were making things even worse. Why should they be allowed to associate with the kids, no matter how pure their intentions, if everyone couldn't? Opinion was divided on the issue when it finally hit the fan.

Garf argued that kids didn't choose a college based on the assistant coach. Except for Pete Gillen and later Dave Odom and a handful of others, head college coaches rarely worked the camp and if they did it was because they'd come up through the ranks. He remembers Jerry Wainwright one year developing a friendship with a kid named Chris Weshinsky. It was a genuine friendship. They just got along. Wainwright taught the kid plenty at Station 13 and they had fun. Afterwards, he recruited Wechinsky diligently for Wake Forest.

"Wechinsky went to Michigan State and that's very typical of what happens," Garf says. "It also happened to Will Rey, who recruited a kid named Mike Lipniski out of Pitt IV very hard and didn't get him. Lipniski went to Western Illinois. Jerry Wainwright and Will Rey are two of the most popular guys in camp history and neither got their man. I once gave the NCAA a list of coaches who worked certain weeks and the kids they successfully recruited who were in camp during the same weeks. The numbers were so miniscule they were to be laughed at.

"It's not that the coaches are bad recruiters, it's simply that they aren't using the camp to cheat. And even if they did recruit kids at camp, it wouldn't matter. They probably wouldn't go anyway, because prospects go to a certain school because of the head coach, not an assistant coach. It's true that our people rub shoulders with prospects for an entire week, but there's just as much chance a coach could turn a kid off as turn him on. I've heard of that happening as much as I've heard anything. Our coaches never hesitate to counsel a kid aggressively, whether he's the best player in camp or just another high school player.

"To be factual about this, Five-Star Camp has never hired a college coach. Will Klein and I didn't hire college coaches in the beginning and we're not hiring college coaches now. Every one of these people were high school coaches or college players returning as counselors who went on to become college or pro coaches. But we don't even see them as that. To us they are our guys, giving up their summers to work hard and improve. That's all. They started with us, we hired them, and we can hire and fire anyone we want. They are our own people.

"As far as I'm concerned, Dave Odom might as well still be a teacher at Durham High. Tom McCorry is still coaching his ass off at St. Dominic's, and Rick Pitino is still the youngest stationmaster in Five-Star history as a junior at the University of Massachusetts. If they moved on to do great things, that's super for them, but we didn't hire them after they made it big-time. We hired them before. If they became outstanding college coaches or, in the case of Rick Pitino, Hubie Brown, Mike Fratello, and on and on, great pro coaches, is that a sin? Are we supposed to not hire them because of that? Are we supposed to fire them because they reached the pinnacle of success in their field?

"Guys like Will Rey, Tom McCorry, Pete Gillen, Brendan Malone, Jerry Wainwright, and all the others helped fill this camp with players when they were high school coaches. They were loyal and they are even more important to us now because they have gained experience and stature. All our coaches teach their guts out on the court. It's very hard to explain to an outsider how important these people are and what they've done for the camp. The teaching and guidance they provide is what Five-Star is all about.

"Not only do they work at stations and Station 13 and give lectures, they work as commissioners and help us run and organize the camp. I can't emphasize enough the fact that the 132—and counting—guys who have moved up in the ranks, some of whom have been with us as long as 25 years, helped build the camp into what it is today. There's no way we would ever give them up voluntarily.

"There are some ignorant people who say that having college coaches working at Five-Star is bad for the game of basketball. Our coaches are among the best teachers and organizers in the sport. They are not bad for the game, they are good for the game. Nothing they do at camp goes against the game. I know I'm not overestimating their ability and value as coaches and teachers whenever I hear them talk to our campers the way they do, the messages they deliver. They can only help the game and make the campers better people.

"If a kid learns something other than basketball from one of our guys, then that kid is better off, and if he spreads his better-offness to other kids, that makes the world a better place to live in. I'm not overestimating the importance of that. I take that very seriously. Is it really bad for the game because there are people who aren't working at Five-Star who are jealous of the people who are? No, it's just bad for the people who are jealous."

Big guns got involved in the verbal shoot-out. Outsiders wanted Garf's Guys outside with them. Either that or change the rules so everybody could go inside and scout whenever they wanted. Opposition to Five-Star's system built slowly but surely. In 1986 a three-man committee comprised of USC coach George Raveling, St. John's head man Lou Carnesecca, and George Blaney, the coach at Holy Cross, asked Garf to voluntarily give up his practice of rehiring college coaches.

"I told them I would think about it and get back to them with an offer," he says. "When I talked to them again I said I would give up my guys if they made it illegal for a kid to go to any college-run camp between his junior and senior year. That's where the real edge is. Either that or call it a paid visit. I suggested they do that if they were really trying to help the sport, but they never got back to me."

In January of 1989 NCAA-member coaches considered regulations that would bar Division I coaches from working or lecturing at camps not run by NCAA-member institutions, Five-Star included.

Observers of the game had mixed points of view.

Al McGuire: "The Coaches' Association and NCAA constantly put Five-Star under a microscope like there had to be something wrong there. They couldn't believe it was like Caesar's wife, beyond reproach. Five-Star is a wholesome experience. It is the first and last of the great teaching camps and the teaching never gets the paint it deserves. Howie's intentions are extremely honorable, but there's an old saying too: 'You can't be a person's friend and a flatterer too.'

"Just because a person's intentions are honorable doesn't mean everything that is done is right. Obviously you prefer certain people to others in your profession and if one of them ends up with some recruit from your camp, either from direct or indirect influence, the other guy is gonna think to himself, 'That guy or that camp is hurting us.' That person and that camp are Howie and Five-Star. That's gonna happen no matter what you do.

"Things change and certain things like TV and videos have come into it. I believe the NCAA had no choice. Garf didn't hire coaches with the intent of giving them an advantage. The loyalty developed because of their dedication. Like anyone else, they moved up the ladder and as they moved up, Five-Star was a part of their world. It is a case where both people were right, but for the good of basketball and the appeasement of the coaches not intimate with or working at Five-Star, the NCAA had to do something. It was the lesser of two evils."

Billy Packer: "Obviously guys have advantages in life. That's what life is all about, to have some advantages. An awful lot of coaches, as you go down the list, who have now become extremely successful on the highest levels didn't start off trying to take advantage. They started out as grunt workers. Over the years guys weren't invited back who came only to look at players. Only guys who gave something back to the camp were invited back.

"Whether you're Dave Odom, Rick Pitino, Hubie Brown, or Bob Knight, who was a fledgling coach at Army in the early days, I don't think any of the guys who have really devoted themselves to camp work did it on the basis that it was a big recruiting advantage. I think there's a real love for the game and I think it's unfortunate that legislation would have to come down that would take away guys who really devoted a lot to Five-Star."

Garf's Guys were not blind to the realities of recruiting but questioned the motives of protestors.

Pete Gillen: "The advantage is not so much whom to recruit as whom not to recruit. If anyone says it's not an advantage that way they are lying. Personally, though, I might get to know a kid from watching him, but I do not sell Xavier University at camp. If I weren't the head coach at Xavier I would still come to Five-Star. I have been coming here forever and I don't think people should deprive me of something I've done forever. Maybe it's not fair, but life isn't fair and I resent people telling me I can't work at camp and make a few bucks and make some contacts."

Dave Odom: "I feel I gain much more personally than professionally being at Five-Star. I love the opportunity to work with and coach eager basketball players. It is a bittersweet position as far as having an advantage. I admit there are many advantages to me as the Wake Forest coach and the university itself in my being there, but there is not only an opportunity to praise and instruct. It is necessary to discipline a kid every now and then and great players do not block out confrontations.

"We are not operating in any dark shadows at Five-Star. I have no problem with people objecting to the rule allowing me to go. I have found that most objections are to the rules, not to me personally doing what the rules allow. I do not deny that we have informal contact with the players, but every situation has built-in advantages. We all have advantages we must play to."

Tom McCorry: "Coaches never associated with Five-Star perceive it as an advantage to work there and most will try to take something away from someone who worked for it rather than try to work for something of their own. You can talk all you want about the advantage I have because of day-to-day contact with kids, but that's not why I've been a part of the camp for 22 years.

"Recruiting is a high-pressure, jealous situation now. There is a lot of flat-out cheating, out-and-out buying of players. Schools cheat on academics and there are always ways around whatever proposition is passed. The lack of ethics is what's at the bottom of it. That is the worst part. Destroying the credibility of another college's coach is a very common thing to do. Power corrupts. Once you've got it your job is to protect it, and those who haven't got it want it. As long as there is big money involved it will be like this."

Garf's closest friends in the business were not necessarily in his corner, including Mike Krzyzewski, a member of the NCAA-member coaches' legislative committee, and Bob Knight.

Mike Krzyzewski: "Coaches shouldn't be allowed to work at Five-Star during the so-called Dead Periods, the NCAA quiet periods. That gives out the wrong vibe because recruiting is a tough business and we have rules we have to follow. It's kinda like when those coaches work there, they are getting around the rules. It's legal, but the intent of the rules is not being followed. I would like to see that not happen or to see the NCAA rule change to allow it to happen.

"I'm not saying anything illegal is going on, but the coaches are there for a week interacting with the kids. It's like they could say to a kid, 'Let me show you something individually that you can work on that the coach at some other school is not doing.' It doesn't affect our program as much as it affects mid-major programs and coaches who really have to develop close contact with a kid. At that level it is a very big recruiting advantage."

Bob Knight: "I've argued this point with Howard and sometimes he looks at things with very narrow vision when it comes to Five-Star, but it all depends on whose ox is getting gored.

"Is it an unfair advantage? Absolutely, and I've told Howard that for years. Any guy who is a grad assistant or an assistant coach or part-time coach, none of those people should be allowed to work at any camp except those on the campus of the institution for which they work, and I feel very strongly about that.

"As far as camps like mine and others, there is a tremendous difference in the quality of players at one of the specialty camps as opposed to a camp for kids on the college campus. We don't get those type of kids. And why is there gonna be any teaching lost? There are so many good high school coaches who work at that camp and, in fact, getting rid of some of those guys is simply getting rid of recruiters instead of coaches. Maybe Jerry Wainwright is a really good teacher and I'm sure that he is, but there's somebody else who can teach extremely well."

Stuck in the middle was the NCAA.

Bob Minnix, NCAA Director of Enforcement: "As far as it being an earned advantage, it may be to Garf because he's employing those people and it may be earned in that sense, in the eyes of Howard Garfinkel, but not necessarily in the eyes of the NCAA. The NCAA's rules don't give out brownie points for working one's ass off at Five-Star. We don't have such priorities.

"On the other hand, it is a question of fairness and trust in my mind. Coaches keep complaining about the extra contact, but we have never deemed it important enough to keep statistics on their complaints. I have never launched a full-scale investigation into activities at the camp.

"Presidents and faculty representatives are the leaders in formulating legislation that runs the NCAA as far as rules with summer camps. I ask them all the time if they've ever observed the camp or talked to a kid about his time there to see if he was badgered by a coach about going to a certain school. I'll bet you right now 10 out of 10 presidents and faculty reps would say no, they never asked a kid that, so how do they know what's going on?

"What happens very often is that if a hotshot recruiter loses a kid he finds it difficult to accept that he got outrecruited that time. He finds it hard to accept that maybe this time the kid didn't like him. Recruiters come back to a college and promote the excuse that there was an advantage, either because some other coach worked the camp and got him that way or because the coach cheated. The offended coach goes to his athletic director, who naturally wants to believe all his assistant coaches and his head coach that that is why they lost a certain recruit.

"Those rumors filter up to the president or faculty rep of the university, neither of whom have most likely ever attended a summer camp of any type. They want to take it for gospel truth because their people are saying it. From personal experience, and obviously I have my job to do, but personally I graduated from Notre Dame. I was a scholarship player, so I have always taken a kind of special interest in Notre Dame. I noticed that when Pete Gillen was an assistant there, there was not an inordinate number of great recruits going there from Five-Star."

The proposed legislation was voted down in 1989 but put to a second vote a year later with different results. Five-Star would cross that bridge when it was built. For the moment, everyone was content gazing at greener pastures and Garf, over the next few days, had some old friends to greet.

* * * * *

Chuck Daly cruised into Pitt like nothing had changed. You wouldn't know it, listening to him and Garf catching up on things, that he and the Detroit Pistons had just won an NBA championship. Waiting to lecture, he was gruff-voiced and dressed to the nines like he always was but still just one of the guys. He could just as easily have been sitting in the Orin Rec Hall with Cingiser and Buckley and the boys.

He and Garf weren't even discussing basketball. They were

laughing about how whenever Daly visited New York, he always dragged Garf kicking and screaming down to Barneys, a high-class Seventh Avenue haberdashery. It wasn't that Garf disliked the place. The problem was Daly and his reputation as one of the best-dressed guys in the business. Every time he was in town, he talked Garf into going down there to help him pick stuff out. "I never buy anything," Daly was saying, "but Garf ends up being broke for the next three months."

The Pistons' coach more than squared things at two o'clock, Five-Star time. He was the afternoon lecturer on Monday, and when Garf brought him out he mentioned that at that very moment he could have been pocketing a few thousand dollars speaking elsewhere. Garf didn't say so at the time, but Daly was getting only a few hundred dollars plus expenses for this gig.

The pay scale at Five-Star has never been what anyone would call exorbitant. The afternoon lecturers, Five-Star prime-timers, get roughly 300 bucks for their trouble plus expenses. The coaches haul in anywhere from 130 to 400 a week depending on the job they do and their seniority. With all the trainers and other staffers, the payroll comes to about 15 grand a week. "There is no way we could ever pay these guys what they are worth," Garf says. "If we tried to we wouldn't have a camp. They have to be flexible."

They are, and Daly isn't the type to forget his roots anyway. There's no way to put a price tag on a thing like friendship or what Five-Star means to him. He wouldn't keep coming back if money were the lure.

There were almost as many coaches as campers in the gym when Daly rolled up his sleeves and got busy. As he talked they tried to keep up with what he was saying, writing everything down in notebooks, but as he got into it more, they put down their pencils and just listened. It wasn't stuff they could read later and under-stand. It was necessary to hear it and let it sink in.

Right off the bat Daly put them on the spot. "Do you know where your players want the ball on the court?" he asked. "When I went to the Philadelphia 76ers as an assistant, I was there about two weeks when Julius Irving asked me that. He wondered if I knew where he liked to get the ball. It had never occurred to me that it mattered, but a player like Doug Collins, for instance, liked shooting from the right corner. He hated the left corner."

It was like another world opening up of players with one or two unique skills and having to create special situations for them and in-corporating their style into a team concept. And for the campers, everything they were learning at stations suddenly made more sense. The whole idea of knowing your strengths and working on your weaknesses to give yourself options was clear. There were so many players with so much talent it was scary, but it all came down to what a person did with it and his ability to adapt.

"Our league is a tough way to go," Daly said. "A lot of people look at the glamour of the NBA, but one of the major differences for any of you guys coming in that nobody thinks about is the lifestyle. You guys are probably saying, 'This guy's full of shit,' but for 18 of the past 21 months, the Detroit Pistons were together nearly every day of the week, between practice, playing games, and travel. That takes getting used to.

"I love it when they bring college players in to training camp as rookies. They think that after they've been drafted it's over. Once they get there, it's just the beginning. When we take a kid in the draft, not one of my guys wants to give up one minute of playing time to him. If they lose minutes, it means money. And I'm not a drug expert and you guys will think I'm full of shit again, but you'll all be confronted by drugs. Some of you are possibly already doing drugs. We don't know much about drugs, but we know when someone is late. What matters most is how you handle your time off."

Game time counts too. "Defense is what wins championships," said Daly. "We were 63-19 in the regular season and 15-2 in the playoffs. We won every series on the road and the only way to do that is with defense. Defense doesn't just happen. You all think scoring points makes you win, but if you get on a team that understands the other side and is willing to make the sacrifices, you have something.

"Defensive success is not just the coach. He's just part of it. On shoot-around days before we'd play a team like the Lakers, each one of my players would get a videotape and watch the guys they figured they'd be guarding. They'd watch their favorite moves, their favorite plays, and then walk through them at shoot-around. While they were going through the plays, you could hear them talking among themselves, saying things like, 'We don't want anybody moving on the court without contact.'

"The main difference is that at the NBA level, defense is not a dictatorial thing. Whenever we had to play the Cleveland Cavaliers, I'd tell Isiah he had to guard Mark Price and ask him how he was going to do it. When he tells me it makes all the difference, and guys like Dennis Rodman and Bill Laimbeer, I let them decide how and when to do things like switch on the low post screens. When they decide, there are no excuses. It's their responsibility."

*   *   *   *   *

Ron Rothstein had a tough act to follow the next afternoon. First there was his old boss Daly and then Garf, who was feeling a bit testy. A morning thundershower had put him behind schedule, the recruiters were still underfoot, and it was so hot you could see wavy lines above the courts. To top it off, the gym was like an oven and the tired campers wanted some comic relief. They wanted Garf to shoot.

He had performed well in the past under more difficult conditions. Syracuse coach Jim Boeheim was guest lecturing one afternoon, fielding questions from the floor. His Orangemen were infamous for their inaccuracy from the foul line and one kid wanted to know how such a thing could happen. Having been to the NCAA finals in 1987, it was obvious they could play the game. What was their problem with free throws?

Boeheim, knowing a blind alley when he saw one, sent Garf in blindfolded instead. He didn't exactly avoid the question, but he didn't answer it either. He said making a wide-open, 12-foot shot wasn't as easy as it looked, especially in a pressure situation, and to prove the point he would challenge Garf to make one shot, just one, with the whole gym watching. Cooler than Calvin Murphy, Garf strode to the line and bagged eight in a row. The campers were delirious.

Shooting in front of Rothstein should have been a cakewalk, but Garf was nervous and cranky. Charging around the gym, waiting for everyone to filter in, he scowled as the campers shouted, *"Shoooot,"* finally telling them, "Knock that shit off." They kept it up, though, and he was beside himself and mumbling under his breath about the schedule until Will Rey, egging the kids on the whole time, reached for his whistle and extended both arms like a butler waiting to take his master's robe.

Garf surrendered, went into his schtick, and buried the thing. He had them right where he wanted them. He signaled it "good" first, punching both arms straight up over his head like he'd scored a touchdown, then poked a defiant fist in the campers' faces, pumping his right hand into his bent left arm. Everyone knew what he was trying to say—"Up yours"—and they howled and accepted their just due. Then Garf yelled, "Top that, Rothstein" to complete the spectacle, and the campers were sufficiently warmed up for the coach of the Miami Heat.

Rothstein got the coaches scribbling again in a hurry. "If not for Five-Star I would not be where I am today," he said. "I made it to the

NBA by working my ass off, but I didn't get there by myself. All my associations, guys like Mike Fratello and Chuck Daly, I met here. You have to pay back and there will always be a place in my heart for Garf and this camp. It is like family to me."

The Five-Star Connection. "I have worked here 21 years and I have known Garf personally for 30 years, going back to when I played point guard for his New York Nationals. This is a tough business. "We are a young, struggling team at Miami, but I am proud to be one of 27 coaches in the NBA. If I could get where I am today, there is no reason any coach can't, but if you're willing to settle for second best whenever you fail, you won't. Are there people working as hard as me not in the NBA? Yes. I worked hard and got lucky. I also had to sacrifice to be able to have an opportunity later on.

"I was very fortunate to work with Hubie Brown in New York and Chuck Daly in Detroit. Chuck had enough faith and confidence in me to let me handle game preparation and basically let me be in charge of the defensive schemes. The bottom line, however, was that he made all the decisions and, believe me, moving from an assistant coach's seat on the bench to the Heat head coach's spot is the longest 12 inches in the world.

"When you have to make all the decisions, it is much more draining. After the first couple of games I coached at Miami, my whole body hurt. I was going from a veteran team to a team never before formed and it was very difficult balancing teaching with working with players. And you have to make more decisions in one pro game than in three or four college games. You have to prepare for sequences, not just games. Each team has a distinct style and the mindset is different. The game is constantly changing."

Rothstein gave the players something to think about as well. "I hope none of you guys in here are sleeping," he said, raising a couple of drooping heads. It was sweltering in the gym and getting late in the week. A lot of the campers were beat or at best nearly drained dry. Some weren't even aware that their eyes were shutting. Others were glad of it. How many times did they have to hear this stuff? It seemed like a broken record. They knew they had to bust their butts, but they could always do that later.

"That's just great," Rothstein said. "I guess you guys know so much you can afford to sleep. Why did you come here, to tell your friends you played alongside some great players? I've seen only one guy out of hundreds of All-Americans who thought he was was hot shit make it. The rest of them could shoot the ball and jump over people, but they wanted to do things their way. I saw one guy in a free agent camp, an All-American, get cut. All his life people had told him how great he was. Was he ready for that cut? There are 312 jobs in the NBA and a hell of a lot more guys than that never even get invited to a tryout.

"Almost every single one of them was a big-time high school player. You gotta open up your heart, fellas, and open your minds. Be willing to learn. Never think you know it all because as you go up the talent levels off. Will you always get where you want to go in basketball? No, but if you try you'll always feel good about yourself. If you fall, get off your ass and try again so that if you don't succeed at basketball you'll succeed at something else. Don't be afraid to dream. The opportunities are there.

"You gotta work, though, and be willing to risk embarrassment. How many of you are willing to work at things you're not good at?" To find out, Rothstein set up a drill, emphasizing the necessity of shooting off the pass at higher levels of play. Good defenders don't just stand there and watch a guy shoot, they are in a guy's face, and the NBA is full of them."

Garf volunteered some campers and Rothstein had them catch a pass and shoot, quickly, with a defender coming on them. One kid, Joe Reid, kept getting his shot blocked. Reid, from University School outside Cleveland, Ohio, was smooth and graceful around the glass but, at 6'8," not used to firing away from 15 feet. He took his time getting the ball set and by then the defender was hammering it into downtown Coraopolis.

After the drill, Rothstein walked around holding a hand over each volunteer's head. He told the campers to make a ruckus when he got to someone they thought was shooting too slowly and they chose Reid. A private and resolute young man, he was noticeably discomforted by the attention. "He shouldn't be embarrassed," said Rothstein, placing a reassuring arm on the boy's shoulder. "He just found out somewhere he can improve his game. There are coaches here who can teach you things you will need to know later on. Ask them. What the hell is there to be embarrassed about?

"Little men, to be a great player, you need to be able to put the ball down and take it to the hole with either hand. If you can do that, you are the ultimate offensive threat. The defense can get no edge on you. Get your ball fake down pat. Take your little sister out on the court with a broom if you have to and have her get after you until you get that shot fake down. And don't apologize for taking the shot if you're open from 17 feet on in. If you can hit it consistently, take it.

"Big men, you are a different breed of cat. It is harder for you to handle the ball. Make your moves so the little men can get the rock in to you. And when you get it, don't move it behind your back and up your ass and out your nose, just up-fake and stay in your stance. Keep the ball up, you post men. Little men, remember, you aren't going anywhere as a team without the big man, but force him to make the moves. If he doesn't, don't give him the ball. He'll get the message.

"This is revolutionary, isn't it, fellas? Of course not. This is a simple game we make hard because we don't think. We want to be the star and we play selfish. You hear it all the time, but it's true, this game is *We*, not *I*. It's important to look at your basketball team as your second family. Learn to care about your teammates. They can become people you talk to when things are going well and look to when they aren't going so well.

"But no matter what happens to you from here on, fellas, the most important thing is your own family. Don't ever be afraid to say 'I love you' to your mom and dad. Don't be pissed off when they discipline you. They love you and they make sacrifices for you without you even knowing it. And don't ever be afraid to kiss your father in front of anybody. That's bullshit."

The last part seemed as if Rothstein hadn't planned to say it at all and it had burst from him. That happened sometimes and the campers always perked up when it did. It was something that came from inside the speaker, whether it was Rothstein or whoever, and moved them. Garf got swept up in it too and usually led a Five-Star style standing ovation or say something fitting, but none of that would do with Rothstein. Garf crossed the gym and embraced him.

*   *   *   *   *

Five-Star has its share of quirks. For starters there is The King, who lives for summer and camp yet dislikes stations. He says he doesn't like repeating himself. He doesn't get involved in the rah-rah and also treats new guys like they have the plague, but the place wouldn't be the same without him. "He's a very loyal guy," Garf says. "He's great for the camp even though I might like to see him tone down his act a little. He is a little too harsh on winning and losing, which I don't think is that important in camp. He does challenge the rest of the staff to go for the win, though, and that's made the competition better. He gets on the kids to play hard and smart, and I think they appreciate it. They know where he's coming from."

There's also this thing about the applause. Campers always applaud when guest speakers and lecturers are finished, but they express different levels of enthusiasm. Sometimes they clap for a minute or so and that's that. Other times they stand or get into a rhythmic handclapping. On certain occasions, they do both and there is a kind of secret competition among the lecturers to get the longest and heartiest ovation. It's like being the first one to go hoarse.

The contest is pointless because Hubie Brown wins it hands down whenever he comes to Five-Star. That's as it should be because he's been there longer than anybody except Garf, Will Klein, Marv Kessler, and Bill Aberer. Brown is a charter member with his lifetime dues paid in full, but he keeps giving more. "He is the greatest hoop clinician alive, dead, or yet unborn," Garf says, settling the matter succinctly.

"If I needed more proof, which I don't, I got it returning home from the McDonald's Classic in the spring of 1990. On the flight from Indianapolis to Chicago, I wound up sitting next to the Wizard of Westwood, John Wooden. Coach Wooden told me he'd seen Hubie lecturing on fast break offense and was so excited he wanted to jump out of his chair and start coaching again."

It's no wonder that tradition demands Brown close the week, to have the last word before the playoffs and the Orange-White Classic take over. It's nothing but basketball and kids being lifted to new heights the final day and night of any session, whether it's Radford or Honesdale or Pitt, but before Brown could captivate anyone or before the basketball magic could start to take place, there were chores to do.

When stations ended on Wednesday morning, most of the coaches had raspy throats, and a number of campers were banged up and bandaged, but Al Rhodes was still down on his hands and knees teaching "One-on-One Moves Facing the Basket." He was kneeling, shifting the kids' feet around, and telling them, "You need to know how to get open with the ball, but make your moves within a team concept." They were knocking each other over setting screens and he was helping them up and urging them to give him just a hair more intensity.

It was vintage Indiana. Rhodes grew up there and takes it wherever he goes. He's almost as bad as The Chill when it comes to basketball fairy tales coming true. He led the Warsaw Tigers to a state title in 1984, one year after his first trip to Five-Star. He took along a gang of kids that first year, including Jeff Grose, "Mr. Basketball" in Indiana his senior year, and Steve Hollar, who later had a role in the movie *Hoosiers*. "The confidence they gained at Five-Star helped them tremendously," says Rhodes.

An unadorned and plain-speaking man, Rhodes doesn't like all the language at Five-Star but loves the way Roundballese is spoken.

"This is the finest basketball camp there is," Rhodes said. "My sons will come here. It is important to me that they get the best of everything. You can sense the competitive nature here for the kids and it adds to my flexibility as a coach. What I learn helps me keep my job back home. In Indiana, you win or you lose your job. That's not right, but that's the way it is."

Reality can play tricks on you. In the late eighties, Rhodes brought an exceptional young man to Pitt. Rick Fox moved to northern Indiana and Warsaw from the Bahamas for the 1984–85 season. Fox was a sophomore but had the basketball skills of a third grader. He had watched North Carolina win an NCAA title on TV back on the islands and decided he was going to play there someday. It seemed like he had a snowball's chance. But that was before he met Al Rhodes.

"I don't believe in discouraging anyone," Rhodes says. "He was a terrible player, but he had a few things going for him. First, he had no bad habits, he just hadn't played much, and second, he was a great listener. He also had a great work ethic." Fox scored 15 points in six minutes in his first game for coach Pete Smith's B team and was benched. Rhodes wanted him rested for the varsity game. He was moved up to Rhodes' A team that same night. Dean Smith saw him at Five-Star the following summer, liked the way he played defense, and made him a Tarheel.

Sometimes that's the way the ball bounces. "It is unbelievable that he made it. It shows you that in basketball, proper knowledge plus repetition is equal to skill," Rhodes says. Other times the ball bounces differently. "I have seen kids at Five-Star hiding behind a tree, crying, because they've discovered the world has more than their little corner. It is worth my time to walk around for an evening to talk to kids like that. Basketball is important, but it's certainly not anybody's world."

Hubie Brown knew that in spades. It was ironic in a way that he remained and still remains loyal to Five-Star. He had seen what being true-blue could do. His father at one time worked at the Kearny docks in Jersey. He showed up every day and did his job, but business got slow and a lot of men were laid off and he was one of them. He managed to get a job at the Singer factory. It was steady work and it was a living.

Things picked up down at the docks and they called him back and out of loyalty he went. Three weeks later they closed and the Singer people said thanks-but-no-thanks, so he had nothing. He was a survivor, though, and managed to make ends meet. When Garf started his little camp up in the Catskills he didn't have to hire him as an assistant trainer, but when he did it struck the man's son deeply. It wasn't millions but it helped.

It wasn't sympathy money. Garf needed them just as much to get Five-Star off the ground. Besides that, there was Will Klein. The way he saved a dollar made Jack Benny look like a spendthrift, but once you got to know him and saw how he was with kids and what he did for people without drawing attention to himself, it meant something. These guys were from the old school. They understood that nobody got by alone. So did Brown, and over the years it got to be like a family thing, tightly knit, and it grew from that. Nobody could say otherwise and if they did they were dead wrong.

It was simple and so is basketball to Brown. He is a very powerful, expressive speaker, almost Shakespearean in his speech and mannerisms. He is dramatic and polished but also raw and gut-wrenching when he has to be. Even The King, who has heard them all in 25 years and can be cynical, gets chills listening to him.

Coachability, having the good sense to learn from coaches and to be or not to be adaptable was the theme of Brown's lecture the final afternoon. "Go back with me to the beginning of Five-Star," he began. "There were 61 players at a little camp in upstate New York and the first MVP was a guard named Ron Johnson from Van Buren High School in New York City. There was another kid named John Roche, who became an All-American and a first-round draft pick of the Denver Nuggets.

"In camp Ron Johnson was better than John Roche. He stuck it up John Roche's ass. His senior year, he took six slugs in the back in a bank job, so when I talk to you, you should understand I'm not impressed with your talent. None of you are Ron Johnson or even Moses Malone, who was the best ever at Five-Star, and if anybody ever worked harder than he did, I want to meet him. If you think you're good, if you think you have it all together, take a look at the MVP's on the Wall of Fame sometime."

The Wall of Fame is Five-Star's testament to itself and its self-made legacy. At Pitt the four walls of the lecture hall are lined with stories about the camp and pictures of the players and coaches who have passed through over 25 years. Most of them are there, the playoff champions and award winners, the NBA stars and the kids who probably hung 'em up long ago. There are stained and tattered old newspaper articles and up-to-the-minute magazine features around the entire room.

"Half of those guys on the Wall of Fame are guys you've heard of," Brown said, "and the other half, some of them the best players this camp has seen, are ones you've never heard of. Why? Because they became uncoachable. You guys couldn't wipe the ass of half those guys, but you never heard of them. What am I telling you? You've been here a week, but have you figured out what Five-Star is all about? Do you know why you're here? What are you taking back home?

"Being coachable is the key. All you guys are no different than Mike O'Koren. He became a pro player with the New Jersey Nets, but he couldn't get into the NBA league at Five-Star for two years. He knew what being coachable was all about. This was your week for exposure. Did you understand that college coaches ask your Five-Star coaches about you? This was your chance for exposure. What did you do with your opportunity? And if I said to you, 'Show me your notebook,' what would you do?"

Brown paused for effect as he spoke, using his hands to embellish a point and his eyes to draw the campers in and force them inward. "When I was hired as an assistant by Larry Costello of the Milwaukee Bucks, they had some great players: Bobby Dandridge, Oscar Robertson, Kareem Abdul-Jabbar. When I walked in the gym my first day of practice I heard a ball bouncing at a side basket.

"I wondered to myself, 'Who could be here before me?' and I saw this 7'2" person shooting a basketball into a rim with a rebound ring on it. Kareem was shooting that little sky hook that you and I always took for granted. For 20 minutes every day before regular practice he did that. He was so accurate with that shot he could hit someone in the ass buying a beer in the mezzanine. Why? Because every day he was out there doing it."

The campers were picturing the scene as Brown talked, and having gotten them that far, he forced them the rest of the way. "Are you afraid to fail? Here's the balls I have. I walked up to Kareem that first day and told him I could teach him 10 back-to-the-basket moves. Did he tell Hubie Brown, 'Forget it, man, I got a game'? No, at the end of 30 days he had two big-time moves because he was coachable.

"Be coachable. All of you guys, and you younger guys especially, add something to your game because if you don't guys like Joe Dumars and Isiah Thomas will suffocate you. With or without the ball, those guys are in your face and they make you change your game. Larry Bird learned to up his free throw percentage. Magic Johnson too was an average foul shooter and now he's one of the league leaders. Magic had no outside game, but he learned to get where he had to go. John Stockton of the Utah Jazz was a skinny kid who was six feet tall on a good day, and Mark Price of the

Cavaliers was small too, but they learned to go from the top of the key to the top of the key faster than anyone else.

"Let me ask you something: Dr. J., Mark Iavaroni, and Bill Russell, what did all three of those guys have in common? They all were late developers. Dr. J. went from 6'2" to 6'7" very late and Iavaroni was a gangly kid who had trouble not tripping over the lines at Five-Star. Bill Russell was on the third team at McClelland High School, but San Francisco University took a chance on him. What am I telling you? That you have no idea how you will develop in your growth, so learn the fundamentals of handling the basketball.

"Get the four basic dribbles down: the crossover, behind your back, between your legs, and the change of direction. And develop a baby hook. I saw Joe Dumars in training camp this year working on a baby hook. Joe Dumars, can you believe it? Coming off those curls and low picks the Pistons run, he got so he could hit it with either hand. You may need it too.

"I hope if you have Five-Star-level talent you ask yourself the following five things before you go to bed every night. Keep these for the rest of your life because if you've got just one you are not going to reach your potential. First, do you have a low pain threshold? Can you play with a cold or after you've been smashed on your head? It's like Michael Jordan says, it's all in the mind.

"Second, do you have a low IQ for what the team is doing? Do you think it's easy to play for the Lakers or Detroit who exert just as much energy on defense as on offense? You have to understand the game.

"Third, are you selfish? Are you worried about your points? Do you really believe in your heart that an assist is just as good as scoring a basket?

"Fourth are the intangibles. Do you take a charge off the ball, something no one keeps stats on? Do you want the last shot?

"That reminds me of John Drew. When I was coaching in Atlanta we got a kid who had been the MVP in the NCAA tournament, John Drew, and he came to me to talk. Drew was playing behind a guy who had a high basketball IQ and he wasn't happy. That guy said to Drew, 'What's your problem? You haven't even had to fix your uniform yet, you're soft.' Nobody had ever told Drew that before. He never had to play like that before. He had never been a substitute before.

"How were you when your coaches here put you in during the first and third quarters? Did you get a little red-assed? Did you say to yourself that obviously this coach doesn't know what he's doing, that you averaged 23 points a game back at school? The competition gets better as you get higher and you've got to have a better game.

"And fifth, do you have a juice or drug problem? We have lost plenty of all-star players because of booze and guys snorting stuff. They all thought they were tough guys, but that is why you won't reach your potential."

The more things change the more they stay the same. "And as for you seniors, when you pick a school, pick one where you'll be coached," Brown said. "Please don't pick one for the goodie package because it's so small in comparison to the goodies you'll get if you take your Five-Star-level talent and come out with a finished product, a degree.

"Let me ask you if you know what these six guys have in common: Elgin Baylor, Bill Russell, Wilt Chamberlain, Bob Pettit, Oscar Robertson, and Jerry West. Maybe you never heard of some of those guys, but Elgin Baylor was one of the greatest small forwards who ever played the game. Russell and Chamberlain were great centers, the Jabbars of their day. If I had to pick the best power forwards ever to play in the NBA, I'd have to put Bob Pettit of the old St. Louis Hawks right up there with Bird. Oscar and West would be Jordan and Magic if they were playing today.

"What those six guys have in common is that eventually somebody took their ball away. Jordan and Magic too, someday someone will take their ball away. Except for Kareem, all those guys retired by the time they were 38 years old. You gotta live on this earth for 30 or 40 years after your playing career is over. Think about that.

"Let's say some guy low bridges you and smacks you into a wall, cracks your ankle, and you can't play the eight weeks recruiters are looking for you. There goes your scholarship, Jack. Or, if they came to you with a scholarship today, could you take it? Can you get into the school you want to, today, right now? Your grades, baby, your grades. Can you get into the school you want with your grades? Don't blame your guidance counselor if you can't. You are responsible for your own actions. Take it on yourself."

* * * * *

The final afternoon and night of camp are always busy and bittersweet. The playoffs pass more quickly than the losers would like and even the winners feel a loss at their ending. It is the final Five-Star fling for some and there is nothing physical they can take with them to preserve the feelings. There is nothing to hold onto except the words of the coaches and their own experiences, the richness of which they have already determined.

Many of the campers are anxious to return home to familiar surroundings, yet they have also become accustomed to newness. There is a sense of relief and exhilaration that the week and the fervor are over, but there is that empty sadness too, that heaviness of heart that can only be lessened by playing and learning and becoming what they have seen they can be.

At Pitt, the campus grounds became swelled with arriving fathers and mothers. Many campers departed with their parents as soon as the all-star game and awards ceremony were completed. Their exodus left the camp strangely quiet and made the few clinking room keys that remained afoot sound lonesome. Other campers waited until the next morning to leave, taking buses to the airport, then spreading in every direction.

Attendance at the all-star game and awards ceremony is mandatory, although most of the campers wouldn't miss them for the world. They have acquired a very clear understanding of where they belong in the basketball scheme of things. There are many who are neither all-stars nor award-winners, but each feels like he has contributed earnestly to the others' success and recognition.

At Pitt, Garf set the tone for the Orange-White Classic early in the evening, telling the campers en masse that it had been wonderful all week watching great players play great. They had done well, cranking it out at stations and in the games and everyone had been raised to a new level. That was all he ever asked. They knew he was sincere. He wasn't the type to hold back, which was a mixed blessing but something a person could rely on, and the approval was mutual.

Before the big game the courts were empty but lighted in case someone finished packing early and wanted to work on his moves. There had been so much activity on them they still seemed to be noisy, as if invisible basketball sprites were playing. The King spent an hour there with young Joe Reid in the shadow of the spruce trees, talking basketball. Reid, thinking ahead to the days when he might go against the Alonzo Mournings and Patrick Ewings of the world, and remembering Ron Rothstein's advice, had unashamedly sought advice on how to feel more confident.

The King said to him, "Part of being a great player is having the guts to take your game out of the neighborhood. It takes a special breed of kid to do that. This game takes nerve. It takes heart and poise. Playing against Mourning and Ewing, the first thing you have to face is your own fear. You could be scared to death, but you just need to slow down. Get them out of position. Make them change to you.

"There are things you have inside yourself that no one can teach you. Find them first. The rest can be shown to you on tape in a gym anytime." He poured his heart out, like he was talking to his kid brother, and Reid drank it all in, thirsting for more. It was easy to misread The King. He was crude and irascible and could be a royal pain if crossed, but he is a Five-Star guy and never wants the well to run dry.

Reid was just one of the excellent players in the Orange-White Classic, which had to be held in the expansive Sewall Center, the university's 5,000-seat coliseum, and even that was jammed to the rafters with parents and recruiters. Actually, there were three all-star games, one for each league, and Garf fretted and fumed over each, but the NIT and NCAA contests seemed like preliminaries compared to the NBA.

That's the one the visiting coaches were anxious to watch. Seeing them peer down from the stands with their player lists and notepads, the unsettling sensation returned that they were staring at and shopping for gifted athletes who are still very much young men. But as much as the next guy, they were there as fans too.

Garf was primed and ready, taking his customary Side Loge, courtside seat with microphone in hand. Making the player introductions, his voice bounced off the bleachers and walls, and for someone with his eyes closed and a little imagination, it might have been John Condon and the old Garden. Garf was in his glory, adding colorful tidbits to each announcement and waiting reverently as each all-star dribbled to center court, pivoted, and rolled the ball back to the bench to a teammate who in turn took his place at center stage.

It was the Five-Star coming-of-age ritual, and when it was over there was a basketball game to be played. The Orange-White Classic brings out the best and the beast in Garf. Every time it is his game of games. He often has a player or players he roots for, and he is the ultimate involved spectator. He is Five-Star's one-man bleacher section, booster club, and alumni association.

It was impossible for Garf to pick a favorite at Pitt because he liked so many of the players. That's his problem, he likes them all. Brian Hopgood was in there muscling his way through the paint for the Orange team along with Lawrence Mitchell, who'd brought his thunder-dunks north from Radford. They had Bill Curley too, a 6'9" soft-spoken slaughterer from Duxbury, Massachusetts.

It took Curley awhile to get to Five-Star. With his red hair, outlet pass mastery, and unselfish play, he brings to mind Bill Walton, but Curley thought you had to get invited to Five-Star and nothing ever arrived in the mail. Someone straighted him out and since he first attended Five-Star, the Duxbury post office has been busy sorting the letters of interest. Curley almost saved the postman a lot of work. He got very homesick on his first visit to camp. He wanted to skedaddle, but instead he stuck it out and says, "I realized that's what the coaches meant when they talked about having to sacrifice. I also knew it would get me ready for the isolation I would feel when I went to college." It was hard for Garf not to pull for him.

Garf didn't even try to hide his enthusiasm for Pat Sullivan, who was teamed with Joe Reid on the White squad. A 6'8" scrapper from Bogota, New Jersey, Sullivan says he developed his game by playing against Bob Hurley's guys from St. Anthony's High in Jersey City. Sullivan says he learned to enjoy every practice and every game by listening to Jerry Wainwright speak. It was quite a combination. He always had it in him though. He just didn't know there were words to describe what he did.

Sullivan's stock had risen immeasureably in the playoffs. In the quarterfinals his team was down by one with just enough time for one shot, which he took from outside and missed. Somehow he got through five defenders to get his fingertips on the rebound to tap it in before the buzzer, which didn't seem humanly possible, but he got it done. It was on Court Two and Garf happened to be sitting there with Coach K. Those were the moments both of them relished.

It took Garf awhile to fully enjoy the play because Sullivan had gone around and through two more of his fair-haired boys, Travis Best and Grant Hill. Best, out of Springfield, Massachusetts, was slightly shy of six feet tall and was the only rising junior on the White team. Garf found him in the NIT league two years earlier and instantly dubbed him a palace guard. "It wasn't hard with him," says Garf. "He kicked ass."

Best was named the Best Playmaker at Pitt II and handles a basketball like it's joined to him at the wrist. He is loyal too and keeps coming to camp even though the recruiters have long since found out his street address. He comes to learn but also because he knows what it means to Garf and Five-Star. Hill is the same way. A 6'7" small forward headed for Duke from South Lakes High in Reston, Virginia, he glides over a basketball court like a ghost floating over a peaceful lake until he roars up suddenly and slams one.

The game was over in what seemed like a blink, the recruiters vanished, and it was just a camp once more. Curley, Sullivan, Best, and Hill would all be at Honesdale when Five-Star moved there at the end of August, but for Garf there were two weeks left at Pitt and the rest of the night to get through. A small group of kids sneaked off campus around one o'clock in the morning and got caught swiping liquor by the local police. They were read the riot act, but they were going home in a few hours anyway and there was only so much Five-Star could do.

Garf changed his policy because of the incident though. He increased the supervision between the all-star game and awards ceremony, which cost him some valuable time but enabled the counselors to keep better tabs on everyone. "There's no way you can stop a kid from leaving the grounds if he has his mind set on it unless you put a cop on every door," he says. "I'd sell the camp before that would happen. Five-Star is not a detention center."

A depression sets in at the end of every session for Garf, which lifts only when the next one begins. His depression is mercifully short at Pitt, with only one day to rest between closing and reopening, but it deepens during the three weeks from the end of Pitt IV in early August until he returns to Honesdale. It disappears for eight days before digging in for the winter.

*　*　*　*　*

The summer of '89 was an exception, at least briefly. Garf didn't have time to get downhearted leaving Pitt. It was all set, he thought, for Jim Hoy to take him to the airport at 5:45 a.m. for a 6:30 flight back to New York. At the appointed hour he lugged his suitcases up the hill outside his dorm, but Hoy was nowhere in sight, nor was he 10 minutes and several frantic cigarettes later.

At 6:00 a.m. Garf appealed to the guard at the main gate. The guard was willing but on duty and the best he could offer was a phone to call a cab. Keeping his wits while clutching his cancer sticks like a prisoner facing a firing squad, Garf mentioned to the guard that he would get 20 dollars for his trouble. He got the point, canceled the cab, and got Garf to the terminal 15 minutes before takeoff.

The race was on. "I reached into my pocket to pay the guy, but all I had was a 50-dollar bill," Garf says. "I ran into the restaurant to get it changed, but there were already three people in line. I ignored them and pushed the bill into the cashier's hand and she didn't even look up, just took it and cashed it, and I ran back out. It was 6:20 and I was panting by then. I heard them announcing my flight as I got to the guy to give him his 20 dollars.

"I looked in my hand and I had a whole bunch of coins. I had no idea why until I realized that the cashier must have thought I was paying for the three people ahead of me. I turned around and they were looking at me like it was the most outrageous thing they'd ever seen, but I paid the guy and just shouted, 'Have one on Five-Star' and ran out of there, hauling my bags about half-a-mile to the plane.

"I found out later that Hoy had been called to France for a clinic on a second's notice and had no time to get in touch. When I got to New York I could barely lift the same luggage I'd carried at a breakneck pace halfway across the airport. But what's the point? It proves that all the guys who lecture at camp are right. People can do things beyond their power when the pressure of thinking about it is off. If Bob Knight or somebody like that is on a player, coaching and inspiring him, it's easier to exceed what he thinks are his limits."

* * * * *

It was high time to get back home. Heading east from Coraopolis to Lake Bryn Mawr, Five-Star travelers pass Penfield, which at an elevation of 2,250 feet is something worth bragging about if you're from there. They make quite a sight with their orange sweatpants in rural Clearfield County before the highway comes back down to earth around Altoona, rising toward Hazleton and then the night lights of Wilkes-Barre below.

It is usually warm and summery that time of year in Scranton, and beyond the outskirts clean lakes begin to jump out again and the sounds and smells of the mountains in July enter through an open car window. They disappear along Route 84 as the air changes abruptly, a telltale sign that home is near. Bearing north, windows closed against the chill, two-lane 191 passes through Honesdale to Fireside Road and Bryn Mawr Camp, where at the end of the dirt road the city kids meet.

Fig's 32 & 33

A STAR IS BORN II: *Two rare and improbable photos of Michael Jordan, who blossomed at Five-Star during the summer of 1980. Above: Mike, as he was known in those days, hustles through Woody Williams' (Lake Clifton H.S.) four-corner passing station with mouth open, tongue in! Left: This photo is a Ripley reject; even **he** wouldn't believe it: Jordan clearly beaten on a jump ball by an unknown kangaroo. Where is Tom Konchalski when we need him? The tosser is Harold Merrit, who took over the head coaching reins at Northern Arizona U. in the spring of '90.*

Fig. 34 Campers salute Michigan State coach Judd Heathcote, 1979 NCAA champion, following his lecture at Robert Morris College.

Fig. 35 **CATCHING THE "RED EYE":** *Five-Star is where the teaching never stops, so Will Rey (Loyola of Chicago) gets the diehards up early for pre-breakfast ballhandling/shooting drills.*

Fig. 36 **"THE WRITER":** *Mike Ryan, not to be confused with Five-Star's attendance man, worked harder at some of the stations during his three-week residence than some of the campers. Here he's taking down impressions of Camp Bryn Mawr in August of 1989.*

Fig. 37 Hall-of-Fame-to-be hoop mentor Bob Knight accepts a plaque from Howard Garfinkel, emblematic of Knight's 20-year association with Five-Star.

Fig. 38   *Alonzo's foes are in mourning as he snares yet another rebound during the Pitt II playoffs, July 1987.*

Fig. 39 Billy Owens, who helped lead Carlisle H.S. to four straight Pennsylvania State titles, learns interviewing techniques from one of the best—CBS analyst Billy Packer—during a camp lecture. This training proved useful when Owens later became a superstar at Syracuse.

Fig. 40 The Knicks' Trent Tucker teaches the two-pointer on a wet Coraopolis morning in 1985. During the 1989–90 season, Tucker became only the eighth player in NBA history to swish over 400 "threes." The pupil on the left wearing the blue Daily News shirt is Duke star-to-be Alaa Abdelnaby.

Fig. 41 Wake Forest's associate coach Jerry Wainright works the triceps of Carolina-bound Pat Sullivan in a manual resistance extension drill during a Honesdale lecture, August 1989.

Fig. 42 Hubie Brown, #1 pro hoop analyst for CBS, left 400 campers and assorted celebrity types spellbound in a closing stemwinder in the "Walls of Fame" Room, July 1989.

Fig. 43 Xavier's Pete Gillen displays perfect baby-hook shooting form during a Station 13 teaching session in Pittsburgh.

Fig. 44 All eyes are focused on John Paxson during his surprise visit to Station 13 in July 1987. Paxson, a three-year Five-Star standout, started every game for the Chicago Bulls during the 1989–90 season.

Fig. 45 J.R. Reid (North Carolina & Hornets) hammers one through under the watchful eye of Larry Brown during the drill phase of a lecture at Robert Morris, Pitt-II, 1985. In 1989–90, Brown prodded the Spurs to the biggest one-season turnaround in NBA history.

Fig. 46 **PRIMAL INTENSITY:** *Paul Pryma (St. Ignatius H.S.) teaches defense Chicago-style to a high-octane group at Robert Morris.*

PART FOUR

Honesdale

SEVENTEEN

Huffing and Puffing into the Poconos

*"To one who has been long in city pent,
'Tis very sweet to look into the fair
And open face of heaven..."*

– John Keats

It is cool and sunny.

Ronnie Sidbury is leaning back in the seat of his tractor contemplating his circumstances. He is a long way from 2nd Avenue and 113th Street in Manhattan, where he spent most of his young years spinning his wheels, but he is starting to feel comfortable in his new surroundings. It is the last week in August, 1989, and he is getting ready for autumn and the cold winter nights that will come earlier and earlier. He is the only one left at Camp Rosemont. Everyone else has gone home.

Five-Star left Rosemont many years before. Sidbury, taking a break from his work, says he's heard of the camp and was told that some pretty good basketball players used to hang around: Moses Malone and Robert Parish, guys like that. He never had much time for the game himself but knows what camp life means to him and assumes it meant the same to them. When he arrived the first day, he had something to prove to himself.

Sidbury says he got out of New York to find decent work and build himself a decent life. "People are going mad in the city," he says. "People are crazy in their minds, shooting each other in the streets." He enjoys living in the country and being his own man and having the place to himself.

Camp Rosemont is still going strong. The new owners, Dave and Barbara Kersch of Oceanside, New York, and their partners, Thomas and Lee Elsbree, changed the emphasis of the camp after buying out Harry Silverman. The camp caters to kids with learning disabilities now and the eight-week program has a reputation as one of the best in the country. But Five-Star memories still linger. "I remember walking into the lecture room in the evening with the entire basketball camp congregated in there," says Kersch. "My eyeglasses used to steam up with the heat.

"What I mostly remember is the size of the youngsters. They were immense. I still walk on the courts sometimes, especially the Green Court where the all-star games were played, and think about how many All-Americans have played there." The courts, vacant by comparison since then, are up a knoll past an open, spacious field dotted white with Queen Anne's Lace. The only hint of Five-Star orange is an occasional Devil's Paintbrush leaning into the sunlight.

A few of the bunkhouses still defy the law of gravity, despite obvious efforts to straighten them. The gym floor looks new, although outside, underneath, there is evidence of carefully laid old shimwork. The slivers of wood are gray with age but still functional. Inside, you can still see the low-hanging roof beams and your breath in the afternoon. Across from the entrance, near the massive fireplace, a hopelessly out-of-tune upright piano collects cobwebs. The stage on the far end is lifeless and cluttered with props and camp paraphernalia all the way up the narrow staircase to the loft. There is not a single basketball in sight.

Sidbury loves it at Rosemont, especially blue Rose Lake, which he says "sparkles." Nature is still new and wondrous to him. He absorbs everything he experiences and talks about it with almost childlike innocence. "Camp life is good for you," he says, perched on his machine with the sun warming his shoulders. "Kids who get to come here are lucky. They learn a lot, like how not to be afraid of the dark. That's a hard feeling to get rid of.

"We've got apple trees here. See, over there? The red over there in those bushes? Guys come by and just pick 'em off the trees and eat them. Over there are blueberries," he adds, pointing into the woods off to his right where the leaves are sprinkled with purple. "I've caught some fish too. Blue gill, I think, yeah, blue gill and some catfish too. I was scared of the catfish, but my friend showed me how to clean them and cook them and they tasted pretty good. Good-tasting fish.

"There are times I just sit under a tree and think about things. I like being alone here but you need other people too. Nobody gets by on their own. You have to think about the next guy, you know? People don't do that sometimes."

*　*　*　*　*

Down the road at Camp Bryn Mawr, Garf is thinking the same thing and feeling fit to be tied. It is only the first morning of camp, Monday, but something is bothering him. It's the campers. They are inattentive and uncentered—not all of them, but enough of them to disrupt the flow. It started at tryouts the night before and grew worse at breakfast. The kids talked incessantly. He didn't mind the kids talking during the meal as long as they quieted down afterwards for announcements and they usually did, but this time he really had to lay down the law and even then he heard scattered whispers. Some of the campers had never been to the country before and were scared and homesick, which had a little to do with it, but that was no excuse for all the childish giggling. It was getting on his nerves and he wasn't going to put up with it very much longer.

He tried dropping a hint just before stations. Everyone was gathered on Court Three, center stage at Honesdale. "I want you to have fun and hopefully be adult enough to know when to have fun and when to be serious," Garf said.

"If you leave here with two new moves, I'll be happy. Take advantage of the learning, then kick ass at your high school next season. If you don't learn here, you've wasted your money. You've thrown away your $300." He stopped at that point. They weren't taking the hint. In the back of the bleachers a small clump of campers was yakking. Wiseguys. Garf lit into them. "I'm not going to allow unserious people to screw up our camp," he said, pausing before continuing.

"There are serious players and coaches here. Ninety-five percent of the players are serious and we won't allow the five percent that aren't to mess up the timing of our camp. This week is the culmination of eight months' work and six weeks of intensity here and at Radford and Pitt." The weeding-out process had begun. It usually took care of itself with the weak ones withering in the wind, but Garf would have to get his fingernails dirty this time. So would his friend Rick Pitino.

*　*　*　*　*

Five-Star had survived inauspicious beginnings in the past. The first year they came to Bryn Mawr, in 1976, Albert King, considered by many the greatest New York City high school guard ever, packed his bags and went home early. He was a camper-worker and one of the rumors going around was that he was a slacker and that's why he left. There were other stories that said he tucked his tail and ran after seeing a rat in his bunk and that rats were everywhere.

The truth, says Garf, was that King fractured his sternum. People could say whatever they wanted, but he wasn't about to risk the kid's future so he sent him home. King did see a creature, but it wasn't a dog-sized rat like everyone claimed. It was a harmless field mouse that happened to wander through the bunkhouse one day, but from then on that building was known as "Rat Bunk." Garf, not realizing how skittish camper-workers could be, moved them into sleeping quarters closer to the kitchen after that, putting an end to the hysteria while at the same time eliminating any possible excuse for getting to work late.

Jeff Ruland was there at the same time, which helped offset all the rodent rumors. Garf could watch Ruland play all day, but he always had one regret. He wished something had shown up in the Mirror that he could have warned the kid about. Ruland was a tough player who had to fight for every inch. All that knocking caught up to him in the NBA and he had to retire early with injuries. "Poor Ruland," Garf says now. "He was never injured for even a second, and then all of a sudden it ended with the knee problems. What a great camper and player."

Five-Star was featured in a Converse highlight film that year too, which made Garf forget all about the varmint nonsense. He showed the kids the latest Converse flick every year anyway and they always oohed and aahed watching the NBA stars doing their thing, so it was a real thrill seeing the camp in there with them. It's the only time any camp has been in the movies with the big boys.

For a while it seemed like Five-Star was everywhere you looked. Al McGuire brought the camera crews in for one of his NBC-TV halftime shows called "Al Goes to Camp" and Five-Star was immortalized again in the film *Hoopla* that can still be seen at the Basketball Hall of Fame in Springfield, Massachusetts. The camp wasn't mentioned by name, but it looked like Will Klein had made a home video with all the familiar faces and scenery and it made Garf feel proud knowing Five-Star was a permanent part of the archives.

That's where they belonged as far as Herb Kutzen was concerned. He couldn't have been happier having Garf and his gypsies stop by Bryn Mawr twice every year, once in mid-June and again at the end of the summer. "I like the tone, the atmosphere of the camp," Kutzen says. "Everything had to be just so, but it was worth the extra effort. If the rims are one-eighth of an inch off, Garf notices it and makes us fix them, but he does that because it matters to him.

"In my opinion there are three guys who should definitely be in the Basketball Hall of Fame: James Naismith for inventing the game, John Wooden for perfecting team play, and Howard Garfinkel for doing more for the youth of American over the past 25 years than anyone else."

It would be fitting. With help from his friends Tom Konchalski and Bob Williams and support from Bill Travers (high school sports editor of the New York *Daily News*), Howie Evans (Amsterdam *News* writer) and Olvin McBarnette (a member of the New York City Board of Education), Garf, in 1989, created the New York City Basketball Hall of Fame.

The new Hall of Fame will honor players, coaches, and overall contributors to the game who either were born in the city or who made their mark there. The first 10 members, with names such as Kareem Abdul-Jabbar, Dolph Schayes, and Billy Cunningham on the ballot, will be announced in September of 1990. Sports commentator Marv Albert, a city boy himself, is slated to be Master of Ceremonies for what Garf hopes will be a gala event.

"It is hard to believe how focused Howard has been on basketball and the kids over the years," says Kutzen, who makes it easier by keeping Bryn Mawr shipshape. It's not Kutzen's fault everyone refers to Lake Bryn Mawr as Honesdale. They don't do it out of disrespect. Old habits die hard.

Garf and Will Klein get misty-eyed talking about the place and what it means to them. Every summer, as sure as green grass, Five-Star heads back to Honesdale. It comforts and becomes the end of one draining journey and the euphoric start of another and is a journey unto itself. Honesdale, with its neat rows of arbor vitae and poplar trees and tidy bunkhouses, is always there, waiting.

Other people also get attached to the place in a hurry. It's been like that since the beginning. After Five-Star settled in and Garf got the rat stuff squared away, all that remained was for The King to christen the premises properly, which he did, winning the first NBA championship with one of his favorite players, Cornelius Thompson from Middletown High in Connecticut. For a New Englander, Thompson had a lot of street savvy. He eventually made it to the pros, serving notice that the terrain may have changed at Five-Star, but the ground rules were very much the same.

Nothing was ever etched in stone, though, except stations, and things were never normal again after Sam Bowie sauntered into Honesdale in 1978. It wasn't so much what he did. He shared MVP honors with Dominique Wilkins, who controlled the space above the rim while he dominated below. That was to be expected. It wasn't the Mirror either, which was sharper and clearer than it had ever been.

Garf really liked the kid, but it was what Bowie represented that made him stand out. At the time he was being courted not only by virtually every college in the country, but also by every camp. Consequently, Garf had to roll out the red carpet in a way he never had or lose him. "It was the first time I had to go head-to-head with Bill Croneauer's BC Camp," he says.

"I still believed that we ultimately competed against ourselves, but I knew what Croneauer was about to do—offer Bowie and every kid from the city a deal to go to his camp. Bowie was the number one player in the nation and he was from Lebanon, Pennsylvania, right in our backyard. I had to get him.

"In the past, I would have sent a kid like him a brochure and made maybe one or two phone calls to his coach, but with BC and other camps hovering out there, it frightened me. It scared me to death, but it also spurred me to work and recruit nationally, which is something I never would have done before. Locally I had done it but I knew then if I didn't get the big-name national players, BC or somebody else would. In the long run, BC moving in made Five-Star flourish and become better. In that regard, Sam Bowie may have been the most important camper in the history of Five-Star."

The store was safe temporarily but the BC Camp, as well as the other camps, would never stop nipping at Five-Star's heels. Bowie had his chances to spread his allegiances, but he remained loyal to Five-Star and in fact formed an unanticipated attachment to Garf. It had little to do with the camp and a lot to do with saving face.

Garf at the time was still co-coaching in the Dapper Dan Classic with Red Jenkins, the coach at W.T. Woodson High in Fairfax, Virginia. The format of the game had been altered. In the past it had pitted Pennsylvania's all-stars against the rest of the country, but it had evolved into a four-team tournament with teams from the Midwest/Far West region (led by John Paxson that year); the South/Southwest (led by Wilkins); Pennsylvania (Bowie); and the East (tournament MVP Sidney Green).

Garf's job included recruiting players for the East (mainly New York and New Jersey all-stars), which he did faithfully, keeping a soft spot in his heart for the big kid from Lebanon. It came in handy. The East won (adding to his career coaching total of 500-plus wins with fewer than 100 losses). "Bowie had a disastrous two days," he says. "The locals booed him and I ended up calling them all assholes. It was unbelievable." The kid heard about it and later told Garf he owed him one, which put him at the end of a long line.

* * * * *

The King too was forming some allegiances. He saw Bowie and Wilkins lighting it up but barely noticed in the glow of "The Rocket," Rod Foster. "Foster was from New Briton, Connecticut," The King says. "He was so naïve he didn't even know who Dean Smith was. It helped him in a way because he didn't realize he was supposed to be intimidated at Five-Star. He burst out of the pack at tryouts and it was the first time I really got close to a kid as a player."

The King did whatever he could to help him with his game and with recruiting. He was even offered a job at LSU to make The Rocket a Cajun but turned it down. He'd seen arrangements like that go sour too many times, especially for the kid. Laid-back UCLA seemed more suited to Foster's style, and it turned out to be the right choice. Foster fired his jets for the Bruins for four years before hitting the afterburners with the Phoenix Suns. His success helped soften the blow later on with heartbreaks like James Blackmon and Lloyd Daniels, although The King would scarcely say as much.

Year after year Garf and The King tried to treat the kids as if they were their own, and there were always a few who for one reason or another became their favorites and stuck in their minds.

* * * * *

In the late seventies and into the early eighties, while Isiah and Paxson and Jordan were making life miserable for everyone at Pitt, things were hopping at Honesdale too. Patrick Ewing was there and Garf badgered him the whole time to go learn an offensive move from Rick Pitino, which did nothing but start trouble.

The Five-Star Connection was persistent. It could show up anytime and anywhere, and many years later when Pitino was coaching the New York Knicks he finally did get a chance to work with Ewing unfettered. They spent a lot of time in the paint. Pitino left for Kentucky after two seasons, and by then Ewing had become a monster inside, which, of course, was mere coincidence.

The King, with Ewing in tow, managed to lose a title. Ed Pinckney had a hand in that mournful memory. Three times Pinckney went head-to-head with Ewing, and each time the Mirror had to be adjusted. If more people had known how to read the thing, they would have known that incredible 1985 NCAA championship game between Georgetown and Villanova was inevitable. Rollie

Massimino wasn't in the picture yet, but there were a couple of other faces in there with Pinckney, young Dwayne McClain and Gary McLain.

The three of them made a pact right then and there, in the camper-worker bunkhouse at Honesdale, to go to college together. If there ever was an argument for the Five-Star Connection being an advantage, there it was. Kids could decide to go to school wherever they wanted, that wasn't the fishy part. What smelled was how Pinckney, McClain, and McLain happened to pick the Wildcats. Mitch Buonaguro, then an assistant at Villanova along with Mike Fratello, was working in camp at the time and it just seemed funny that afterwards everyone ended up in the same spot.

A person could build a case if he wanted to. After closer examination, it didn't hold up. First of all it was not mere chance that Buonaguro was at Five-Star. He had been a camper, and a pretty good one, while still at Bishop Loughlin High in Brooklyn. That was in the early seventies and he was a counselor after that and kept coming back when he got into coaching.

The real reason the advantage thing didn't hold water, once you started poking around, was the 1985 NCAA championship game itself. It's true that practically every guy on Villanova's starting five and half the guys coming off the bench were ex-campers, but the same thing was true for Georgetown with Ewing and the others. It was a regular Five-Star reunion except for one thing: None of John Thompson's people worked at Five-Star. They hadn't since the Hoyas' coach had his falling-out with Garf.

The complaining about Garf's Guys continued, though, even after Reggie Williams rubbed elbows with every coach in camp for two years and still chose Georgetown. Williams first arrived in camp in 1981 with a reputation for being good with a gun. He had to share turf with hombres like Len Bias, Hoya teammate David Wingate, future Big East rival Walter Berry, Notre Damer David Rivers, and Duke-bound Johnny Dawkins among others. If it had been anywhere but low-down-and-ornery Honesdale, there wouldn't have been room for everyone, especially Dawkins.

"The first time I saw Dawkins," says Garf, "it was raining at Honesdale. We were inside, standing on the sideline watching his game and the court seemed too small for some reason. Every time Dawkins jumped, it looked like he was going to land right on top of you. He was so quick and so explosive, it was like he was in your face all the time." If he wasn't, his Blue Devil backcourt mate-to-be, Tommy Amaker, was.

Sidewinder Keith Gatlin was in camp then, too, lurking in the shadows and alleyways. He ambled in from North Carolina and was a magician with the basketball. Gatlin became one of Garf's sidekicks. They were like Pancho and The Cisco Kid. "Gatlin and I were very close when he was in high school," Garf says. "When he got to Maryland University I didn't see him much. That happens all the time. When they go to college you don't see them again. You have to live with that but it's hard, very hard, because you think you've made a relationship with a kid.

"It's probably not normal because I'm an adult and they're kids, and it figures after they leave the camp they're supposed to go their own way. A lot of the great campers come back and pay their dues, and some of the great players do, but many don't. It sometimes leaves a bitter taste in one's mouth, especially a kid like Gatlin. We used to do a 'Hook 'em Horns' football thing for no reason whatsoever whenever he did something good. I have a picture of him and me doing that."

Billy Thompson and Milt Wagner, both headed for Louisville, were campers in those years and didn't exactly back down from anybody, but Reggie Williams was the one left standing after the dust cleared, and rightfully so. He was the only player in the history of the camp to attend three sessions his final summer and win three all-star game MVP awards. "No one will probably ever do it again," Garf says. "It is as rare as DiMaggio's 56-game hitting streak, but not quite."

The way Williams rode off into the sunset after his second summer in camp was what made him legendary. Honesdale sheriff Tom McCorry was there. "It was the summer of 1982 and Reggie was getting ready to start his senior year," says McCorry. "It was in the Orange-White Classic. It's a tradition to play the game outdoors and if it's humanly possible Garf will have it there.

"It was cold that night, about 40 degrees, I think, and the wind was blowing. The kids were bundled up in blankets around Court Three and you could see steam coming out of their mouths it was so cold. Court Three was right there, right next to the mountain and it was already well established that it was tough to shoot there, even on a calm day. It was awful that night.

"Reggie came out and started shooting from 15 feet and hit his first couple. Everyone figured he'd cool off, but he kept hitting so they had to get out on him. He just kept moving back to 18 feet and then 20 and he hit about nine in a row. The rest of the campers were coming out of their blankets, jumping up and down and going crazy. That was a very special evening."

In Garf's mind, scenes like that were the substance of Five-Star, one kid lifting all the others and they in turn willingly supporting him. It was the ebb and flow thing and it was pervasive. It didn't just happen anywhere and it wasn't something that could be done by anyone alone. It took everyone. Forget the rest of the stuff, being seen and the recruiters and having an advantage and even *HSBI*. They were important, but they weren't the essence.

* * * * *

Not everyone was convinced of Garf's sincerity.

Honesdale, in the years before Radford was added to the fold, was always the first site to be affected by any new NCAA regulations, and when the Garfinkel Rule was passed in the mid-eighties and the Live/Dead Period followed shortly thereafter, Garf figured his basketball palace in the Poconos was in trouble. He didn't understand the problem. He had always been willing to make changes if you could prove him wrong. Granted, that wasn't easy to do, but he wasn't inflexible. Show him in black-and-white terms what the difficulty was and he'd eliminate it.

He had proof of that. In July of 1983 he and Will Klein received a letter from an irate parent criticizing the coaching at camp. The coaches had always been Five-Star's crowning glory, but the writer of the letter had a point. Garf had a long-standing policy of hiring college players as counselors and coaches, not only to lend some glamour to the camp and keep up with the times, but also to give them an opportunity to get their feet wet. Most were interested in continuing in the profession and it usually worked out fine.

That year, however, one counselor got in over his head. A kid in the NIT league questioned his knowledge and he told him it was his first crack at coaching. He said he was doing his best, but the kid wasn't satisfied and told his parents about it when he got home. His parents told Garf they resented paying $225 to have their son coached by such a rank amateur. They were right, Garf said, and from then on the number of counselors was reduced and more assistant high school coaches, young guys with a few years under their belts, were added to the staff.

The Garfinkel Rule and the Live/Dead Periods were different. They backed Garf up against a wall, blindfolded him, and tied his hands. That first summer was an anxious one. "I knew the days of coming to Five-Star primarily for a scholarship were over," Garf says. "If all we were selling was exposure and coaches lining the courts, I saw nothing but problems ahead. I couldn't see why any good players would want to come to camp.

"I really shouldn't have been worried and deep down I knew that.

I had always put exposure as a third priority. First was the teaching and having fun and a good time in an organized situation. Second was the competition, kids learning to become better players so when they went back to their high schools and the college scouts came to look at them, they would be ready. Third was exposure. I put them in that order for almost every kid I spoke to over 25 years and I never changed. I never believed a kid should come to camp for a scholarship, but very few believe me when I say that.

"The deader it got with the NCAA regulations, though, the better Five-Star became. I am very proud of the fact that even after the Garfinkel Rule and in that first Dead Period, there were seven McDonald's All-Americans in camp, kids like Rony Seikaly (Syracuse and the Miami Heat) and Tom Sheehy (Virginia). That gave me confidence and showed me the kids weren't coming just to be seen. I always thought that, but this proved we were doing things right. The only thing dead about Honesdale was the silly notion that good players wouldn't come there without the college coaches."

Hubie Brown never needed additional convincing. He had no misgivings about Five-Star, then or later, and he always returned. "Going all the way back, the key to Five-Star has been the competition, the purity of competition," Brown says now. "I remember in the early days at Rosemont, refereeing an all-star game. It was a gorgeous night and there were nine *Parade* All-Americans on the court. It was a three-point game and everyone was playing their hearts out and I was thinking that it was unbelievable what those kids were doing.

"Along with competition, the whole theme of the camp has been teaching. Do you think Mike Fratello or Ron Rothstein or Rick Pitino or Brendan Suhr would have gotten where they did if not for Five-Star? You have to look back and understand, they all got a chance to be seen coaching and teaching at the highest levels because of Five-Star. It broadened the horizons of a lot of those guys and that created a tremendous sense of loyalty."

The bickering over Five-Star is in large part a matter of perspective. "The problem is once a guy has been to Five-Star he feels that he should be the next person to get a major break," Brown says. "That creates hard feelings among the coaches. And there are always cliques. There are always guys that get along and don't get along, inside the camp or outside it. The real students of the game are the ones who listen to other people and keep expanding what they already know.

* * * * *

Five-Star, given half a chance, could grow on you. Bernard King found it hard to leave when he dropped by to lecture in the mid-eighties, and not only did the NBA scoring dynamo fully clear the family name (absolving little brother Albert in the Rat Bunk escapade), he provided one of the most unexpected high points in camp history.

"I always say a leopard doesn't change its spots, but Bernard King was an exception," Garf says. "During his career with the Knicks and the Bullets, he changed from having an alcohol problem and being found nearly dead in his car to one of the classiest figures in pro sports. When he came to camp with his agent, Bill Pollak, I figured he'd do his hour and drive off. Instead, he did something totally unbelievable.

"After he talked, he offered to sign autographs for anyone who was interested. Almost every kid in camp got in line. We had to break it up so the schedule wouldn't be thrown into chaos and he sat there for an hour and 45 minutes until every camper eventually got an autograph. He didn't just hurriedly sign his name, he took the time to write 'To' and then each kid's name and he signed them 'Best Wishes, Bernard King.'"

The Riverside kids slowly grew found of the place too. They were among the last to trickle into Honesdale. They came in dribs and drabs at first because their coach, Ernest Lorch, was leery of Garf and the whole Five-Star Connection. He'd heard the camp was one of basketball's smoke-filled back rooms. He didn't want his kids getting messed up in the politics of recruiting. They had enough to deal with already.

"At first, I was not a supporter of Five-Star," Lorch says. "I was under the impression a kid had to go there to get decent ratings and I resented that. I found out, though, that it is a very affirmative situation. Now I support it and help kids get there. If you're a real player, you want to go to Five-Star, but I would send a kid there who wasn't even a Division III level player just for the experience. Garf is totally immersed in it all."

Lorch's kids are from Riverside Church in the Morningside Heights section of Manhattan. He is more than a coach to them. He is everything imaginable: father-figure, benefactor, advisor, and somebody to talk to. He gets all kinds at Riverside and has learned to go with the flow. He was a city kid himself and played a little hoop. He wasn't necessarily pro material, but he loved the game and when the church, in the early sixties, asked him to help get a new program underway, he accepted the calling.

"At one time I'd thought of joining the ministry, but I couldn't hack the economics of that situation," jokes Lorch, the president of a private investment and operating company. "Riverside had always been known for its social involvement and its great preachers. In the late 1950s, they saw that the community was changing, that more minority groups were becoming a part of it, so they brought in a black minister, Bob Polk, to be ready.

"I knew Reverend Polk through a mutual friend and he asked me to run their new after-school athletic program in the gym down in the basement. We wanted to give the kids an alternative to the streets, so the first thing we did was go out and try to get the gang leaders. Kids in New York are sophisticated. When they see a program that is credible they go to it, especially minority kids looking for discipline. If they didn't have it at home or in school, we supplied it. When kids see something stable, they will be there."

Riverside was flooded in no time. It was amazing how many talented kids were out there drowning in the streets. Basketball was only part of the daily agenda, but Lorch soon found himself coaching a juggernaut. It was like a reincarnation of Garf's New York Nationals and by the mid-sixties Riverside ruled the outside all-star team waters along with Lou d'Almeida's Bronx-based Gauchos, the modern-day Gems.

As the program grew to include 300 youngsters from ages 9–19, Lorch gradually became deeply involved with two teams, the Juniors (ages 15–16) and Seniors (17–19), traveling around the country and even overseas with them. Sixteen of his players have made it to the NBA. Chris Mullin, Ed Pinckney, and Mark Jackson all passed through Riverside. So did Walter Berry, although he nearly missed the boat. Berry was near and yet ever so far from St. John's and the New Jersey Nets when Lorch first set eyes on him.

"I was sitting on the hood of my car on The Hill out behind Yankee Stadium," Lorch recalls. "I was actually waiting for another young man to show up so I could take him to a game. Walter was just shooting around over in the park. He looked awkward, but everything he put up was going in. I went over to talk to him and he hemmed and hawed about where he went to school until he finally admitted he wasn't going regularly. He's done a super job since then.

"He was abused in terms of the media and his academic background, but he overcame all that. He was six hours short of his degree when I last saw him. If not for basketball he might be on welfare today. Now he's a hero to the kids, but at Riverside his is just one story. Every year it's just his story multiplied. A lot of kids have achieved more than he has.

"Coaching the Riverside team gives me a tremendous sense of satisfaction," Lorch says, "but if all I wanted was another 'W' I wouldn't still be in it. I've got plenty of wins. If I weren't involved with the kids, involved in their lives, I would stop doing it. Basketball is a weapon, a means to get from here to there. If you look at it as an end it will kill you. We've had kids killed by the game because they thought of nothing else.

"I love working with the basketball players, but the most important kids to me are the ones we call our Winter Seniors, the kids who have used up their sports eligibility and know this is their last chance. I believe it is important for somebody like me to relate to them. I am a white businessman. Many of them are coming from primarily black neighborhoods and black schools, but they will have to go out and relate in a very different business world. Hopefully I can modify their improperly perceived notions of that world in some way.

"I try to do the same thing with the kids who do well in basketball. Over the years there have been accusations made that I tell the kids where to go and what schools to choose, but that is not the case. We talk about recruiting, but I never tell a kid where to go or where not to go. They seek my advice because they know I don't want or need anything from them. I might tell a kid what he should look for, a feeling of comfort, but then he has to find it for himself. A kid should go where he's comfortable because once he is in the program, he is part of the program."

*   *   *   *   *

That was the whole point of Garf's little speech the first morning. He wanted everyone to get with the program. It wasn't aimed at any of the current Riverside kids, like Adrian "Red" Autry, or Brian Reese, or Lee Green. They'd seen enough of the underside to know what was up. Autry, a senior at Tolentine High in the Bronx, would earn the Mr. Stations plaque by the end of the week, and Reese, also a senior at Tolentine, would become just the fourth camper to get the 30-for-30 Award following in the footsteps of Rumeal Robinson, Ed "The Chill" Schilling, and Drew Philips, one of Colonel Mullis' kids.

Autry and Reese didn't need to be told. Neither did Lee Green, the hands-down choice as Honesdale's Best Defender in 1989, or any other time for that matter. Green's basketball talents had already taken him from the South Bronx projects to Cheshire Academy in Connecticut. It was not an easy haul. His father played at Missouri two years before falling on hard times and there were times he unloaded his miseries on his family.

"I got my strength to stay out of trouble from my mother," Green says. "In the projects, all you talk about is getting out of the projects, getting your mother out. It is definitely not the place to be anymore. It used to be the best place to grow up and play basketball, and whenever I go back now, kids in my neighborhood remember me. They pat me on the back and look out for me. A guy told me once to get off a bench in the park near the courts because I would be mistaken for one of the drug people and get marked. That's why a lot of kids play basketball, to get away from the projects."

A three-year camper, Green says, "I can't stay away from basketball for too long. Even when I rest I find myself trying to get out there. I might come back to Five-Star someday as a counselor because I would like to help the younger guys. I would like to give something back. This is my last year and I will miss the camp and I will miss traveling with Riverside. I will miss all of it. I'm going to remember everything."

That's what Garf was talking about. That's the kind of thing he was looking for, an appreciation for what was unfolding right in front of their eyes. Every kid had it in him to understand and add his part. It didn't make sense that some of them would choose not to, but Garf would keep after them, not just for their sakes but for his too. He knew that the success of Five-Star depended on them. It always had and always would and for him there was nothing else.

EIGHTEEN
Home Again in Honesdale

"If you are lucky enough to have lived in Paris as a young man, then wherever you go for the rest of your life, it stays with you, for Paris is a moveable feast."

– Ernest Hemingway

Garf was hoping the energy level would pick up once the games got underway, which it did. The city kids love to play ball. They are still in the majority at Honesdale, and the reason Five-Star expanded in the first place was to save a spot for them. They have never been thrilled with the camaraderie stuff, and sometimes the stations and lectures sound like a broken record to some of them, but they love the "comp."

Nobody has to tell them how hard life is and what they have to do to survive. It's easy to talk, but they live it every day. They come to play basketball, not to listen to a bunch of old guys yak. Garf understands that, but he also knows that the kids who figure out the fastest that they need both—and more besides—are the ones who tend to make it and stick around the longest. That's why he keeps after them.

The King realizes that too, but he might be the worst offender. He's just like the kids. He's there to get it on. The summertime has long since become his most important season. It is that simple and so is his philosphy: "Just play good in the games." He coaches on and off at Pelham High, near his hometown, whenever there is money in the school budget, and otherwise seems content to subsist over the winter in order to return to Five-Star.

He paces the sidelines before the opening tap every session, impatient for stations to end, and when the jump ball is tossed all else ceases. There is no esprït de corps, no Five-Star Connection. He would as soon accuse a friend of cheating on the clock as look at him, particularly in a close game. There is no before or after, only the moment, although he does make exceptions, particularly where referees are concerned.

* * * * *

Mike Feinberg has probably made one questionable call, no more than that, in 20 years at camp even though The King swears there have been hundreds more, all against him. Feinberg was a counselor at Rosemont before Five-Star got there and quickly became part of the family. A mathematics teacher at New Rochelle High now, he has officiated in the New York State high school tournament and reffed Rick Pitino when he was a rising senior. He's made a call or two in his day.

He still refs at Honesdale and has called fouls on the best of them, and every year The King cries a river to him. Feinberg barely hears him anymore. The tears, after all, started with Moses Malone, when Feinberg nullified one of his dunks. Everyone booed, but there was no doubt in his mind that Moses slammed it and rules are rules. The King's team wasn't even involved and it happened how many years ago, but that never stops him from bringing it up. If a kid even gets a fingertip above the rim and Feinberg doesn't call it, he wails, "You didn't let Moses do that 16 years ago," or something less civil.

He does it practically on cue every year, so when Garf heard him working Feinberg, about two minutes after the games got going, he felt better. Maybe things would get back to normal and maybe all the kids needed was a chance to adjust to the different time zone. Every August the clocks are turned ahead at Honesdale, and apart from the sensation that arrival at camp and departure a week later seem unseparated, there becomes Five-Star Time and time in the rest of the world.

Garf started stealing time in the early years when, more and more, with the addition of stations and more campers, late games lasted past dark. The daylight saving plan confuses the campers at first and bums them out all week, depriving them of precious sleep until the lost hour is returned the final night. Garf's eventual goal is to steal a month, flipping the calendar back along with the clocks when Honesdale ends.

Even without Garf's tampering, there is a constancy about Honesdale that makes it a thing of beauty. The camp was bustling and busy so no one noticed when Itchy and Twitchy arrived. Garf wasn't about to disturb the flow to announce them, and if he had he'd have been met with a lot of blank stares. If it were Michael Jordan and Isiah Thomas, it might have created more of a stir, but only Garf and Will Klein, who was occupied elsewhere, knew who the twins were and that they, as much as Air and Isiah, were the fiber of Five-Star.

It always lifts Garf's spirits when kids come back, regardless of their position in the world of basketball. Andy and Jeff Diamond always return to see if the place is the same and how it has changed and how they have changed. They did all right for themselves after their camping days were over. They both got into law and stayed with the game, playing college ball together at New Paltz, New York, and refereeing in the Continental Basketball Association for a number of years.

Twitchy got into broadcasting, becoming the voice of CUNY radio and television games and figures it's safe now—he's too old for the Alligator Pit—to talk about one of Garf's camp classics. It happened when he and the Itch were at Rosemont. Then as now, Garf had a camera wrapped around his neck like it was part of him, snapping pictures of anything that moved. The campers kidded that he looked like an Oriental tourist, but he ignored them and kept adding to the family photo album. One morning Garf jumped up on a bench to get the proper angle and met with misfortune.

"It had rained the night before and he slipped and fell flat on his back into a puddle," Twitchy said. "He was very cool about it and got up like nothing happened, but we were screeching. You can't help but admire the guy, though, for all he's done. My brother and I were never great players, but I know being at Five-Star put a certain fire in my system. It gave me an intangible desire to succeed because I knew I was sticking it out against guys bigger and stronger than me, that I was able to function in that land."

The Fireside is perpetually down the road. Old Fuzzy is usually there mornings in his full-length white apron and suspenders, wiping down the bar and inspecting the glassware. One way or the other, even when he's gone, he'll be there. He says they're always yelling at him to retire, but he doesn't mind helping out in the morning, when it's slow.

His son, Joe Ranner II, remembers when Moses Malone sneaked out of camp one night and came in for a brew. He didn't serve him but was impressed by Malone's maturity. For a kid, he sure seemed to have seen a lot of the world. The Five-Star coaches still come down at night, he says, but it isn't the same. The college Dead

Period sure did cut down on the noise on Saturday nights in late August.

The fireplace wall is lined with autographed pictures of some of the bigger names who have warmed themselves and eaten there, like Bob Knight. "It's funny the way we got that one," Ranner says. "My grandson asked him for it and Knight said, 'How come you didn't want a picture of me when I was a nobody?' My grandson looked at him like he was crazy and said, 'Who wants a picture of a nobody?' and Knight just shook his head and laughed and gave it to him."

* * * * *

The nights at Honesdale, after lights out, are perhaps the least affected by time. The air can still get nippy and there is often a mist that surrounds the bunkhouses like an aura in the reflected glow of the camp's scattered floodlights. The bunkhouses are dark well before midnight but voices carry easily from them through the mist long afterwards. On the second night of camp a few of the campers were talking in bed, working things out. "Word," said one voice that sounded inner-city. It was street vernacular for the truth, the way things really are.

"There was this one dude I know who got shot in the face and then some guy shot him six more times. Seriously, man, I saw that and got out of there." Another voice said, "I know, man. You know that wilding thing in the park? I knew one of the guys who did that. I knew him, but that isn't the kind of stuff you wanna be doing. Those boys be crazy." And there were other voices in the darkness that sounded low and muffled like they were coming from inside a confessional.

* * * * *

Tuesday morning Garf treated the campers to some Cole Porter. He selected "Begin the Beguine," hoping they'd get the hint and also get an impromptu history lesson. He informed them that the tune had probably outsold anything Michael Jackson ever had on the charts, as if at 7:15 a.m. they really cared. They never know what's in store when he starts messing with the PA system, blowing into the microphone and turning dials. Every day it's Benny Goodman or somebody else they never heard of, and meanwhile there's the countdown.

Every 60 seconds or so he announces how much time is left before the morning workout, and little by little the campers trickle out of the bunkhouses until he calls "Everybody up" like some Five-Star rooster, and then there's nothing but screen doors slamming and sweatpants being pulled up on the run. The counselors make one final sweep, shooing along any late risers and the camp is in full swing again.

After stations the campers still weren't upbeat enough to suit Garf. They weren't even after him to shoot. Will Rey, getting his first taste of Honesdale after several visits to Radford and Pitt, joked that it had nothing to do with the energy level, they'd just given up thinking he'd ever make a basket. But the truth was Garf wasn't happy. He just scowled and told them to pipe down whenever they even tried to start anything and it was obvious he was serious.

It went on like that all afternoon and night. He didn't need them jumping for joy. He would have been satisfied with constrained excitment, mild delirium, anything to prove they were alive and well. The next morning he made a scene before stations, haranguing the kids about the turnout at one of Will Rey's Morning Mini-Lectures on defense. "It was a great lecture and there were only 35 people there. Twenty-eight of them are already Division I players," he said. "Where the hell were the rest of you?" It was the borderline players he was after, the marginal players who needed Five-Star the most.

"This is the Dead Period. The college coaches are not going to come here and line the courts. If you're waiting for that to turn it on, you're wasting my time and yours. Tom Konchalski is here and there are other scouting service guys here, but they aren't going to get you a scholarship. What kind of enthusiasm do we have here? Nothing! This is the worst Five-Star session ever!" Maybe it was for effect, like a coach purposely getting a technical foul to fire up his team. More probably it was pure and utter frustration, but to accentuate the point, Garf wadded up a sheet of paper and hurled it to the ground.

It stayed there quite awhile before anyone dared touch it.

The outburst made something click, or perhaps Garf was out of his mind, because there was no lack of interest at the NBA league's "Man-for-Man Defensive Pressure" station. It's hard to imagine what the results would have been if the campers had not livened up. Not that Garf is a pussycat, but coach Gene Thompson would have been extremely upleasant to be around had the campers been anything short of ecstatic.

Thompson is a bulldog of a man who has coached Wilmington High of Wilmington, Delaware to three state championships, and they're still counting. Thompson's assistant was Tom Herrion, the coach at Rindge and Latin, Patrick Ewing's high school alma mater, and the son of Jim Herrion, Garf's former envelope stuffer from Friendship Farm. Thompson got the campers going before turning over the reins to Herrion. That's how the coaches have always done things: The veterans teach the rookies, then sit back, listen, and learn. It goes around and around like that until everybody gets it right.

"Nothing great," Thompson began, "has ever been accomplished without enthusiasm." He was quoting Ralph Waldo Emerson, who never set foot in Five-Star and would have had to overcome frailty if he had, but whose outlook on life would have made him one of Garf's favorites. "Defense is fun and today we're going to have some fun and learn how to put pressure on a man bringing the ball up the court.

"Defense doesn't build character, it gives you the opportunity to display the character you already have. Now I want you all to listen up. I don't want to repeat myself. When I say 'Get,' I want you to get in your defensive stance. Get! Bend those knees; we don't want stuff dripping on those new sneakers. OK, good. Now, when I say 'Feet,' I want you up on our toes, running in place and I want you shouting, 'Defense is fun, defense is fun.' Feet!"

The campers responded, sounding like charging marines, and Thompson continued, "Let me hear you! Good, now make a quarter turn. Turn quickly. Be quicker than quick and turn back to the front. Keep those feet moving. Let me hear you."

It could be heard all over the camp: *"Defense is fun, defense is fun,"* but nobody was laughing. "OK, relax," Thompson said. "Now we'll do some slides. Follow the direction I point. Good. You over there, bend those knees. Don't cross your feet. Show me some enthusiasm. Next we'll do advance steps and retreat steps. To advance, start with your left foot forward. Step with the front foot and slide the rear foot up. Don't bounce. That takes too much time. To retreat, step with the rear foot first and slide.

"Every time you step, I want to hear you yell, 'Hey.' Keep your eyes forward. Don't bring your heels together. That knocks you off balance. Maintain your balance. Now add a swing step, as if your man is trying to go past you. Pivot and stay down. Don't stand up. That takes time. You want to keep constant pressure on the man. Make sure you don't cross your feet. Good.

"When you do this drill, do it as if you are actually guarding someone. Imagine he is there so you can adapt to game situations. Keep yourself at arm's length from your man and keep your head on the ball. Harass him. Flick at the ball. You aren't always trying to steal it, but you want to harass your man. Use your inside hand. If you slap at the ball with your outside hand, the ref will call it a foul 90 percent of the time."

The campers were primed and ready for Herrion. Thompson had shown them how to pick up the scent. Herrion was going to teach them how to follow the trail. "Your goal as a defender is to get the basketball and score," he said. "In a man-to-man defensive press, there are several ways to go about it. Let's assume the stance. Get! Feet! Let me hear it: 'Defense is fun, defense is fun.' Don't stroke me, fellas."

While the campers stutter-stepped in place, Herrion continued, "One way to get the ball on defense is to look for the charge. When you hear me shout 'Charge,' I want you on your backs. Get those feet set first. Charge! OK, now up, quickly. Keep those feet moving. On a loose ball you want to get down on the floor after it quickly. When I say 'Down,' I want you on your bellies after it. Down! Now up, fellas, quickly. Charge! Make it look good. Make the ref buy it. OK, good, up quickly. Down! Turnovers are what it's all about, fellas. OK, everybody up and listen.

"When the offense has the ball out of bounds, your goal is to get a five-second call, make them throw it away, or go for the steal on the inbounds pass. If you get the steal, score and get right back on defense. If the offense receives the ball inbounds, your goal is to make the dribbler turn three times before he reaches the 10-second line. You want to create as many opportunities to get the ball and score as possible.

"Don't reach guarding the dribbler. That's bullshit. Remember what Coach Thompson said about the flick. And if you get screened, fight through it, don't step behind it. Step up and over it by making your body small. Bust your ass to get your leg in front of that screen. The guy guarding the screener has to help out too. Take a step at the man with the basketball to delay him. Hedge at him without losing contact with your own man. It's a team thing, fellas, and it takes enthusiasm."

The campers had defense coming out of their ears, but the fundamentals were becoming part of them too and the camp was starting to hum. Even Garf could feel it. He could almost start to enjoy himself watching some old reliables. Tom McCorry was at his familiar post, the low post, Pete Gillen was pounding the rock on Court Three, and right next door was another Five-Star regular, Bill Donlon, the assistant coach at Northwestern University.

Garf calls Donlon "Lon Chaney of the Hardwood, The Man of a Thousand Drills." Donlon was the one who came up with the idea to set up a footwork station to teach the players how to set screens, post-up, move without the ball, or anything else that would help them get a step on their opponent. He has more ways of cutting to the basket—back-door cuts, V-cuts, L-cuts, circle cuts—than Mack the Knife.

Donlon was into footwork at Honesdale, teaching them to save time and space and making the campers do things they wouldn't dream of doing back home, not in broad daylight anyway. They looked more like guilty ne'er-do-wells than basketball players. He had them up on their toes creeping from sideline to sideline like they were sneaking out of a china shop, stolen goods in hand. The plan, though, was to make them quicker, not slicker.

He had them jumping in place with their knees bent, landing and pushing off on their toes to help make them light-legged. They were hopping on one foot, then the other, keeping their hands up for balance the whole time, and they were drawing squares and X's and triangles with their feet that would have made Pythagoras envious. That was just for starters. Donlon was loosening them up for their introduction to plyometrics.

Plyometrics, Donlon explained, is the science of explosive jumping. European high jumpers have been using it for years, but it is helpful in basketball too. It's good for blocking shots and rebounding and increasing vertical leap—in other words, dunking. "The principle is to go from negative work to positive work as quickly as possible," Donlon told the campers. "The first thing you need to know is that you should always be supervised by a trainer or coach and be in good shape before starting to do plyometrics."

Then they need to find some boxes. Big ones. Donlon had three of them approximately 12 inches, 20 inches, and 24 inches square. This was the first time he was using them in camp and they were sturdy little buggers. The staff at Bryn Mawr built them out of heavy plywood and painted them Five-Star orange. They did a great job, but some of the coaches told Garf they looked like huge orange ice cubes that wouldn't melt even if he nuked them for a week.

But Donlon wanted them solid because the kids had to jump on and off them rapidly, sometimes all three in succession, and he didn't want them wobbling. Showing the campers an assortment of drills, he just called them Box One, Box Two, and Box Three, respectively. Everyone else referred to them as Garf's Folly.

There was no question they were beneficial if used correctly and Garf loved them, but it created quite a stir when Donlon unveiled them. The rest of the coaches had a field day. Every morning they laid bets on which one Garf would be hiding under and all week they busted Garf's chops about how expensive they were. They said he could buy a beautiful home in the nicest part of town for the same amount of money and still have money left over.

But the boxes were innovative and worth every bit of $675 in Garf's mind (Will Klein managed to cut the cost in half after considerable debate), plus he figured he'd already saved a bundle at the "Weak Hand" station. For the price of a few rubber gloves, Pat Quigley had the kids doing things with a basketball that would pay huge dividends in their game. He was forcing them to do things against their will, but Five-Star guys had a strange habit of doing that.

Quigley, the coach at Bishop Loughlin, where New York Knick Mark Jackson learned the game, first had to convince the campers that he had their best interests at heart. They took one look at his rubber gloves, which in reality were foam pads with finger holes cut out, and said to themselves, "No way, dude." Quigley expected them to put the stupid-looking things on their strong hands, which would basically render them useless, except for the exposed fingertips. It meant they'd have to rely on their weak hand, the one they couldn't pass or dribble with to save their lives.

The right-handers would be forced to use their left hands and vice versa, which is something they'd always tried to avoid. They didn't enjoy looking silly in front of their peers, but Quigley relieved the pressure in a hurry. "You have to have a willingness to change and work on your weaknesses," he said. "You have to be willing to risk embarrassment. I remember when Dominique Wilkins was a camper here, before anyone knew who he was. He blocked one guy's shot five times in a row and the guy left camp.

"If you get your shot blocked at Five-Star after you've made your best move, the one you eat them alive with back in your hometown, it's not because you're weak. It's because this is a strong place. Even the best get their shot blocked and there will be times you will need to adjust your game." The kids saw his point and slipped the things on and were better for it immediately. Quigley made them play monkey-in-the-middle first, with the passer at each end using his weak hand and the kid in between defending.

"When you make a hook pass, make it directly off the defender's shoulder," Quigley said. "Did you ever see a guy try to block a pass with his face? Hell no, so fake low and then go right at him. He'll shy away. On a curl pass, fake up, then go low. If you make that pass with two hands, there will always be somebody quick enough to steal it. Use one hand. Whichever hand you use to make the pass, use the other hand to ward off the defense."

Quigley forced the kids to catch passes, go to the triple threat position, dribble in for layups, grab rebounds, and make outlet passes all with their weak hand. Campers in nearby stations had to keep one eye peeled for errant tosses, but at the end of 15 minutes things were basically under control. Then Quigley had to ruin it by making campers shoot hook shots: sweeping hooks, half hooks, and jump hooks. It was like they were shooting medicine balls.

Quigley knew it was good for what ailed them. "On the sweeping hook, bring it from the hip. Make sure you sight your target. Turn you shoulder and head so you see the basket and keep two hands on the ball until you are ready to release the shot. You guards especially, the half hook is good in close to the basket. Keep the ball close to your body. When you practice these at home, start out with no basketball. Go through the motions. That's a good way to practice something new. Don't be afraid to look bad in order to improve."

That was one way to put it. Over at the "Executing Special Situations" station, Jerry Wainwright was saying much the same thing but a tad differently, more like a Chicago hit man. "There are no secrets in this game," he said. "If you do something shitty, you better work on it. In stressful situations you go to what you do best, and if all you have is a bad habit, that's what you go to. Right here is where all the stations come in. If you paid attention or if you didn't, this is where it shows."

The campers love Wainwright and practically hang on his every word, but he has a major problem. He can never tell when he's at Wake Forest and when he's at Five-Star. He was supposed to be teaching the kids how to handle the critical moments during a game when split-second execution is absolutely necessary, easing them into it, and yet here he was out in the middle of nowhere acting like he was going for all the marbles.

This was camp, not an ACC showdown. The kids couldn't figure him out. He was all buddy-buddy one minute and down your throat the next. Which was it, Five-Star or the real thing? "We lost five games last year because we weren't mentally prepared for special situations," Wainwright said. "In one of those games a very good player froze in the heat of excitement. We were ahead by three points late in the game and the other team had a one-and-one. The shooter made the first one and we called a time-out.

"We thought the shooter might try to miss the second shot on purpose, so we told the guy responsible for boxing him out to just face him and bar him out. Don't just step in front of the guy, look right at him and keep him out. The kid said he understood and went out and just stepped in front of the shooter with his back to him. The guy missed the shot, went around our guy for the rebound, scored, and we lost in overtime. Our kid lost his poise. I'm trying to show you how to avoid that."

Wainwright showed the campers what he termed a "simple play," calling it "Wake Forest." It was designed to get a good, open shot in a minimum of time with built-in options. He separated the campers into five-man teams, then outlined the play. It was a typical 1-4 setup with the point guard on top of the key and the other four players spread out, with the post players on opposite wings. He diagramed a series of cuts and screens and was Mr. Nice Guy. Everyone said they understood it and could run it anytime he asked, day or night.

He decided there was no time like the present. He motioned the first five onto the court and they self-consciously walked out, and without warning he was Mr. Hard Ass. "You guys get off the court," Wainwright said. "There's a chronic bitch in America. All I hear is, 'Aw, this coach is screwing me.' That's bullshit. There isn't a coach in America who won't play you if he has confidence in you. I can't have confidence in a guy who walks onto the court. You guys get off the court and the next time I call on you, try to show me something."

Two more teams tried to run the play, hustling out but failing miserably. Wainwright could only shake his head. "You're all gonna be big-time players, right? You've got a lot to learn about being big-time." It was back to Mr. Nice Guy after that. He walked one team of five through the play, bodily moving them from spot to spot. "This is the easiest way in the world to learn a play," he said. "You guys will never forget that play again. Maybe it's not fair that the rest of you just had to watch, but in the heat of the game sometimes that may be the only chance you get."

He gave the campers another chance. He was all sugar and spice until one group massacred the play, bumping into each other like rush hour subway riders, and there was Mr. Hard Ass, lambasting them, especially the point guard. "This guy is killing me," Wainwright said. "Let me explain some things to you. I do this for a living. Coaching basketball and winning is how I feed my family. When I hand the ball to my point guard, I'm not just saying, 'Here's the ball,' I'm saying, 'Here's my job, here's my family.'

"Is that fair to the kid? I don't care and if the plays don't work I'm going to get all over his ass. Point guards, you are in charge on the court. If you see a teammate out of position, tell him. And you other guys, if the point guard is screwing up, let him know. Do you think a teammate will remember if you help him out? You bet your ass he will. Five men being tight is the only way a team wins. It seems obvious, but basketball is a game of mistakes and the team that makes the fewest usually wins."

* * * * *

Wainwright didn't know when to quit. He was the two o'clock lecturer later that afternoon and chose as his subject "Manual Resistance Training," which tied in with his whole weight-training and
conditioning program. The campers weren't sure they appreciated
his timing. It was the middle of the week and the middle of a hot
day, and this maniac wanted them to yank towels and try to do
situps with guys pushing on their legs making it almost impossible.
But they went along with him. He hadn't done anything to hurt them
yet.

Pat Sullivan, still worn out from Pitt, was his first victim. In front
of the whole camp he had to do reverse pushups on a bench and
then stand up and put his arms over his shoulders and yank on a
towel with all his strength with Wainwright holding the other end. It
wasn't until well after he started wishing his arms would fall off that
Mr. Hard Ass let him stop. "This may seem ridiculous to you,"
Wainwright said to all the campers, "but what we just did could
mean a better outlet pass for Pat, or some guard's stronger dribble.
For everyone it could mean a good, strong shot extension."

Jamal Mashburn was his next prey. Mashburn, a 6'8" power forward out of Cardinal Hayes High in the Bronx, is not a young man to
be trifled with. He looks like he eats backboards and eggs for breakfast. But for the moment he was just a shy kid standing alone in the
middle of 400 campers. He got red as a beet when Wainwright told
him do do pushups, then straddled his back and held him down
while he was pushing up. He got crimson when he had to lie flat on
his back and bring his arms straight up from the side with Mr. Hard
Ass applying steady downward resistance.

"I don't give a damn what the rest of the campers think,"
Wainwright told Mashburn as he strained and turned redder.
"Don't worry about making an asshole of yourself in front of other
people. Right now I'm the only one you have to answer to." But
Mashburn was the one grunting and groaning and having his arms
shake like a weakling. It was humiliating. He gutted it out and got
a nice round of applause when he was finished, but Wainwright
wasn't through, not quite.

"Don't tell me how hard it is to be embarrassed," he said. "Don't
tell me how hard you've got it. I've seen guys in cities trying to learn
how to play basketball dressed in the same clothes every day. Try
living with that. There have been times I've talked to kids in the city
with cocaine crack vials on the ground all around us and people
hawking drugs. What the hell does being embarrassed have to do

with it? You don't ever have to let other people drag you down because you're afraid of what they might think. The bottom line is you have to answer to yourself."

Wainwright hadn't said much, he figured, just shown the kids some exercises and spoken a few words from the heart, but it was the last time he would speak to them and the campers wanted to give him something to remember them by. They gave him a Five-Star ovation, rhythmically clapping as they rose to their feet. It died down after a minute, but then that "other thing" began happening. Garf started to announce the schedule for the rest of the day and the applause started up again, sporadically, from the back of the gym. The kids were off their seats again until it died down gradually and they sat down.

Garf was ready to talk, but the emotion welled up anew and the kids were standing again, clapping as one body without saying a word. Garf hesitated after they sat down the third time, just to be sure they were done, which was a good thing. Once more they stood and showered Wainwright with love. That was the only thing it could be after so many spontaneous outbursts and they weren't ashamed. Mr. Hard Ass soaked it in until he couldn't help it. He got teary-eyed and wanted to turn his face away but didn't.

* * * * *

Thursday morning Garf wanted more. Mike Fratello was coming in later that afternoon, if he could get out of Georgia, and Rick Pitino was due Friday and Saturday for a Double Bubble, two straight days of lectures and juking the campers out of their Air Jordans and Cons. The names on the sneakers had changed, but Pitino hadn't. Garf didn't want anybody messing up the works and there was still a handful of kids not completely consumed.

Garf had one ace left up his sleeve: Dennis Burke. In August 1971, Burke, a 5'9" lefty guard from St. John's Prep in Brooklyn, was on the list to come to Honesdale as a two-week camper-worker. Two weeks before opening day, he called Garf to tell him he'd broken his left wrist in a motorcycle accident. He said he was ambidextrous and still wanted to come, but Garf told him he was full of ambi and told him to stay home.

Burke insisted. He was one of Garf's discoveries, so he got his way, and besides Garf knew he was the type to get something out of the stations at least. He had already won the Playmaker Award in June. He showed up in soft cast, and playing right-handed all week he won the Playmaker Award again and made the Orange-White Classic. "That's the difference between kids today," Garf said.

"There isn't one kid in a thousand who would do today what Burke did. They would be too afraid of losing a scholarship.

"You can never tell what will happen though. Burke went to Florida State where something went wrong. Maybe it was injuries, I don't know. That had to be the most shocking non-make in the history of the camp. There wasn't a thing wrong with that kid, but I never heard from him again. I wish there were more like him." Garf tells the story to inspire kids from time to time and he tried it Thursday morning on a camper who'd injured his thumb. The trainers had advised him not to play and Garf hoped he'd stick around for stations after hearing the Burke story, but he went home.

*   *   *   *   *

Some kids never listen. Some can't. There was one Burke-like camper that Garf was satisfied with, Jan Struhar, a 5'11" guard from Monroe-Woodbury, New York. Struhar became the first deaf Five-Star camper ever when he went to Pitt in 1988 and won the Mr. Hustle Award. It wasn't a sympathy vote. Struhar was the second-and-fourth-quarter point guard on his team and led them to an NIT league championship. It takes more than sympathy to get that done. He also made the Orange-White Classic, which he didn't at Honesdale. People don't just hand you things at Five-Star.

There is something about Struhar. He plays in utter silence. It is difficult to understand what he's saying too unless he writes it down, and then it's easy. "The whole game seems beautiful, and when I watch I become a little excited," Struhar said. "I always dream about being like Rex Chapman. I like his style. The first time I watched him on TV he was with Kentucky. He was a very good shooter and could fly down the court quickly on the fast break. Then I read in the newspaper that Rex went to the NBA.

"I am amazed at how fast he moves and also Michael Jordan, the quick speed. They both are so smooth. I dream of becoming as skillful as they are. My dream is to play in the NBA. I don't have any sure plan except to work hard improving my skill in basketball. I know about deaf people not going to the NBA. I have a friend, Walter Gribbs, and we always wonder why it is so hard for deaf players to make the NBA. I think one reason is people who can hear have trouble communicating.

"At Five-Star my teams always have a secret. Communication is hard, but we manage with special signs. The whole team knows them. One sign might mean to pass the ball to a team member or go ahead and try to make a basket. When the coach needs to talk with me, there is a friend who knows some sign and helps me out, but yes, it is all very difficult. I feel inside many times that I wish I could hear and be the same as my friends. I would love to someday have hearing and deaf people play together in the NBA. That is my dream for the future."

Struhar has that little something extra and people are drawn to him. They are nervous about talking to him at first because it is so different, but they adjust. It was the same way when Kyle Domar came to camp one year. He was from Ohio and nobody bothered to tell Garf he had only one hand when they enrolled him. Garf screamed bloody murder, not because he was prejudiced, but because he was afraid the kid didn't know what he'd gotten himself into.

Domar was a real scrapper, though, and won the Mr. Hustle Award. Having one hand didn't alter the fact that he was a Midwesterner. Struhar was made of the same stuff. It was hard enough playing at Five-Star without needing someone to do your listening for you. There are worse things in life, but the campers truly liked Struhar's spunk and at the awards ceremony Saturday night they got together with Coach Wainwright and gave him a gift. It wasn't any big deal, just one of Wainwright's jump ropes, but Struhar said it made him feel "happy and proud of myself."

Garf gave a jump rope to Doremus Bennerman that night too, tabbing him "the greatest ballboy in the history of Five-Star." It wasn't degrading. He meant it. Bennerman, a fine player from St. Joe's in Trumbull, Connecticut, who later committed to Siena College, was paying his way through camp. There were supposed to be other kids helping, but they didn't show up and he had to do their jobs too. He could have whined but he didn't, and Garf truly appreciated that. Little things like that made life simpler.

*   *   *   *   *

The campers still had places to go and people to meet before all that would happen. Bob Mackey, the coach at Tolentine, and his assistant Bobby Gonzalez had the "Post Defense" station in the NBA league. Standing in the paint Mackey said, "When you play defense, nobody should get through here easy. Your best tool to stop them is your forearm. Make contact with your man and use your elbow as an antenna to deny him the ball cutting through. Once the big man gets the ball inside, the show is over. Get to that spot first. Don't let him get there and set up."

The Development League campers were getting much the same message from John Sarandrea, an assistant at the University of Pittsburgh. He wouldn't start until everyone was clapping their hands and then all he talked about was their feet. "Playing good defense means getting to a spot before the other guy and that is accomplished with your feet," he said. "You have to keep your eyes open too and sometimes, down low, your hands become your eyes.

"You have to stay in touch with your man. Don't hold him, but keep in touch. If the ball is on the top of the key, get good defensive position, low and balanced. Play between the ball and the man with a hand and foot in the passing lane. What is the passing lane? It's an imaginary straight line between the ball and your man. Find it and straddle it. You won't stop every pass, so when the ball gets inside, don't leave your feet. Make your man take the toughest shot possible and box out after the shot."

And at the "Rebounding, Blocking Out, and Pitching Out" station, Kevin "Butterfly" Jones, an assistant at Canisius, was curing the campers of White Man's Disease. An ex-camper, Jones has been known as Butterfly since he tried out for the team his sophomore year at Truman High in the Bronx. "I must have looked uncoordinated with my long arms," he said. "I guess the other kids thought they looked like a butterfly's wings."

Butterfly put his wide wingspan to good use later at Dartmouth, where he got more than his share of rebounds. Never a great leaper and thin as rail, he made up for it by boxing out beautifully, and despite his ebony hue feels he has much in common with others similarly afflicted, Caucasian and otherwise. White Man's Disease: the unexplainable inability to jump high, grab a basketball, and hold onto it all at the same time.

White Man's Disease. Butterfly knew he could get away with calling it that at Five-Star. He is acquainted with racism but knows it is barred from camp. That was taken care of long before he came along and his only interest was ridding the basketball world of the dreaded malady. He had been been healed and wanted to heal others.

His panacea was Total Concentration. Butterfly is a unique teacher. He sounds like a Jamaican version of William F. Buckley, Jr., singsong and concise, and when he speaks he accentuates each syllable. He is very eloquent. He is also a rip. The campers are always in stiches when they leave his station and a kind of metamorphosis takes place at the same time. It can be seen in their eyes. "Total concentration is the key to rebounding," Butterfly said, and to emphasize the point he made the campers do punishing pushups whenever they messed up.

They didn't merely push themselves up and down. At just the right moment, when they had almost reached their limits, he made them hold their trembling bodies two inches off the ground until he was darn good and ready to relieve their hilarious agony. After they understood the basics—and the penalty for forgetting—he supplied the details.

"You must want rebounds and go after them with total concentration," Butterfly said. "You must let your opponent know you want them too. Let me hear you growl!" The kids self-consciously purred and he stopped them. "No, no, not like wimps! Imagine if Mr. T. were going for a rebound. How would he do it? Growl!" They put a little more into it then and he put them through a drill, tossing the ball against the backboard. They had to get the rebound, and if they didn't growl to his satisfaction, they did pushups.

"Yes, total concentration," Butterfly said. "Use two hands to catch the ball, or if you must, grab it with one and bring it quickly into the other hand. Then chin it. Now that you have the rebound you must make a good outlet pass. Turn to the outside and release a strong pass. What do we call someone who turns to the inside where the defense can strip them and score an easy layup?" Met with blank stares, he told them.

"An asshole." Just to make sure they understood, he asked again, "What do we call them?" The campers, cracking up and looking around to make sure nobody was going to cuff them for cussing, answered, *"An asshole, sir!"* Butterfly was soaring now and the kids were totally at ease. They thought they were having fun, but they were effortlessly learning a tough job. "Yes, an asshole," said the teacher. "You must have total concentration and not be an asshole. Then you are free from the curse of White Man's Disease."

It was time to test the cure in a spirited game of Monster Rebounding. The object of the game was for one camper to beat two other campers to the glass and not only get the rebound but score. There were two rules: no undercutting and no grabbing of shirts. Everything else was perfectly legal. The losers had to do 10 pushups and the winners had better growl or they'd be pumping too.

It was a man's world more hideous than anything Moses Malone could envision. It was like a Mr. T. convention gone rampant. The faint of heart were hiding, trying to avoid getting involved, and Butterfly was making sure they did, laughing and standing well out of harm's way. Meanwhile, two kids, Dana Dingle and Pat Flynn, were crushing the boards. Dingle, from St. Raymond's in the Bronx, was doing it with athletic style. Flynn, a 6'6", 15-year-old from Osbourn Park High in Manassas, Virginia, just wouldn't take no for an answer. He wanted the ball, period.

Both Flynn and Dingle wound up in the Orange-White Classic,

which was a minor miracle because by the time Garf blew his whistle ending stations, they were in the middle of a madhouse. They were lucky to get out of there in one piece. Butterfly had the situation well in hand, however, and before he dismissed them, he huddled everyone up and reminded them what the camp was all about. It was about learning and doing the right thing, and rebounding was about pride and hustle, not athletic ability. With their hands joined in the center they all said, *"Five-Star"* and *"Word"* and went on their way, forever changed.

If Garf had seen that he probably would have felt more at ease about Mike Fratello's upcoming visit. If he had looked in the middle of the pack and seen Laray Hardy he might have totally relaxed. Hardy, from Cardoza High in Queens, showed up in camp the first night dribbling the ball between his legs and making sure everyone knew he was there. He injured his foot the next day and couldn't play in the games but stuck around for stations and participated where he could. His team won a league title and he was there all the way.

Wherever he went he carried a copy of *Five-Star Basketball Drills* with him. Garf gave one to every kid as a bonus for coming to camp. The book (which might be the largest-selling tome of its type in hoop history) has many of the same drills taught over the years at camp by all the coaches, including Knight, Pitino, Hubie Brown, Larry Brown (long since forgiven for his flight from the Nationals), Gene Keady (Purdue), Jim Lynam (Philadelphia 76ers), Mike Krzyzewski, and you name him. Hardy clung to it like it was lifeblood. He didn't want to let go of what he was feeling. He didn't realize yet that Five-Star is a moveable feast. It would always be in his system.

Garf probably did notice, but he had a lot on his mind. As a matter of fact, he was panicking. Mike Fratello was having trouble getting out of Atlanta. The Hawks were embroiled in sticky negotiations involving Jon "Contract" Koncak and Fratello had to be there. If he made it at all it was going to be on the bull's tail.

NINETEEN
Waving to the Caboose

"You can't leave the place a mess."

– Will Klein

It was a long way from Hackensack to the Atlanta Hawks and Mike Fratello remembered every mile.

Garf was in a frazzle all day but he knew there was no way Fratello was going to be a no-show at Honesdale. Somewhere else, maybe, if he absolutely had to, but never Honesdale. As it turned out, Fratello arrived halfway through his introduction and was gone before the applause died down, but the campers knew he'd been there.

Garf began his intro after Fratello's car was spotted less than a mile from camp. Time was of the essence, and it was also a perfect excuse for drawing it out. "Mike doesn't have to be here," he said as the car rolled in. "He's up to his ears in contract talks with the Hawks and shouldn't even be here. He's been a loyal worker for 20 years and should have missed a year but he didn't. He knows the meaning of ethics. How do you thank someone for that? You can't."

Fratello knew the feeling. He wasted no time telling the campers that he hadn't made it to the Atlanta Hawks on his own. "There is no question Five-Star is one of the main reasons I've gotten the opportunity to work in the NBA," he said. "What Garf and Will Klein have done in the past 25 years for coaches and players alike is awesome and mind-boggling. When a young coach can work with thoroughbreds and experiment with ideas with players of that caliber, it makes him look very good.

"As players you should realize that this camp makes everyone look better. That is very important because right now, at your age, you are beginning to influence how other people perceive you. What they think they see will not always be the truth, but it's how people look at you that ultimately determines how they treat you. You've got to understand what makes people tick and how they perceive you. It can make a tremendous difference."

There was also basketball reality to consider. "You need three things to be considered as an NBA or major college player today," Fratello said. "The first thing is shooting. If you're a shooter they'll always find a place for you, but don't believe it's easy street. All last summer, Doc Rivers, a very established player, and Roy Marble, one of our draft picks, worked out to develop the strength and flexibility we told them we needed. Every day they did stretching exercises, worked with the medicine ball, worked out on the stationary bike, and took a thousand shots a day after practice. Those guys are in the NBA. Are you better than them?

"The second is dribbling. At the higher levels your game comes off the move. You need to be able to go off your dribble to a place where you can get your shot. Let me tell you a story about getting your shot. For a long time, guys like Doc Rivers and Spud Webb and Dominique Wilkins took it personally when someone like Robert Parish or Bill Walton or Kevin McHale would block their shot. Those guys were used to taking the ball underneath and pounding it through the basket.

"It's not like that in the NBA. I remember Dominique, in one game against the Bullets, getting his shot blocked something like 16 times by Jeff Ruland and Manute Bol. He'd go inside and try to double pump and hook dunk and Ruland and Manute would just stand there and swat it. Manute is a kick. He loves talking shit to guys. They'll come in and he just stands there and says, 'Take that shit outta here.'

"Well, Wilkins and the others finally got the messasge that they had to give those guys some respect. They started to develop their middle game, their in-between game from about 8 to 12 feet and even further, out to 15 feet. From there, they could make the defense commit and then go jam it down their throats.

"The third thing you need," Fratello continued, "is to be a thinker. Thinkers make good decisions on the court. You can't play the game at the higher levels unless you know how to think basketball. You have to know what you're capable of doing and do it the best you can. There are two categories of players in the NBA: specialists, guys who are very good at one or two things; and skill players, guys who are solid all-around. Think about what you are and play to your strengths.

"Now I know guys miss shots, so the next thing you have to think about is rebounding. It's a combination of hard work and understanding. I don't know if your coaches have told you about angles, but it is very important to understand them.

"If you are on the strong side or up high when the shot goes up, use whichever leg is extended to step toward your man and make contact," Fratello said. "I used to teach guys a pivot move, but they were confused most of the time. By the time they got through saying to themselves, 'Aw shit, which foot do I use?' their man was history. The main thing is you've got to make contact and prevent guys from flying in toward the basket.

"Down low, when you turn to box out, get your arms up high so your man can't pin your arms down. Get your ass on his thighs too so when he tries to roll off you can feel which way he's going and prevent that explosion to the basket. On the weak side take a step at your man and if he stays out there, turn and look for the ball. It's a physical battle every night, but it's also a mental battle."

The campers were just starting to enjoy themselves, but Fratello had a plane to catch. "You know, you guys are part of the greatest game on earth," he said. I'm sure you've heard this before, but you should try to take advantage of what you have here at Five-Star and appreciate the things your families try to do for you.

"I remember overhearing Doc Rivers and Isiah Thomas talking once about their sons. It was after the Dominique Wilkins All-Star Game and they were in the shower soaping up. I happened to walk past and I heard them saying how it wasn't until they were grown up that they realized how smart their own fathers had been, that it was incredible that so much of what the old man had told them was right. There they were, stars in the NBA, and it finally hit them."

* * * * *

Shirley Bassey was the featured artist Friday morning so Rick Pitino had a tough act to follow. He would do the first of two lectures that afternoon and finally put a stop to the camper's shenanigans. Maybe the Kentucky coach had been forewarned or maybe he picked up on it on his own, but either way he would have no time for their nonsense.

It had been a grueling few days for Garf. Try as he might, he couldn't make the camp come together to suit himself. "Maybe I'm just having a bad week, but it bothers me," he said. "When the kids don't behave or when they act like jerks in the bunks, which once in awhile they do but not very often, I think they don't approve of the camp. That depresses me."

Garf seemed to come out of his shell with his friend Pitino in camp, and when the kids exhorted him to *Shoooot,*" he did. Besides, Garf had his reputation to think about. Pitino would never let him live it down if he refused. He hemmed and hawed as usual and paced and twitched until Will Rey bowed down to take his whistle and watch, but then he was all business. He swished the first shot and, like an old tap dancer, issued a challenge to the young highstepper.

Pitino knew he was being hornswoggled. It was Garf's home court and he hadn't even warmed up. He tried to bluff his way out but the campers were all over him. All he ever talked about was how good he could shoot and now it was time to put his money where his mouth was. He put one up and missed and the campers moaned, *"Ooooh shit!"* Garf didn't say a word, just looked at him like, "You never could finish, Richie boy." Chalk one up for the Five-Star guy.

Being an old huckster himself, it made sense that Pitino started out talking about odds. He told the campers the chances of making the NBA were the same as being struck by lightning. "Less than 200 players out of more than 20,000 from this camp have made it," Pitino said. "But you should still dream. Patrick Ewing made it, Mark Jackson made it, and at one time they sat here just like you are doing right now."

Pitino was rudely interrupted by a handful of kids tittering not 10 feet away from him. He was stunned hearing it and the words shot out of his mouth faster than he could think them. "What's wrong with you guys? Why don't you just shut the hell up?" It was the campers' turn to be shocked. This wasn't Howard Garfinkel, some strange guy trying to tell them what to do out in the boondocks, this was Rick Pitino, the coach of the Knicks and Kentucky.

It stung and they stopped, and whether it made a lasting impression or not, only they could tell. Pitino wasn't the type to wait around and see. Pitino knew it was the same whether he said it or Garf did. He'd be there if they smartened up, but in the meantime there were other people patiently waiting to hear what he had to say. "Some of us didn't make the big show as players so now we coach and we want to see you make it," he said. "When you don't because of your attitude or drugs or bad grades, a piece of our hearts is cut out. Don't screw up and look for the easy way out. Take advantage of your opportunities."

Pitino always did. To this day he swears he never hustled kids out of their sneakers when he was a camper, not as a card shark anyway. In one-on-one maybe, but not cards. It was easy to believe that, watching him work the audience. His usual gig was to come in and burn the campers one at a time. He was a real hustler, letting them win at first and then doing a face job on them.

He asked Garf for a volunteer, gave the kid the basketball, and told him to shoot. Before the kid could release it, Pitino barked at him to freeze. The kid did, and Pitino told him to walk in the direction of his front foot. He led himself in a steady path about 10 feet wide of the basket.

"When you shoot, you need to have your foot pointed at the target," Pitino said. "And as you bring the ball up, tuck it. Keep your elbow pointed down at your foot as you bring your arm up and don't let your head move. When you practice, practice one-handed. If you can't shoot one-handed, you can't shoot. Remember the sequence: foot, tuck it, and your head not moving."

The campers listened intently, but also seemed to figure they'd seen all he had. The proof was in the pudding. They wanted to see him perform. He asked Garf for a second volunteer, someone who was a deadeye. Travis Best, up from Pitt, fit the description. Pitino watched him shoot a couple of times, then guarded him. Best missed four out of six. Pitino didn't get right in his face. He noticed right off that Best was pointing his foot toward the bleachers, and as long as he did that he'd let him shoot all day.

Best is a helluva player, and Pitino didn't let him walk away thinking otherwise, but a chain is only as strong as its weakest link. Pitino is shrewd. He can take one look at a guy and size him up and know how to stop him.

Anyone who needed further convincing got it when Pitino asked for another guinea pig and was given Ken Blakeney, a 6'4" rising senior from DeMatha High. Blakeney is a smooth, powerful, scoring machine. Pitino hounded him but Blakeney hit seven in a row. He even had the audacity to say, "And one" after a particularly humiliating basket. He faked low and put one up from the top of the key with Pitino hanging all over him. He shouldn't have rubbed it in. That was Pitino's game.

The Kentucky coach got Travis Best back out on the court and told him to force Blakeney, a righty shooter, to his left if he could. Best did and the DeMatha Kid suddenly went cold, rimming six out of seven. Good defense stops good offense. Great offense is another matter. "If you want to play beyond high school, you have to get in the lane and be able to go one-on-one," Pitino said. "You have to be able to go body-to-body and drive the lane.

"If you drive off a screen, show the shot by looking at the rim. To get your shot you have to get the defensive guy to react to you. Look at your target. That will get the defender standing still. And unless you're under six feet tall, you will have to post up at the higher levels of this game. Post up at the first marker. That way you have the perfect angle for the board game on a turnaround. Be a wide body with your legs spread and arms out. Going to the basket, drive your shoulder toward the rim. You are harder to block that way."

The next day Pitino showed the campers Moses Malone drop steps, Bernard King low post turnarounds, and Kevin McHale up-fakes like he'd taught all those guys everything they knew. He even told how he had been able to help Patrick Ewing become a better offensive threat.

"Patrick had a reputation for having bad hands with the Knicks. That was not true even though he dropped the ball a lot. His difficulty was he was losing sight of the basketball going into his hands," Pitino said. Ewing, an NBA superstar now, might have learned that much sooner, but such is life.

It wasn't until he was nearly finished that Pitino finally admitted he was a flimflammer. "Yes, I'm a con man," he said, "and I teach my players to be con men. Not bad con men though. They learn good cons so they can deal with adversity, not bad cons so they can bullshit their professors and coaches. Organize your lives, guys, and think beyond graduation. Put yourself in the best position to be educated so you can adjust to whatever comes along in your lives. And don't put down the basketball, guys. When you do, you put down the dream too."

Dreams are Pitino's real forte. That's where he operates best. Any true basketball son of Garf would have to be that way. It was the Dead Period and he couldn't stay at camp to watch the games and the stations and take in the atmosphere, but he could talk about old times and catch up on what was new. Old Fuzzy's was the perfect place and down at the Fireside the old school and new school were breaking bread.

Larry Pearlstein was there with Pitino. Pearlstein is still "Scout" to anyone who knows anything about the game. He still bird-dogs for the New Jersey Nets too and was traveling with Pitino. They have much in common despite the difference in their years.

"Rick likes to pick on you," said Pearlstein, "but only if somebody else is there to hear it. Otherwise he's too busy trying to pick your brain. He has always been one of Howard's fair-haired boys. Howard picked him out right away to be a great coach, and from the very first it's been a battle royal to see who's the master and who's the apprentice. Rick was a cocky little thing as a camper. There wasn't room for both of them in the same camp. He is a sleep-in-the-gym kind of guy, though, and will never be too big for Five-Star."

Taking it all in, amused and respectful, Pitino said, "Garf is a Damon Runyon-type character and all the kids love to have fun with him. He and Will Klein have been my friends for almost 25 years. That's the main reason I come back, but I also just really enjoy coming back. Five-Star still teaches the game the way it should be taught.

"I got my start here and so did a lot of other guys. It was a stage for all of us in a highly competitive environment. We used to work for $100 a week because all we wanted to do was coach, talk, and live basketball. I was the baby in the family back then. Those were great times. I'll always have a place in my heart for Five-Star, even though a lot of the guys I coached with are gone now."

The past is not Pitino's cup of tea anyhow. He doesn't mind learning from it but he can never be happy there. The past has its place, but his place is the future. Part of him is always there. He dreams and then becomes his dream and in the summertime shares it at Five-Star.

* * * * *

After the lectures were over and after the playoffs were decided and before the Orange-White Classic, there was much left to do. For everyone there were duffle bags to pack and addresses to exchange. Some of the campers would immediately begin again to think in terms of time in the rest of the world. The clocks wouldn't be set back until nearly midnight, but for those who arrived with false expectations or had given less than everything, it was time to face reality. The task had been set before them starkly.

Many others have discovered they were more than they knew. On the surface they had always projected self-assurance, but deep down they were unsure. Now they were sure, at least more than before, and it was something no one could take from them. Five-Star time would continue for them and for the other campers with one game left, especially those in the camper-worker bunks for whom the Orange-White Classic is a way of life.

Most of the camper-workers, barring something unforseen or unless they mess it up for themselves, will be top Division I college players. One or two will become pros. The places they'll go and the people they'll travel with are the stuff of dreams for most young players. Old ones too. But the growth process is the same for them as the rest, with one notable exception.

The camper-workers who have been to Five-Star several times understand that they set an example for the entire camp. They set the example and the other kids look up to them as a young boy might to his big brother. It is not necessarily a role they relish, but most accept it and deal with it accordingly. That burden of responsibility, passed on year after year, is what keeps the camp on solid ground.

Back in the bunks, they could relax and be kids without upsetting the balance. Resting before the all-star game, sitting amid socks and sweatshirts that hung like stalactites everywhere, they ragged on each other. An hour or so earlier, Travis Best had almost single-handedly knocked Grant Hill and his teammate Dan Buie, a 6'8" rising junior from Harrisburg, Pennsylvania, out of the playoffs.

Hill and Buie were saying Best cheated. "It doesn't do any good to box Travis out," Hill said. "He just throws you out of the way." Best, smiling as usual, countered, "Yeah, but I do it in a nice way. You're my boys. When I'm out on the court you'd better believe I'm trying to win."

"Travis was good tonight, I gotta admit," Hill said. "It looked like he was dribbling down the court thinking to himself, 'Well, should I score or pass this time? Hmmm, I guess I'll score.' It was like he owned the court—but there will be other times."

Best and Hill were both snakes in the grass as far as Buie was concerned. "Travis is nasty, but Grant hooks you every time you go near the basket even if you're on his team. Don't even try to get a rebound 'cause the refs never call nothin' on him."

Everyone agreed the ultimate pirate was Garf. "I know he messes with the alarm clocks in the morning," said group spokesman Best. "There was one day, I swear, I woke up and heard him say, 'Three minutes until the morning workout.' I swear I took about two steps and the next thing I heard was, 'Fifteen seconds to go.' I was pulling my sweatshirt on as I ran out the door and ran right off the porch into the bushes. I know he had to be lying."

It had been a good week, they all thought, despite Garf's overall dissatisfaction. "The best week for me, though, was when Jamaal Faulkner was here," Hill said. Faulkner, out of Christ the King High School in New York, had a lot of cute moves for a 6'7" kid, including a baby hook that drove opponents nuts.

"Jamaal was funny," Hill said. "He was here when I first started coming and I remember him going up against Billy Owens. Owens was the main man then, and he took Jamaal to town a couple of times, but Jamaal got him back and told us the story of how he did it.

"He lowered his voice real deep when he told the story and said, 'Now I ain't no ballplayer, and Mr. Owens came down low and treated me bad, so I had to reach deep into my bag of tricks for him. I reached deep, deep into my bag of tricks and put the crossover on him and put up the And One! That was all it took. It was over.' I really miss Jamaal."

Hill, the only camper to be named Outstanding Player of the Week and all-star game MVP in the same session twice in the same year (at Pitt and Honesdale), is not the type to forget his roots. "I was lucky growing up in the suburbs because I think it helped me learn the fundamentals," he said. "I was lucky too because a lot of guys want to make it to the NBA to get their families out of the projects. I don't have that pressure.

"When I first came to camp I used to imitate guys like Jamaal and Billy Owens. I learned a lot and after a while I found out they were human, just like me. It was very strange after I left camp the first time. I started to get recruited and it shocked me. I couldn't believe it was actually happening to me. I was discovered here and even though I don't need the exposure anymore, I come to Five-Star to learn and out of loyalty to Garf."

*　*　*　*　*

The coaches also use the interim between the playoffs and the all-star game to slowly slip back into ordinary time. Their work was mostly done, and over at the Manor House there was laughter coming through the screen door. The front room was crowded with guys like James "Healer" Ross who goes everywhere Five-Star goes, and Will Rey and John Sarandrea, who cracks everyone up whenever Jerry Wainwright lets him get a word in edgewise, and a few others.

Wainwright was doing all the talking. "Over at the old Rosemont site," he was saying, "there used to be this deep kind of dip in the ground in front of the dining room. Everybody used to call it the Frog Pit. It was no problem on dry days, but whenever it rained it filled up with water. There were never any lights in front of the place and one night it poured like hell and Garf was walking past and forgot about it. He fell in up to his waist and couldn't move. We had to pull him out and for years after that, every time I saw a big puddle I laughed.

"There was another time right here at Honesdale, over on the hill by the gym. It was probably the funniest thing I ever saw. It had rained for something like three days and Garf was trying to make it down the hill to go into the gym. He started slipping and it's a good thing he always walks fast and pitched forward like he does, because he started sliding and he looked like somebody in one of those silent movies. He was off balance all the way but made it down without falling and slid right in the gym door. He just stood there for a minute and then said, 'Only a great athlete could do that.'"

There was some serious conversation. "Trying to coach and have a good marriage at the same time can be tough," Wainwright said. "Coaching drains you, you know, and you come home tired and drained and no good to anyone. Then the phone rings and maybe it's one of your players or some parent on your case and suddenly you have to be 'on' again after you just got done being a pain in the ass to your wife. Some wives might resent it and I can understand that. It's not easy for anybody.

"Coaching is a tough business. One thing I always remember about Bob Knight is him saying he never ever felt that his teams played as well in a game as they did in practice. I can still see him putting his hands at two levels to illustrate the point. I always made it my goal to bring the practice level to the game level. There's never the same flow in the game as there is in practice. Coaches have very little control in the game. We literally sit there observing things out of our control."

* * * * *

It was brisk and windy for the Orange-White Classic, which is as it should be. Grant Hill was his usual self, seeming to vanish from sight downcourt and then reappear without warning above the basket on his own end, and Travis Best did things with the ball that can't be done and then did them again, but otherwise the game was anticlimactic.

The game was downright sloppy. The players were smashing shots off the rims and bending them so badly Garf almost stopped the proceedings at one point to put the No-Dunking Rule back in effect. Even usually placid Tom Konchalski was in an uproar, shouting from the sidelines for the players to get into the game. It was a side of him seldom seen outside the camp.

Garf was mostly disappointed because it was the final Five-Star curtain call for kids like Hill, Bill Curley, Ken Blakeney, and Riversiders Lee Green, Adrian "Red" Autry, and Brian Reese. Autry would walk away with Playmaker of the Week and Mr. Stations honors, which pleased Garf, but Reese, who was taking home the

Sportsmanship Award along with the prestigious 30-for-30 Award, was injured and didn't even suit up.

All in all, it wasn't a classic Classic. The kids were tired, and not just tired but worn to a frazzle. It was the end of a very long summer. Travis Best, for instance, had been going nonstop since the end of the school year. He played in a tournament in New Jersey in June, went to the Nike Camp and Pitt II in July, took in an AAU tournament in Las Vegas, rested a week or so, then squeezed in a tournament in Philadelphia before coming to Honesdale. A lot of his friends had similar schedules.

That could explain the lack of continuity all week. Even Garf got pooped once in a while. He never let it show at camp, but it was there. The kids tried; they just didn't have anything left. It wasn't as bad as he thought. A lot of campers sitting along the sidelines were dragging but ready for more.

Kevin Moore, a rising senior from East Side High in Paterson, New Jersey, had improved his rebounding and even liked the food. "I just dogged it down," he said. He might be the first camper to ever make that statement, but it had to be taken with a grain of salt. With his mother out working, he does most of his own cooking back home.

Akim Hall, a rising junior from Mount Saint Michael's in the South Bronx, was out in the country and at Five-Star for the first time in his life. He got to see a bird's nest up close on his bunkhouse porch, which was great, he said, and so was sitting on the shore of the lake at night, but it didn't feel good sitting on the sidelines for the Orange-White Classic.

His attitude may have been what kept him out. "I got mad because my team wasn't winning," said Hall. "Before the playoffs the team practiced one play for 20 minutes and we were still messing it up. I got mad and walked off the court. If I had known it would come between me and the all-star team, I probably wouldn't have done it. Next time I won't."

* * * * *

At the awards ceremony, Garf knew it was risky, but after he asked the campers if they'd learned two new moves, like he told them to on the first day of camp, and after Jan Struhar and Doremus Bennerman got their gifts, he asked Duffy Burns to give the Five-Star cheer one last shot. It could have been a disaster, but Burns, haggard and hoarse as always and worn out after a summer of doing the thing, got the gym rocking when he said, "Whooooo, are you?"

The campers responded, shouting, *"We are, Five-Star"* loud enough to be heard in the next county. The parents in the audience looked on, mesmerized, and even Garf showed a little more zip.

Later, when the car lights headed down Fireside Road and out into the rest of the world and faded beyond sight, the camp became bare again. A few stragglers remained, but only the wind stays all year at Honesdale. Leaves were falling, drying, and sweetly dying on the ground. It was the end of the growing season at Five-Star.

*   *   *   *   *

Sunday morning, Will Klein was one of the last to go. Garf was already gone. Pacing the sidewalks between the bunkhouses, Klein's arms were laden down with pillowcases and sheets, medicine bottles and notebooks, and sundry other items. He was thinking about who to tell to do what. Rooms had to be cleaned and the premises had to be checked to make sure the camp was left the way he'd found it. "You can't leave the place a mess," Klein said. He could, but then it wouldn't be Five-Star.

"I think the secret of our success is that we care about the people who come here," Klein continued. "I always felt they should be comfortable and Howard genuinely cares about the kids. We both work very hard at what we do. We don't just delegate things to someone else, but if we have to we aren't afraid to pick good people.

"In the beginning I think it was a matter of timing—there wasn't any competition. Then the mystique mushroomed and people wanted to say they'd been here. Maybe, with all the other camps, the AAU, and the NCAA regulations, we will never be as strong as we once were, but we are still very strong."

Out at the main gate, ready to confirm Klein's beliefs, were four of the last campers to leave. Waiting for their parents, Neil Laurine of Hicksville, New York and three West Islip, New York schoolmates, Jim Austin, Michael Keenan, and Dave Hudzik, had mixed feelings about going.

When their parents arrived it was obvious they were a sight for sore eyes, but before they got there, Hudzik, speaking for the group, said, "When you look at it, Five-Star is the best camp in the country, which makes it the best camp in the world, doesn't it?"

TWENTY
End of the Line

"The whole thing is unbelievable."

– Garf

Nothing lasts forever, nothing physical anyway. In January of 1990, the NCAA-member Division I coaches, close to 300 strong, approved legislation barring anyone in their ranks from working or lecturing at non-institution camps. It was done by paddle vote and resulted in "a clear majority," according to Rick Evrard, the NCAA Director of Legislative Services.

"The feeling was that individual coaches selected to work at privately owned business institutions were receiving a tremendous recruiting advantage by being with top prospects," Evrard said. The regulations, voted down a year earlier, were put in place immediately. Five-Star was not the only basketball camp involved, but it was deeply affected.

It was a bitter pill for Garf. "I suppose we are little more than a speck of dust in the overall scheme of things, but to me it is a national disgrace," he said initially. "No one has ever shown where there is any edge being gained. It's a decision born of jealousy and ignorance. The whole thing is personally upsetting at best and ignorant at worst. It makes no sense at all, but when did college presidents or athletic directors ever do anything that made sense? They are the same people, don't forget, who refused to repeal freshman eligibility."

After the bad taste wore off, he added, "Taking the college coaches away is a classic case of biting the hand that feeds you. I fed these schools a near exemplary service with *HSBI* for almost 20 years. I sweated and worked for those guys and gave them all legitimate ratings, very sharp ratings. I wrote about sleepers, kids nobody knew about, and also wrote about overrated kids who might bring a program down.

"For the past 25 years at Five-Star, we have showcased some of the best high school players in America. The only true measure of a kid's ability is how he performs with his own high school team, playing for his own coach, but outside of that, the camp was the greatest basketball stage in America. The colleges were invited to send a representative or two to any session and were never charged a dime to get in. The coaches came to evaluate the talent and it was presented to them in a manner as closely resembling a high school game as possible with regulation size courts and balanced talent. We enabled the coaches to evaluate the prospects in the summertime better than anyplace else."

How quickly people sometimes forget. "Apparently the colleges who have gained the most from Five-Star, as measured by the number of campers who have graduated and gone to those schools—notably North Carolina and Georgetown—are among the most vocal against the college coaches working. But in the whole 25 years of Five-Star, there aren't five Division I prospects who have chosen their school because of a coach who worked at this camp. I'm serious about that. You would have to make a thousand phone calls to find just one.

"I've laid my guts on the floor for 25 years for all these schools. With the little power that I have had, first with *HSBI* and then with Five-Star, maybe I was able to help a few young coaches move up, if it actually was a move up, or I could go beyond that and pick up a phone and maybe help get a kid a scholarship. Coaches and players have used the camp as their stage but that's all. Nothing more. We've been beneficial to all the coaches. Players from Five-Star have gone to all their schools.

"When you get down to it, the biggest advantage of all is held by the college coaches themselves who run camps on their own campuses. They bring youngsters in for a week and the kids feed on nothing but that school all week long, and don't tell me they aren't good players, which some people will tell you. There are schools that for years have fed off the Division I players who went to their particular camp. Why that isn't considered a prospect's paid visit I'll never understand.

"We will find a way to carry on bigger and better than ever. How can you replace the experience of the college coaches? How can you replace their teaching and speaking powers and organizational skills? You can't. There are only 20 or so of those guys still working the camp, the 20 or so everyone is complaining about, and we will miss them deeply.

"But we have a tremendous backlog of very talented young and veteran high school coaches who are the best in the country. To me high school coaches are king. They are the greatest group of people in America. A lot of high school coaches think it's a step up to go to college, but I don't necessarily think it is. To me, the Morgan Woottens and Bob Hurleys and all the rest are as big as or bigger than any college or pro coach who ever lived.

"Truthfully, though, what bugs me more than losing the college coaches as workers is the idiotic rule that college coaches can't lecture at the camp. It is mind-boggling to me to think that a Bob Knight or Mike Krzyzewski or Rick Pitino and the rest, at this point in time, will never again lecture at Five-Star. Bob Knight doesn't need to come to Five-Star to speak. He could go fishing all summer, but he finds time to come to Five-Star and forget the fact that he has a big name. What matters is, does he have anything to say to the kids? You bet he does. He talks about life and how to play this game in the simplest of terms and that's got to leave its mark. The kids leave with something they didn't have when they got there.

"Fortunately, Mike Krzyzewski, who was on a key committee involved in the legislation, is against that part of the rule. I believe he will get a lot done in January of 1991 to get it changed. It is a very sad state of affairs that we have to live in this climate. I know that our camp hurts none of the coaches, but if they perceive, in their own minds, that it does, they should swallow it. Their decision will come back to haunt them because Five-Star, with a lot of help from a lot of great coaches, has taught America how to play this damn game and taught the kids how to act while they are playing."

The future of Five-Star was placed in doubt by the new rulings. Garf had often stated privately that if the college coaches were taken away he would give up the camp. However, when the time finally came, he and Will Klein's first move was to ask the NCAA for a year's grace period. It had all happened too fast for the camp to put new plans into effect, they said, and contracts had already been sent out and returned by the college coaches in question, raising potential legal hassles.

"The year of transition," they wrote in part, "will allow us to: (a) avoid a huge financial loss, (b) meet our obligations to run the camps at the agreed upon dates and sites, (c) train a replacement staff for our camps beginning the year 1991, and (d) develop a new format."

It was an expected request under the circumstances and one that was reviewed by a legislative subcommittee. The validity—and timing—of all the contracts would be reviewed individually and approved or disapproved on its own merits, said Evrard. "That is fairly routine in regard to legalities surrounding contracts. Generally they are honored for the one-year period involved."

Garf, for his part, was gracious in semi-defeat, at least for the time being. "Once again the NCAA has been very cooperative with us," he said.

* * * * *

The new legislation may or may not balance the recruiting scales more evenly and when it comes right down to it, when ties are loosened at NCAA headquarters, Five-Star is not such a horrible place. It is not necessarily the den of inequity it is cracked up to be. "The goal of the legislation," says Enforcement Director Bob Minnix, "is to get outside entrepreneurs off NCAA campuses, all of them. The NCAA rule-makers feel the camps are exploiting the kids and want to cut off the gravy train. They can't control private businessmen like Howard Garfinkel and the rest, but they can control the member institutions.

"Working at Five-Star gives a coach this advantage: He is able to show his personality to the kids. Most kids choose to go to a school because they like the coach, either his coaching style or him as a person. The coaches working Five-Star get to talk to the kids every day and have the kids feel comfortable with them, whereas coaches not working there don't have that opportunity.

"As far as coaches who have camps on their own campuses, like Bob Knight or Dean Smith or any coach, they very seldom get the heavy hitters. As an example, the NCAA headquarters is in Kansas and I have noticed that the kids who attend the University of Kansas camps are pretty much Kansas kids. A handful may be recruited down the road by a Division I school, but they are mostly kids learning the game for the first time. Any kid worth his salt seeks out the specialty camps to get the very best competition he can get his hands on.

"I like Five-Star. Howard has always been very straight-up with me, an on-the-table kind of guy, and that's my style too. Many of the kids I talk to who have gone to Five-Star say that it is the highlight of their careers. I ask them all the time and when they are in college and even afterwards, they still have fond memories of those times. To me that is a good thing."

* * * * *

Fretting over the future has never been Garf's lot in life. Things have to be dealt with as they arise, but he's always found plenty to panic about in the present and would be the first to agree that it's been one shot in the dark after another since day one with Five-Star.

"The whole thing is unbelievable," he says. "It all happened by accident, but as far as our basic philosophy and teaching the game in the best possible way, we have changed very little since the first minute of camp. As far as my personality and image, I haven't changed my ways in 25 years. I might be an anachronism if I started out today, an outside guy helping out, but there are reasons I do the things I do. It's my business, my livelihood. It's what I do.

"Mainly, though, it's because I'm in your corner, a kid's corner, anybody's corner. If I could do something for a kid and didn't do it, would that be right? That'd be wrong, wouldn't it? What are we put on earth for anyway? I thought we, everybody, has a purpose in life. My role is to help people in basketball. Why else am I here? What else am I doing?

"I can't help people get out of jail. I admire lawyers and doctors because they help people, but I flunked algebra 10 times. I didn't even look at geometry, so I'm not going to be a rocket scientist. I can just about put a plug in the wall and turn my TV on, so I'm in a business where I can help people and if I didn't, I would have wasted all those years.

"While you're here you try to do the best you can for yourself and the people around you, and if you don't then you are not a good citizen, not a good person, and that's what I've always tried to do, be a good person, and I'm being serious for a change.

"Helping people is a kick I get. It's a nice feeling helping kids and adults try to better themselves. Five-Star is a great vehicle for that because you get a kid for a week and I always figured that kid or that parent or whoever is paying for the kid is owed an obligation to give that kid more than just basketball.

"I'm not the only one who tries to help. Most people in my position would do exactly what I have done. Whether they could have done it with the skill I did is another thing, but if they wouldn't try to do it, at least try, then they are wastrels."

* * * * *

Maybe eight days of camp life just brings out the best in a person, or maybe Five-Star does, but eventually larger questions will have to be asked and answered. Rick Pitino foresees the days of Five-Star team camps and Five-Star fantasy camps, where former campers of all ages return to mingle with alumni who made it to the pros. He is seldom shortsighted.

There is already talk of spreading west to California, where the Rockfish boys, among others, eagerly await their arrival. It would save them considerable plane fare. Rockfish, a beachcomber's version of Garf's Nationals, was organized in the mid-eighties by David Benezra, a longtime outside coach and since 1986 the head coach at Crossroads in Santa Monica.

Never a great player, Benezra has been coaching since he was 14 years old. It is more than coincidence that his path eventually led to Five-Star. "Wherever there was good basketball being played, that's where I went," Benezra says. "I'll never forget the first time I saw the New York City and Big East kids play. Out in L.A., we play a finesse game. At Pac 10 games it seems like the fans sit on their hands. The Big East games were packed and the fans were raucous. The kids played like there was a burglar breaking into their house and they were trying to stop him.

"The Rockfish kids wanted to be a part of that scene. Whenever people hear the word 'Rockfish,' they think of the TV show 'The Rockford Files.' We actually came up with the name watching Ed Pinckney and Villanova play. The kids said Pinckney was as solid as a rock, and out on the coast at the time, if somebody was hip or cool, they were called a 'fish.' First it was just Rock and then both. We had Chocolate Rockfish and the last phase was All-Encompassing Chocolate Rockfish. It was pretty tough to be that kind of player."

Five-Star was full of them and in 1985 Benezra brought his kids east, kids like Scott Williams (who later went to North Carolina), Kevin Holland (DePaul), and Earl Duncan (Syracuse). The main reason they traveled 3,000 miles was not to be seen but to get smarter. "I already knew enough guys in the business and in one week at camp the kids got what they could never get elsewhere," Benezra says.

"The coaches gave equal training to stars and to kids who probably will never play beyond high school. But even those kids will always have the thrill of remembering what it was like to have their shot blocked by J.R. Reid and Alonzo Mourning or to have Rex Chapman's navel up by their forehead on one of his jumpers. It is a nice, uncomplicated time for them. The thing that always gets me the most is Garf. It's like he still remembers what it's like to be a kid and somehow he reaches the little boy in all of us."

* * * * *

That is Garf's gift. California is ripe for Five-Star and there is also talk of taking Texas by storm. In the early eighties the first Five-Star girls' camp opened and there are three franchises now, at Shepherd's College in Shepherdstown, West Virginia; Pittsburgh; and Radford. Garf and Will Klein loan several coaches to the operation, get a small cut of the profits, and highlight Reneé Ackerman, the coach of Champion High School in Warren, Ohio, and Virginia University's Debbie Ryan in *Five-Star Basketball Drills*, but otherwise are involved in name only.

That is good enough. After 25 years and who knows how many yet to come, the good names of Howard Garfinkel and Will Klein may prove to be Five-Star's final, insurmountable obstacle.

Things like that don't just grow on trees. "I see major problems for Five-Star after Howard and Will are gone," says Hubie Brown. "They go hand-in-hand. Will is the administrative part and maybe that would still be there with his son, but Garf's contribution will be a very, very hard thing to replace."

Will Klein views the matter stoically. "Without Howard, the awards ceremony might be shorter, but I learned a long time ago, in the school system, that no one is indispensable," Klein says. "After a while, no matter who it is, people will be saying, 'Will who?'

"In my mind, Howard's piece of the business might be more difficult to replace than mine. He is truly a character. Perhaps Tom Konchalski could do the job if he wanted to. He knows the coaches maybe better than Howard now and can get along with almost anybody, even if he doesn't have the same flair.

"As far as the financial end, we've raised it to the point where we could make a living at it and if I were offered a million dollars today I might not take it. It's a lot of work, but my son Leigh has been groomed for it. The only additional advice I could give him is, 'Watch your costs as you go and be careful.'"

Leigh Klein was broken-in right. A true Five-Star baby, his parents packed him up with the rest of the family valuables and carted him off to camp a month after he was born. He has been there every summer of his 22 years. Even as a tyke he showed he was a chip off the old block. His father used to pay him a penny apiece to pick up scraps of paper around the place. He did that for a spell, slowly pinching his pop for more until he got it up to a nickel.

He was going nowhere until a year or two later, when he figured out that big pieces could be torn into several litle ones. Nowadays he handles key checkout everywhere except at Honesdale, where nobody locks their door, and runs the canteen, a task he inherited from his older sister Robin. She used to run it and would fire little brother every so often, just to keep him in line. He didn't mind because it freed him to go bug some of the players, but during the all-star game one night Robin quit in a huff. Garf panicked, but Leigh got everything squared away in record time and has been in charge ever since.

He says he can do it in his sleep. For most of his youth Leigh was a self-designated assistant coach for any team that was winning at the time, and when he came of age, he pestered his father to make him a bona fide camper until he finally got his way. "I was terrible the first year," Leigh says. "I had a mind for the game but my body wasn't hip to it. I wasn't too bad the second year. I was a scrappy player and won the Mr. Hustle Award at Pitt. It was legit. I remember hanging my head after we lost in the playoffs and noticing that my legs were all scarred."

He paid his own way through college, earning a business management degree at the University of Texas and one summer, to help himself along, created a Five-Star hat. There had never been one before, so it was good thinking on his part. He designed it, had it made up, and for a while was sitting in the catbird's seat. It was a perilous perch.

"They sold like hot cakes," Leigh says. "But I was sitting in the canteen one night admiring my loot when my father walked in and asked for his cut. He said the Five-Star logo was what made them popular. I stared at him with my mouth open and all I could say was, 'But dad, I'm your son.'"

Business is business, and the fiscal heir apparent to Five-Star had to fork over a third of the profits. Determining Garf's net worth, by all accounts, is not such an easily done deal. That's not the way Garf sees it, but then he's never seen things the same as the rest.

"I see the toughest part as replacing Will Klein," he says. "You'd need to hire 10 people to do his job and then they all probably wouldn't get along."

As for himself, "I'm not on my deathbed yet, but when the day comes I hope someone is interested enough to carry it on, maybe someone like Frank Marino or Tom Konchalski. It could be done if they were interested.

"Or maybe I'll do what Everett Case did. In his will he left shares to all his players, the hundreds of players who made him. I'll leave shares to all the coaches who made the camp and as long as they continue doing what they were doing when I died, they keep getting their share. Once they bow out, it's over. If the NCAA takes the coaches, which it looks like they have, then their shares go to someone else, maybe all the campers."

It's the only thing that makes sense. Better yet, maybe everyone should get a piece. Will Klein has said time and time again that divvying up Five-Star 28,000 ways is at best unfeasible, and he would know better than anybody that anyone who ever enjoyed the game with passionate innocence and never wants the game to end should get a share. That's the only fair way.

"The whole thing started out as sort of a dream in Garf's mind," says his old sidekick, Dave Pritchett, nowadays a scout for the NBA Minnesota Timberwolves. "He's just a hell of a guy and for every five-star player he's helped, God only knows how many two-star kids he's gotten scholarships for and been there when they needed him. They can just call him anytime of the day or night and he's there.

"It's hard to explain why the guy does it. I guess it's sort of like a cancer, you know, and it's like a train leaving Boston. It's not like that in football and not like that in anything else, but people will tell you you can get on a train and go collect 20 people in every city who are just obsessed with this basketball stuff. Garf has to be right there as the engineer."

EPILOGUE

"A career is a curious thing. Talent isn't always enough. You need a sense of timing and an eye for seeing the turning point, recognizing the big chance when it comes along and grabbing it. A career can rest on a trifle, like us sitting here tonight, or it can turn on somebody saying to you, 'You're better than that. You're better than you know.'"

– Norman Maine to Vicki Lester in *A Star is Born*

I only want to set the record straight. It's a trifling thing really, unless you put stock in such things. It has to do with Garf and Nadav Henefeld and is not widely known and is something Henefeld may not even know himself.

Much was written about Henefeld during the 1989–90 college basketball season and how he helped put the University of Connecticut on the NCAA map, spearheading the Huskies' drive to their first Big East title and a trip to the NCAA's Sweet Sixteen. By the end of the season every hoop fan this side of the Sea of Galilee knew the freshman sensation was from Israel and had been a soldier in the Israeli Army before heading for foreign soil.

How Henefeld got from Israel to New England in the first place is typical of how Garf enters people's lives and changes them. It started to happen quite by chance on a Friday afternoon in the spring of 1989, right around the time the final plans for this book were being made.

Garf got a telephone call from Marv Kessler, who told him about Henefeld. He said the kid was interested in playing in America, preferably in the Big East. Kessler had no self-interest. For many years he had given clinics in Israel and coached in a pro league there, but he wasn't coaching anywhere else. He was, and still is, working for the Portland Trailblazers as a scout. One of his ex-campers at Five-Star, Brad Greenberg, had helped him get the job.

Kessler had seen Henefeld in his travels and raved about him to Garf, telling him the kid was "The Larry Bird of the Gaza Strip." That became Henefeld's nickname, "The Gaza Stripper." Garf had had never heard of Henefeld, but Kessler was Kessler and besides, he'd already spotted Mickey Dorsman, the coach of an Israeli club team that Garf had hired and been very pleased with, so he listened.

Plus, it reminded him of a story. In the summer of 1987, there were three campers from the Middle East at Pitt, one from Israel and two from Kuwait. They were seen in coversation late in the week, and one of the coaches, curious, went to them and asked what they were talking about. "Peace," he was told. "That is so much what Five-Star is about," Garf says. "That's where it's gonna start, anyway, isn't it—peace in the Middle East, I mean—with the kids talking?"

Henefeld could cut it without a doubt, Kessler said, but he was having trouble deciding where to go and running out of options. He'd already visited St. John's and loved the team and Lou Carnesecca but had envisioned something different, more of a campus scene with rolling hills and classmates strolling the grassy commons. St. John's was great, but the kid had his heart set on somewhere else although he didn't know where that was.

There was another problem. Henefeld had a plane ticket back to the Middle East that he had to use or lose and it was good for only two more days. Realistically, he had 24 hours to find a school and Kessler had no idea where to turn.

When the call came in, neither did Garf. "Kessler gave me the details and I asked him if he was positive about St. John's," he says. "I didn't want to have a hand in hurting Looie. I just wanted to help Kessler and he said he was sure Henefeld was not going there. So I started going through all the schools in the Big East, one by one.

"I hit them all in about eight seconds. In my mind Syracuse had too many good players already and Georgetown, which needed a 'three-man,' wouldn't have listened anyway, and on and on down the list until I said to myself, 'Eenie-meanie-minee-mo-catch-a-Huskie-by-the-toe' and came up with Connecticut. I figured it was not top,

top Big East and that if Henefeld was at least decent, he would play eight to ten minutes a game and be happy."

It was all arranged. Garf and Kessler called Evan Pickman, who worked as a volunteer assistant for Connecticut, and he agreed to contact head coach John Calhoun. Henefeld stopped at Mitch Buonaguro's Fairfield College on the way, which was nice but not the Big East and he continued north. To make a long story short, Calhoun wanted him for the Huskies.

"After I talked to Kessler on the phone and got ahold of Pickman I said I wanted to be kept out of it," Garf says. "That was the last I heard about it until about eight months later, in November, when I saw the kid playing on TV. I was stunned. You'd think someone would have told me or at least mentioned it to me.

"A lot of other things happened between the original phone call and Henefeld going there, but what made me remember it was after he started to do well, all the reports said how all his life he'd wanted to play in Storrs, Connecticut. The kid had no idea. He thought "stores" was Lord & Taylor. I often wonder what would have happened if I'd said 'Eenie-meenie-minee-Massachusetts' or anyplace else."

* * * * *

Garf says he doesn't believe in dreams, not the ones people have in their sleep, but I still don't believe him. The final words in this book—these words—were written in the spring of 1990, nearly a year after I agreed to undertake the project, a month or so later than the publisher wanted them, and long before I ever imagined they would be.

They never would have been written if I hadn't taken that nap at Radford and had my dreams invaded. It is totally factual, although Garf maintains I'm making it up.

I think he knows it's true. It sounds bizarre, but I think he has a way of being able to see inside a person instantly and understands how to meet them at every corner. If he doesn't, he makes you think he does, which works out to be the same.

Great coaches and teachers do that, get you to do things you wouldn't normally be able to do without you even knowing how or why. Great parents do that too. I agree with Hubie Brown who says that the man has a way of preying on your conscience until you can't resist any longer, and I think it goes even deeper.

The reason I think it goes deeper is because of a phone call I got from Garf when I was about halfway through this project. We talked at least twice a week throughout the winter and one time, trying to get his goat, I told him I had another dream and that I was including it in the book.

I told him I'd dreamed that I was playing in a pickup game somewhere with Chris Mullin of the Golden State Warriors. I was the only one on the team passing the ball to him. When I asked why, everyone else claimed he couldn't shoot, and that I should ignore Mullin and dribble upcourt and drive the lane as often as possible. I analyzed it to mean I was afraid of getting the facts all wrong in the book.

When I told Garf the dream he got impatient and upset, and said he'd heard enough of my absurd talk. A few weeks later, however, he called very early in the morning to tell me he'd had a strange dream of his own. Maybe he was trying to be comical, but this is what he told me.

He said he dreamed he had taken me out to dinner to celebrate the publication of the book and had deliberately poisoned me. He said I had it coming. I had forgotten to include Jeff Ruland in the book, never mentioning how close Garf was to both Ruland and his mother and how great a camper and counselor he'd been.

In his dream, Garf was sentenced to the electric chair for killing me, which was only right, but I guess he was worried too, panicked you might say, that things would go wrong (and he has the nerve to call *my* dreams weird).

I was struggling at the time and it made me relax. I realized there was no way I could ever totally please him, which was something very much on my mind. It was very comforting in a way because I knew I would always try to anyway, and that could only make me a better person. It also made me understand that I didn't have to please him. If this book ever sees the light of day, and even if it doesn't, it will prove I am right.

*　*　*　*　*

I feel different having written the history of Five-Star. The camp is not perfect. Normal people work there and normal kids play there and do normal human things, but altogether they make it a remarkable place.

Being there made me think of a Moose Club basketball tournament I played in when I was 12 or 13 years old. I remember it because we lost and after the game my coach told me there was a man who wanted to speak to me outside the locker room. I went and it turned out he was associated with the old St. Louis Hawks. He said I was a good little player and that I should keep playing hard. That was all he said.

I didn't believe him. I forgot about it, or at least put it way back in my mind, and there was no one else around me who was able to see what he had seen, so the moment was lost. I thought about it in passing over the years and there are fewer and fewer regrets, but to me that's what Five-Star is all about, moments like those. Saving them.